COSTUME
JEWELRY
Identification and Price Guide

COSTUME JEWELRY

Identification and Price Guide

2nd Edition

Harrice Simons Miller

The CONFIDENT COLLECTOR™

AVON BOOKS ◆ NEW YORK

Important Notice: All of the information, including valuations, in this book has been compiled from the most reliable sources, and every effort has been made to eliminate errors and questionable data. Nevertheless, the possibility of error always exists in a work of such scope. The publisher and the author will not be held responsible for losses which may occur in the purchase, sale, or other transaction of property because of information contained herein. Readers who feel they have discovered errors are invited to *write* the author in care of Avon Books so that the errors may be corrected in subsequent editions.

THE CONFIDENT COLLECTOR: COSTUME JEWELRY (2nd edition) is an original publication of Avon Books. This edition has never before appeared in book form.

AVON BOOKS
A division of
The Hearst Corporation
1350 Avenue of the Americas
New York, New York 10019

Copyright © 1994 by Harrice Simons Miller
Cover photo by Kenneth Chen; Linda Rodin, stylist

Cover jewelry *(clockwise from top)*: Miriam Haskell necklace, Trifari frog pin, Schiaparelli pin intertwined with Miriam Haskell necklace, Trifari pin, all courtesy Robin Feldman Collectibles, New York, NY; Schiaparelli dangle pin (unsigned), courtesy Carol Moskowitz, New York, NY; Kenneth Jay Lane tiger pin, courtesy Norman Crider Antiques, New York, NY; Eisenberg Original pin, courtesy Carol Moskowitz; Kenneth Jay Lane and unsigned Italian Lucite cuffs, courtesy Robin Feldman Collectibles; Joseff bee pin, courtesy the author; 1920s store mannequin courtesy Norman Crider Antiques.

The Confident Collector and its logo are trademarked properties of Avon Books.
Interior design by Martha Schwartz
Published by arrangement with the author
Library of Congress Catalog Card Number: 90-648685
ISBN: 0-380-77078-4

First Avon Books Trade Printing: January 1994

AVON TRADEMARK REG. U.S. PAT. OFF. AND IN OTHER COUNTRIES, MARCA REGISTRADA, HECHO EN U.S.A.

Printed in the U.S.A.

OPM 10 9 8 7 6 5

To Sloane, Kate, and Max — the future.

Be yourself, be daring, and above all have fun!
—*ELSA SCHIAPARELLI*

Acknowledgments

A very large thank you to everyone who contributed their time and knowledge and to those brave souls who entrusted me with their jewelry!

Special thanks *again* to Pam Smith, research assistant and general person extraordinaire, who helped get me through another one!

To my agent, Ruth Nathan, and everyone at Avon Books who helped make this book happen, I salute you!

Many thanks to photographer Kenneth Chen, who has the patience of a saint.

To my extended family—thanks for being there when I needed you and leaving me alone when I "vanted" to be.

Contents

AN OVERVIEW

Introduction

So much has happened in the world of costume jewelry since the first edition of this book was published in 1990! Prices have continued to rise—after pundits predicted there would be no more room at the top. Collectors have become even more sophisticated, seeking the finest, the rarest, and both the most well-known *and* the most obscure designers' work. More people have become more knowledgeable and sought out more information. For some collectors, buying a pretty piece of vintage costume jewelry has become a beginning, not an end.

On a five-week-long trip to Europe in the autumn of 1992, I discovered that American costume jewelry has truly become an international language. While I knew that many of the European dealers came to the United States to buy, and I had met many of them while doing shows and markets in the New York City area, I hadn't realized the breadth of the market outside this country. The first weekend I was there, I went to an antiques fair at the Kensington Town Hall in London. I felt like the most popular girl at the prom! I knew so many of the dealers, and the ones I didn't know quickly heard I was there and asked excitedly if I had brought jewelry with me to sell. It was thrilling to me that so many people had my book and asked me to sign their dog-eared copies.

Paris was a hard place to be—so many antiques shops and a flea market that goes on forever. I didn't know whether to buy or sell or just be a tourist. Often I'd walk into a tiny shop and there'd be one little section of vintage American costume jewelry and I'd feel totally at home.

In Geneva, I appeared at the launch of a new shop specializing in vintage costume jewelry, where I signed books and answered questions about American designers and styles and had the best time talking about one of my favorite subjects. In their shop, my gracious hostesses displayed each piece of jewelry as a small work of art on its own gray velvet pillow in a beautiful glass case.

One of the nicest serendipitous experiences happened in Venice. After Paris, I had packed away my jewelry, thinking that it was high time to take a little vacation. In every city I had scurried around, looking for new dealers to list in the Dealers' Directory, or to buy from or sell to. I was traveling with my daughter, who was going to be staying in England for her senior year of college, and Venice was our last stop before she had to check in at Oxford. About a half hour after we got to our hotel, after an amazing but scenic ride in the wrong direction up the Grand Canal in a *vaporetto* (water bus), we wandered into a little *campo* (square) right around the corner and there was an outdoor antiques market! It took about three minutes to find the dealer with the most American vintage costume jewelry. When I introduced myself, I was told I had missed Kenneth Jay Lane by about two hours and that a dealer from California had just been there as well. Talk about a small world! The next day, after concluding our business, the dealer covered up his cases and he and his partner and friends, the California dealer, my daughter, and I trooped over to a tiny restaurant along a narrow canal and had a wonderful, long Venetian lunch. What a great way to do business!

THE ENGLISH AND EUROPEAN MARKET

Shah Mohamed is one of the busiest costume jewelry dealers in London. His shop at Alfie's Antique Market is always jumping with dealers from all over the world. He sells mostly to the trade but also has a devoted following among collectors. We spoke at length about the European market when I was in London:

> I've been in the business for about ten years. When I first started buying costume jewelry everyone thought I was crazy and said I should be

buying gold! I had always loved things that were different. I was buying Dior sets and Art Deco and French jewelry from the Twenties and Thirties. Trifari pieces cost me two or three pounds ($3–$5) and I was selling Dior sets for thirty-five to forty pounds ($45–$60). I bought a lot of Haskell and couldn't give it away. I was buying all of my jewelry in London then.

It's been about seven years now that people have been asking for pieces by name. Prices on lower end jewelry have gone up two and a half to three times and the higher end eight to ten times since I started. This year, because of all the publicity about the "Jewels of Fantasy" show, dealers and collectors are looking for the top pieces—Trifari, Chanel, Dior, Schiaparelli, and others. The American books also help people to be more discerning. Five years ago, I sold anything and everything. Fifties Trifari gold and pearls and Coro gilt and pearls were really cheap then—they always have sold well. Now there are more collectors on the scene and they want rarer pieces, possibly for investment.

I have about ten or twelve collectors who buy directly from me. I always tell them the most important thing is they have to love what they buy. Usually they wear the pieces as well. Some collectors buy just to collect because they love the designs. It's important for collectors to read the books and go to the exhibitions so they can see which pieces are held in high esteem by curators and other collectors and dealers. They must shop around and not overpay. Unsigned, unusual pieces are also excellent. Their value is in the beauty and rarity of the piece.

We don't see much costume jewelry made in England before the Fifties, probably because of the war. Attwood & Sawyer (marked "A & S") makes fine quality costume jewelry like Ciner. Butler and Wilson is another popular English company that's being collected because of their book—even their new pieces are being bought and saved. Sphinx is low end but quite popular with Italians and Japanese. People buy it to wear. Ciro is very much an English thing—excellent quality.

The English taste is quiet, slightly curtailed, very tailored and elegant. Even if it's a large piece, it's still finely made, not cabaret-ish. English buyers like elaborate pieces with a lot of work. Sixties and Seventies jewelry never got off the ground here. It's not an English taste.

Art Deco is essentially a European taste. Small, geometric designs in Bakelite and chrome or paste are preferred by French and German dealers, less so among Italians. They like more flamboyant jewelry. If it weren't for the Italians, business wouldn't have grown the way it did in London. London is the center of everything for Europeans. Now with the European Community, there are no more customs charges. They can buy as much as they like. It's good for our commerce.

Recently, I had a few very big sales to Japanese dealers who have shops there. They buy Trifari tailored pieces. well-known designer names such as Chanel and Nina Ricci, and lots of pieces made with pearls. They are interested in the best quality. They got interested at about the same time the Germans did.

Most of my customers know I now buy everything in America, but it's worthwhile for them to come and sit with me for three hours and buy everything they need for the season. My associate, Steven Miners, travels thousands of miles buying jewelry for the shop. We find dealers we like in America and buy heavily from them. We have done a lot of research and put a lot of time into finding our sources. I have about fifteen or twenty dealers I buy from in bulk, mainly "middle of the road" pieces. The top pieces get very high prices in America, and if we buy them, it's hard to sell them here.

When customers ask me what they should buy, I tell them to buy pieces they know are special, like Chanel script pieces, Schiaparelli sets or figurals, the best of Coro Duettes, or fine Trifari. The prices stay up there on the best pieces. I always tell my customers an investment in costume jewelry isn't like buying gold, because there's no intrinsic value. It's purely a fashion thing, not a liquid asset. The value certainly goes up, but they can't count on putting it in the bank and taking it out with twenty times more value. I can suggest to my customers to buy pieces, but only certain ones that I think will hold their value.

The pieces have gotten harder to find at reasonable prices. I believe the whole costume jewelry scene will stay strong; people will always buy costume jewelry—it's their nature.*

THE SECOND EDITION

Why a second edition? From a really personal standpoint, I wanted an excuse to continue to research and learn about this exciting collectible that many of us have watched being born. What makes it so viable is that anything goes—there's still room for the new collector to discover beautiful pieces at little out-of-the-way markets at small prices as well as for the more seasoned collector who sends out faxes to all the major dealers looking for rare museum-quality pieces that cost a small fortune.

At an antiques show, I watched a dealer's shaking hand write out a check for seven thousand dollars for a single fabulous piece of

---

* Shah Mohamed died in July 1993, at the time this book went to press.

Thirties Trifari. Within a week she sold it to another dealer for even more money, who then sold it to a collector who was glad to buy it at any price! I've had the thrill of finding a piece of rare, early, unsigned Haskell for $22 late in the day at the Twenty-sixth Street Flea Market in New York City after all the dealers had been and gone and overlooked it. The fact that both extremes exist in this still-young field of collecting is why I have more to write about and illustrate in a new edition. And then there was the woman who told me she just loves the old bracelets, particularly the ones made of cellulite!

Unfortunately, there is a little downside to all this popularity of costume jewelry. There has been a commensurate rise of fakes and forgeries. In every form of art and antiques, as the pieces become more valuable, there is more of a temptation to reproduce the archetypes and sell them as originals. I have no problem accepting honest reproductions that don't pretend to be anything else; copies of good design have always been produced in furniture, clothing, fine art, and other fields. The way that forgers can be stymied is through education and the dissemination of information. If someone doesn't call a halt to it somewhere along the line, people's reputations and wallets can both be hurt!

February 22, 1991, was an auspicious day for lovers of costume jewelry all over the world. It was the opening day of "Jewels of Fantasy—Fashion Jewellery of the Twentieth Century" at the Museo Teatrale alla Scala in Milan. It was the world's first comprehensive traveling exhibition of important European and American costume jewelry of the twentieth century.

There were approximately 610 pieces of extraordinary costume jewelry on loan from museums, public institutions, and private collectors, including Gianni Versace, Christian Lacroix, and leading dealers from Europe and the United States. Chanel, Schiaparelli, Dior, Trifari, Coro, Eisenberg, Kenneth Jay Lane, Miriam Haskell, Marcel Boucher, and other important designers were represented, tracing the impact of social, economic, and historical influences on their designs.

What was most interesting to collectors and admirers of costume jewelry was that this exhibition legitimized nonprecious jewelry as an art form worthy of worldwide recognition. It gave Europeans an

expansive look at American costume jewelry and gave many devotees the impetus to broaden their collections or, in at least a few
instances, start a business.

The exhibit went on to Zurich, London, Cologne, Berlin, and
New York, gathering followers wherever it went. This exhibit, sponsored by the Daniel Swarovski Corporation in Switzerland, created
more interest in American costume jewelry and showed American
collectors a wide range of jewelry created by leading European
designers. "Jewels of Fantasy," which came to the Fashion Institute of
Technology in New York in March 1993, galvanized the costume
jewelry world. The fun, the fantasy, the glamour all came together.

The costume jewelry market certainly has its vicissitudes. "Miriam
Haskell is dead," we hear. Three months later she has a miraculous
Lazarus-type return. Jelly bellies seemed to have hit a peak, gone
through a price correction much like the stock market, and now new
collectors have pushed prices up even further. Chanel script pieces,
with precious little known about their provenance, are hard to find
and high priced. They are bought mainly by collectors rather than
the casual fashion buyer. Trifari is always big—Europeans like the
simple textured gold-and-pearl pieces from the Fifties, sterling silver
crowns, and "fruit salad" pieces. Large, gorgeous, old Trifari, particularly sterling silver, is prized on both sides of the Atlantic. Schiaparelli
is harder to find and holding its price, particularly pieces with large
cabochons in wide bracelets with matching necklaces and large earrings. In 1992, Melanie Coe-Sharman's Schiaparelli Boutique at
Harrod's in London brought "Schiap" costume jewelry into the
international limelight. The HAR genies, buddhas, and dragons we
all were so crazy about at the beginning of the Nineties seem to have
disappeared. Once in a while a set pops up, but it's quickly gone. Old
Marcel Boucher pieces with the MB mark are very popular and high
priced, Kenneth Jay Lane pieces always have their fans—the more
outrageous the piece the better. Reja figurals, Eisenberg figurals,
Joseff elephants, roosters, sun gods, and other figurals are always fun
to collect and wear, and older Hattie Carnegie "HC" pieces, Hattie
Carnegie primitives, and Nettie Rosenstein sterling silver and figurals are collected.

What's greatest about this pursuit is that there's room for everyone to express themselves, whether through their vast collections or with just one treasured piece.

How to Use This Book

The book is divided into chapters by decades, with each manufacturer's pieces presented alphabetically. The chapter on collections contains photographs not only of portions of people's collections but also photographs that represent more than one collector's pieces. We find it fascinating that collectors' treasures are so varied, and thought it would be fun for readers to see what collections are out there—maybe as an inspiration!

The chapter on designers and manufacturers is as complete as possible for the moment. We are always seeking out new information about companies we haven't been able to find. If any readers have knowledge about someone we haven't included, we'd appreciate hearing from them. Manufacturers' marks have been obtained from original pieces of jewelry, or reproduced from material given us by manufacturers. We've concentrated on the manufacturers who are most collectible now.

Following is a chapter about fakes and forgeries, which are even more of a problem than when we wrote the first edition. Next are care and repair hints and techniques, which should help collectors protect and preserve their pieces. As costume jewelry gets more expensive, it's particularly important to maintain the beauty of each piece with proper storage. The last decade chapter covers the Nineties, with photographs of many of today's most talented costume jewelers' pieces. Costume jewelry collections needn't be comprised of only vintage pieces—some of the most savvy collectors are buying the best of today to put away for tomorrow.

Our dealers and promoters section is greatly expanded. We contacted over one thousand people to find listings that would be appropriate. If we didn't know them personally, we asked for pertinent information regarding their inventory, and for the promoters, we asked the number of costume jewelry dealers who participated in their shows. Again, there are, no doubt, many more people out there who should be included in this section. Please contact us if you would like to be considered for the next edition.

The glossary and bibliography are meant for readers who want to expand their knowledge of professional terminology and literature on their favorite subject—"jools"! Please note, that while I tried to be as accurate as possible in regard to prices in the text and addresses and phone numbers in the reference chapters, some information was not available at the time this book went to press.

How It's Done in the First Place

Each piece of costume jewelry that's manufactured goes through many steps. Even jewelry made today using the advances brought on by new technology is still handled by at least four people. Swarovski, the company that for five generations has produced crystals (rhinestones) used in the finest costume jewelry, has been manufacturing its own line of jewelry since the mid Eighties. It uses the following procedure in creating a new design:

1. A master designer creates a detailed drawing.
2. Skilled artisans handcraft a sculptured model from the original design.
3. White metal is hand-casted into a custom mold replicating the original model.
4. Pieces are individually hand polished in preparation for the plating process.
5. A three-part plating process is performed: copper is applied as a sealer; nickel for a hard, shiny surface; and gold or rhodium is electroplated for the finish.
6. The stone-setter hand sets the crystal stones.

We interviewed Al Cerbo, vice president in charge of all manufacturing at Charisma, a Rhode Island company known for producing high-quality costume jewelry for a number of leading designers. Nick Reinone, the product development troubleshooter at Charisma, was Cerbo's teacher in the Seventies when they were both at Monet. Reinone, who contributed valuable information about the older

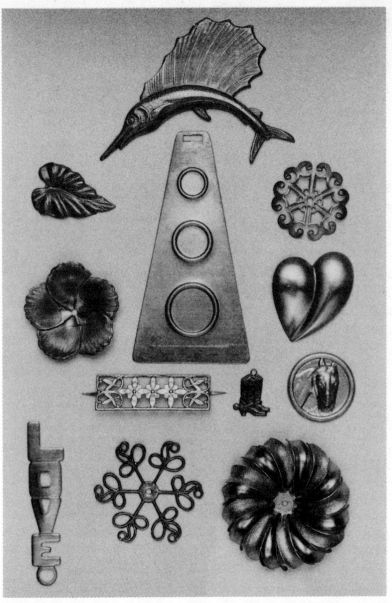

Brass stampings used in the manufacture of jewelry, 1920s–1970s. *Courtesy of Salvadore Tool & Findings, Providence, RI. Photograph by Kenneth Chen.*

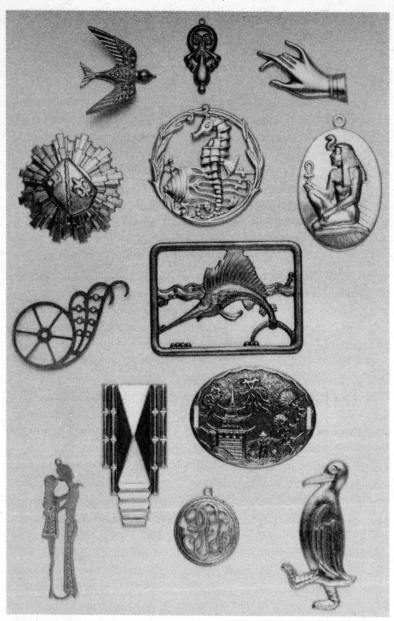

Brass stampings used in the manufacture of jewelry, 1920s–1970s. *Courtesy of Salvadore Tool & Findings, Providence, RI. Photograph by Kenneth Chen.*

methods of manufacturing, started in the manufacturing business the way many people do, as a polisher. He worked for Westminster Jewelry, a wholesaler, for eighteen years and for Monet for twenty-one years. He came out of retirement to lend his expertise to Charisma.

Cerbo started working as a young teenager for his mother, who had a little job shop. She did contract labor for various companies in Rhode Island, including gluing for Coro and assembly for Monet. While Cerbo was a student in the early Sixties, he went to work part-time at Monet. He first worked full-time as a polisher, then in the lacquer room, and then cleaning casts. He worked at Monet's first facility with a woman manager in the early Seventies.

Cerbo and Reinone have seen changes in manufacturing methods over the years. Cerbo recalled that when the Chernows ran Monet, all the backs of the jewelry were hand polished. Then in the Seventies, the Rotofinish machine used centrifugal force to burnish and polish the jewelry. In the Fifties, prong setting stones was replaced by gluing. They still used airplane glue, which wasn't as effective as the epoxies used today (epoxy is a two-part resin system that produces a more pliable, more secure setting for the stones). In the Seventies, epoxy painting replaced enameling, and companies greatly expanded their colored jewelry lines.

Enameling that was done in the Thirties was cured in ovens after it was hand painted on each piece. The enamel was a powder that was used on brass. The cavities were filled with the powder, which melted at 1,500 degrees, and filled in the spaces. The white metal pieces were all hand painted. Workers made twenty cents an hour. Today's epoxy paint is air dried for twenty-four hours and cured for seven days. It's still done all by hand—using a hypodermic needle and air pressure. The paint is put into a syringe and used to fill in the lines.

There's been an improvement in the pin backs. Previously the joint and catch were on one box; it was one piece of metal and the pin was already on it. Sometimes they were riveted on; now both the joints and catches get soldered on.

Rivets were used in the old Coro days, through the Fifties. Tool men at that time were making two or three dollars an hour; now they

Nettie Rosenstein Siamese dancer pin, shown next to original drawing by designer Lois Carol. *Jewelry and drawing courtesy of Dr. Raymond Carol. Photograph by Kenneth Chen.*

make fifty and sixty dollars an hour and one stamping tool can cost $3,500! In the old days a tool cost $150 at the most. White metal is 92% tin, some cadmium and lead. It also used to contain zinc. New rules coming in are attempting to eliminate the lead. Without the lead, it's difficult to give a good finish, according to Cerbo.

The plating was different in the past. In the Thirties and Forties, gold was cheap and the platers used a thick plating that lasted longer. Today plating can be as little as three millionths of an inch, as compared to twenty in the past.

Cerbo said that one of the biggest changes in the costume jewelry industry happened in the early Eighties, when large corporations started buying out the private, usually family-owned companies. Originally in Rhode Island, the immigrants from Europe created the jewelry with their hands—they were the artists. With the next generation that arose in the Fifties, there was less hand work and more automation. Once the corporations took over, the goal was to make the jewelry faster for less money. Before that, the goal was to make beautiful jewelry.

Today there are many immigrants involved in the field again, mostly from Central and South America. They come in as laborers who aren't trained for jewelry work. Cerbo has artists and model-makers at Charisma he has trained and promoted. He has taken people like Reinone and his mother out of retirement to teach the newcomers the old ways. He says, "Jewelry is jewelry, the basic methods haven't changed since the Thirties. My goal is to make the top-quality pieces."

Nettie Rosenstein knight pin, shown next to raw casting. *Jewelry and casting courtesy of Dr. Raymond Carol. Photograph by Kenneth Chen.*

Nettie Rosenstein blackamoor pin, shown next to original drawing by
designer Lois Carol. *Jewelry and drawing courtesy of Dr. Raymond Carol.
Photograph by Kenneth Chen.*

Jim Triano, also formerly of Monet, is the number-one quality
consultant at Charisma. He says, "Good quality is in the compo-
nents—how a piece of jewelry is put together. For an earring, it's
how a clip works, how it holds and balances. A necklace's quality is in
how it drapes, how it lies on the wearer's neck. Quality has to be
designed into a piece of jewelry—it's a combination of the design and
the materials. The original drawing, the weight of the piece, how it's
cut out—it all goes together to make an aesthetically pleasing piece."

COSTUME
JEWELRY
by
OSTBY & BARTON COMPANY

IF, as they say, art is a way of expressing one's feeling about things—then Style is the most intimate of all the arts.

And just because style is such a personal thing, the woman with a *flair* for costume is delighting in the new Costume Jewelry—with its vivid color, its infinite variety, its air of high personality.

She selects her jewelry to emphasize the dominant note of her costume. She cannot wear the characterless jewelry one sees everywhere.

But only in the little shops with their fortunate connections in the Rue de la Paix has she been able to find *individuality*—unless she had her Ring, her Brooch, her Pendant designed specially, and at prohibitive cost.

Some twelve months ago the eminent House of Ostby & Barton originated the idea of making Costume Jewelry available to women everywhere.

With designs created by the leading jewelry designers of America and Europe, this new Costume Jewelry is *individual* to the last shade of distinction, alive with character and color, and—*contemporary*.

Executed solely in genuine precious and semi-precious stones set in 14K yellow gold, green gold and white gold (*with the color and lustre of platinum*).

This distinguished jewelry may be had of representative costume shops and department stores in the larger cities, and of first class jewelers. Ask for it by name—*Costume Jewelry*.

OSTBY & BARTON COMPANY, PROVIDENCE, RHODE ISLAND

"Costume Jewelry by Ostby & Barton Company," a look at the "new Costume Jewelry" of 1917, with designs that are both "individual" and "contemporary." Precious and semiprecious stones are set in 14K yellow, green, and white gold. *Original advertisement courtesy of David Iovino.*

Pricing, or Read This Chapter First!

The question I've probably been asked the most since the first edition was published is "How do you arrive at a price for a particular piece of jewelry?" Actually, that is the polite form of the question. What people really want to know is either how come the prices are so high, or how come the prices are so low? Either way, my answer never seems to satisfy anyone. In the first edition, many of the pieces in the photographs were on loan from shops—the prices were on the price tags. But, as many of us know, in the antiques business there is always some flexibility in prices even in fancy antiques shops!

However, this time, many of the pieces we photographed are from dealers' and collectors' private collections. As one dealer/collector put it, sometimes her prices are based on the degree of unhappiness she'd feel if she sold the piece! Thank you, Robin Feldman! So, for example, if we give a price of $2,200 for the Eisenberg mermaid pin, it is perfectly valid because we know that one was recently sold for that amount. That doesn't mean that another mermaid can't be bought for $900—or less, with a little bit of luck. But by saying it's "worth" $2,200, the new dealer or collector will know that it is a special, rare, collectible, sought-after piece.

The problem here is that if we give an extremely wide price range and tell all the reasons one piece of jewelry can be worth so many different prices, the book would be interminably long. Since costume jewelry has no intrinsic value—the amount of gold, silver, and rhodium is negligible—the market value is based mostly on supply and demand. Other factors that affect prices range from the logical to the laughable. The ones we all know about are how much a piece cost the dealer or the original owner; how rare the piece is; its condition, design, and workmanship; and the specific designer or manufacturer, among others. The more creative pricing decisions include how long a dealer has had a piece, how badly the dealer needs to make a sale, whether the buyer is buying a single piece or twenty, and whether the buyer is a one-night stand or a steady beau, to mention just a few.

For the dealer, profit is never simply the difference between the selling price and the buying price. Dealers have to allow for all the costs of running a business—rent, phone, shipping, employees, and show fees, for example—plus the *time* it takes to buy pieces. Pricing a piece has to take all these expenses into consideration, and they vary from piece to piece. Some pieces show up by magic, others take a tremendous amount of effort to find. It's sort of a wonder anything ever gets priced!

So, readers, please know that the way these prices have been arrived at is first through the owners' evaluation of each piece photographed. Next, we talk to other dealers, as well as use our own experiences and research at the hundreds of shows and flea markets we attend, to find out recent prices at which pieces have been sold. Then we assess how factors such as geography, market fluctuations, and overall collectibility affect these prices. Finally, we give a price range that respects the owners' original evaluation and encompasses our appraisal.

Price guides invariably lead to the following scenario. You're at a show somewhere in rural America and there is a person selling some old farm tools and bric-a-brac. You spy a glittering piece of costume jewelry—it's an Eisenberg Original! You congratulate yourself for being so clever and finding a gem that's going to be very underpriced. The dealer quotes $350. When your jaw drops, "THE BOOK" is mentioned, as in "THE BOOK says it's worth $350." It doesn't matter whose book, it seems any one can always be used against you. When you try to *sell* a piece and you mention "THE BOOK," invariably the potential buyer says he or she just bought one for half the price and won't pay a penny more.

But the good part is, we all, buyers and sellers alike, look at the prices and can use them as a general guide, not gospel. Here are some of the problems of pricing the pieces in this book that had to be dealt with—this won't be the most exciting part of the book, but it might answer some questions. The process, for those of you who didn't contribute pieces or photographs, went something like this. First, we asked each person to evaluate their own pieces and to suggest a range, usually either what they'd buy and sell a piece for or what they'd charge either a dealer or a retail customer. Next, we would evaluate each piece based on the thousands of pieces we've seen and handled. If there was a huge discrepancy between the two evaluations, we'd try to strike a happy compromise.

Evaluating pieces poses certain types of dilemmas for their owners. Sometimes pieces are from private collections and are not for sale. Nevertheless, there is an approximate market value because someone else might have the same piece for sale. Another situation is one in which a piece is priced too high, so that everyone who has one or something similar will raise their prices, making it hard for the original collector to buy anything at low prices. But if a piece is valued too low, that same collector will not be able to get a decent price should the piece be offered for sale!

Knowing all these potential pitfalls, contributors to the book were still brave enough to allow prices to be published, and for that I am grateful. What would a price guide be without prices? Please always keep this in mind: these prices are suggestions, not covenants!

But How Old Is It?

For the first edition, in order to help collectors tell how old a piece is, we went to the source—Providence, Rhode Island. We found out that a fairly reliable method is to examine the functional parts—the closures, pin backs, earring backs, and clasps. That method works as long as the parts haven't been replaced with newer ones. We were shown how various manufacturing methods had changed over the years, but we also saw machinery that was over a hundred years old still producing stampings!

We saw stampings that were designed at the turn of the century and are still available to be used in modern jewelry. Settings have undergone changes; pavé, prong-set, gluing, nicking in—all can denote different decades. Most companies don't hand set stones anymore, but there are still those that do! To add to the confusion, we found that manufacturers can keep successful styles in their line for thirty or more years!

Revivals take place regularly—Victorian, Egyptian, Renaissance, Art Deco, Art Nouveau regularly have new incarnations. Even the most savvy dealers aren't right 100% of the time, in our experience. Some companies, such as Hollycraft, Chanel (sometimes), Christian Dior (sometimes), and Mimi di N (starting in the Eighties), actually stamped the date into the piece of jewelry. Others, such as Hobé, changed their logos from time to time and kept records of these changes and their corresponding decades (see the Hobé section in "Designers and Manufacturers We Know and Love"). Some pieces have a patent number stamped on the back—this method can be misleading, however, because it might be the earring back or the closure that was patented decades before the piece was actually produced.

The most fun way of learning the decades is to go to a library and spend lots of time looking at the old fashion magazines and jewelry manufacturers' trade magazines. It's a real kick to find an old advertisement or editorial that depicts a piece you own! Generally, the best way to learn is through hands-on experience. The quality of workmanship, the design, and the "feel" of a piece are often the best indicators of age.

> **NOTE:** There is a company that does not buy, sell, or appraise antiques. Its specialty is retrieving information relating to an antique's provenance, genealogy, and other pertinent knowledge that may be useful to dealers and collectors. The results are presented in report form, with a list of sources and a photocopy of relevant data, if possible. Their fee is $35 per hour with a three-hour minimum. For information, write Antique Researchers, P.O. Box 79, Waban, MA 02168; or call (617) 969-6238.

Fakes, Forgeries, and Reproductions

As a collectible gains in stature and worth, so does the possibility of skullduggery! When Eisenbergs fetched over $500, fakes started showing up in the marketplace. Jelly bellies went wild over the past couple of years, bringing prices up to a few thousand dollars for the rarest ones, and dealers were offered everything from brand-new pieces marked "Original Jelly Belly" to exact copies of Trifari sterling jellies *with* patent numbers intact. A bold move, indeed!

The patents probably have long run out on the old designs, and in the case of the really old pieces there may never have been patents or copyrights in the first place. So, legally, there may not be a problem, but from the collector's point of view, there's obviously a big issue and possibly a lot of money at stake. There's probably not a dealer around who hasn't made a bad buy—but usually only once. So, since it can happen to the most experienced dealer, the new collector or dealer needn't be embarrassed. Once it has been established that the piece isn't "right," it should be taken back to the person who sold it. (Manufacturers are usually very grateful if you bring the piece to their attention. They will attempt to trace the originator.) Here comes the tricky part. Assuming it was an honest mistake on the part of the seller, it can be righted. But if the buyer can't get anywhere with the seller, either by way of a refund or a credit, the only recourse is to take legal action. We know of at least one case that has gone to small claims court and was won by the innocent buyer. Unfortunately, it takes a lot of time and effort to gather expert opinions as evidence, as well as time in court.

The best way to avert this problem is to educate yourself—look at lots of pieces closely, examine the findings (pin backs, earring clips, chains, etc.) and the materials, look for signs of wear with a loupe (jeweler's magnifier), and examine manufacturer's marks, enameling, and stones. Your best assurance is knowing the seller and his or her reputation.

Reproductions are another story altogether and one that has a number of chapters. There are reproductions done by the same company who did the original pieces. For example, a number of companies have a "retro" line that attempts to re-create pieces that were done in the past. Miriam Haskell has a beautiful line that sells in the finest shops at very high prices. Each piece is made to order, by hand, using the same methods used for the past seventy years, sometimes using the original findings. The pearls are not the same as the originals and the pieces look a bit brighter. The same Miriam Haskell oval logo is used that was used in the 1950s. Trifari did a "retro" line of its Jewels of India, originally produced in the 1960s. The line was not shown very long in the stores and is hard to find today. Most of the pieces had a little *R* to show they were "retro" pieces, but I have also seen pieces that had just the usual Trifari imprint. Confusing? Kenneth Jay Lane produced a line of reproductions of 1960s pieces marked "KJL" with the year. Some companies, such as Ciner, Panetta, and Kenneth Jay Lane, continue to manufacture pieces as long as they sell, which could be thirty years. As some of you know, in 1992, I licensed my name to a company that reproduced vintage costume jewelry to be sold exclusively on QVC, a home shopping television network. Each piece was marked with my initials, "HM" or "HSM" and the year, so that it could never be confused with the originals. We were very careful to reproduce only those pieces that were unsigned or produced by companies that no longer existed. Fashion constantly reinvents itself, and reproductions or copies and "knock-offs" have always been part of the fashion game.

Taking Care of Costume Jewelry

It's happened to every collector or dealer. We bought a beautiful amethyst-and-pearl Victorian revival 1940s bracelet-and-necklace set at a flea market. As we unwrapped it at home, the pearls fell apart, losing their outer "pearlized" casings, exposing the inner beads. Unfortunately, the jewelry had reached its "critical threshold" somewhere between the flea market and our apartment.

Phyllis Magidson, associate curator of the Costume Collection of the Museum of the City of New York, said that prevention is the key, rather than trying to repair something after the damage has been done. If a collector plans to keep costume jewelry more than ten or fifteen years, and it's been exposed to normal wear and tear and temperature changes that may affect stones, materials, and plating, certain measures should be taken to protect it.

Any extreme that any material is exposed to will cause expansion and contraction, either from heat or moisture. All substances that are incorporated into a piece are affected. If rhinestone jewelry that had an adhesive used in setting the stones is discovered in Grandma's attic, chances are the stones will be loose. Even if there's no evidence of it at first, it should be checked very carefully before it's worn or sold. When it's brought into a different environment, the change in temperature may trigger a loosening of the stones. Jewelry may be perfectly fine up to a certain point and then whatever has been accumulating hits it, and changing the environment may just be the one factor that causes it to break down.

A noted conservator who works free-lance for major museums observes that since people originally considered costume jewelry as "cheap throwaway" it has an "inherent vice" that can give it a time bomb quality. Sometimes the material will fail on its own, no matter how it is treated. Some of the early plastics were made with an unstable formulation, which is also true of early adhesives. Always check prongs, if they exist, to make sure they are restraining the stones in case the adhesive gives out. Pieces with adhesives should not be dipped or cleaned with water. If the electroplating is not done well originally, delamination of the outer plating can occur or there can be migration of the precious metal exterior plating (gold or silver) into the base metal. Rubbing, through wear or using an abrasive cleaner, can harm the thin coating. The metal parts of costume jewelry are actually damaged more easily than is fine jewelry and require more care, not less.

Costume jewelry is particularly vulnerable to hostile environments. Lead was often used in its manufacture, making it susceptible to corrosion. Even something as seemingly harmless as storing lead-based jewelry in an oak drawer can lead to corrosion, due to the interaction of the high-acid oak with lead. When pieces are placed in a closed showcase for storage, it must be determined whether the case is generating volatile acids that can harm the jewelry. All metals should be protected from acid environments.

Self-closing plastic bags are fairly efficient in keeping out moisture. Silica gel is a further protection from dampness. Some plastics, however, exude fumes. The best way to store costume jewelry is to cover it with a soft material, such as a washed muslin that does not have sizing, starch, or surface finishes, or acid-free tissue. Then either wrap it loosely in plastic or store it in boxes. Acid-free tissue is made of abaca fiber and does not interact with materials used in jewelry. To buy it, contact your local museum. In addition to preservation, if a piece is wrapped in this manner and a stone should fall out, it will be easily found.

In general, don't wear costume jewelry on bare skin that's just been sprayed with perfume. Oils and chemicals in the perfume can cause damage to any kind of metal. When handling important pieces or ones that are designated to be preserved, use either white cotton gloves that are readily laundered (they can be purchased at photography supply stores) or plastic gloves that aren't treated with oil or lanolin-based emollients. In this way, no traces of body oils or perspiration are transferred to the various materials that make up the jewelry. Natural body chemistry can affect all of the materials adversely. Plastic pearls or stones cannot take much abuse and are damaged by exposure to excessive light and ultraviolet rays, which can cause them to yellow. When glass is manufactured, it is produced under high temperatures, then annealed. If it is not annealed properly, it can fracture very easily due to internal stress. In costume jewelry, glass is cut and then polished, which adds duress to the stone. If it is annealed incorrectly and then manipulated, the stones can be damaged by a slight bump or even a change in temperature, so glass stones should be well protected. If a piece is harmed, it's a good idea to backtrack and try to figure out what caused it in order to prevent a recurrence. Incorrect storage, a hostile environment, or mishandling can lead to serious damage to a piece that cannot be replaced.

Repair of Costume Jewelry

To fix or not to fix is often the question. Each piece has to be looked at individually and a decision has to be made about how damaged it is and what is important to preserve. From simply replacing missing stones to soldering, replating, or re-enameling, the answer depends on many variables. If a piece needs professional attention, see a professional conservator, who normally charges upwards of $25 per hour. Contact your local historical society or museum for a list of conservators in your area.

The first rule is: don't buy it if it's broken, unless you intend to wear it or sell it "as is." The materials used in costume jewelry are more difficult to handle and more fragile than those in precious jewelry, and repairs are more complicated. Generally it is difficult to find someone to solder a broken piece of costume jewelry because repairs on base metal are risky. Replating can be done, but a good plating job can be costly because it is necessary to clean the piece thoroughly and check for failures in the original plating. Few people today do repainting or re-enameling, and it's very hard to match the original colors.

Costume jewelry has two functions: adornment and investment. Today's rising prices verify that often it's not a casual purchase. Making major repairs changes aspects of the jewelry that may change the value.

Here's some advice from a restoration expert at the Metropolitan Museum of New York:

Always use a conservative approach. Look at something carefully before you do anything. For example, when cleaning a piece with an enamel finish, an unnoticed chip can get caught and pulled off, ruining the enamel. Buy a loupe (magnifier) at either a jewelers' or photographers' supply store and use it to examine every piece. Replacing missing stones is usually not a problem if it entails round, square, or marquise shapes. They can usually be found at hobby shops or, if you live in a large city, at a supplier in the costume jewelry wholesale district. An easy way to build up your own little storehouse of rhinestones is to buy inexpensive bits and pieces of broken jewelry at yard sales or flea markets and save them for the stones. When you replace stones, be careful to match both size and color, because even with clear stones, if a stone is too gray or too yellow it stands out and will decrease the value of the piece. Many dealers use cyanoacrylate (Krazy Glue), which is not very good in an alkaline environment such as glass, so that eventually it breaks down and the glass stone will fall out. Epoxy is longer lasting, although it tends to yellow. Better quality epoxies discolor less. Two common mistakes are using too much adhesive and not cleaning it up properly afterward. Use acetone or a solvent after setting the stone to remove any excess. If plastics are involved, test the acetone on a part that doesn't show to make sure it doesn't ruin it. Do not use acetone on Bakelite.

To replace a stone, use either a pair of jeweler's tweezers or wet the tip of your finger, pick up the stone, and carefully drop it into its setting that already has a drop of glue or epoxy in it. For foil-backed stones whose foil has begun to erode, don't attempt to remove or replace the foil. When the original foil is in place, even if damaged, there is an indication of what the original craftsmanship had been.

For metal that is tarnished, first try polishing it by using a clean cotton cloth. An old, clean, soft T-shirt is perfect. A lot of dirt and tarnish will come off by just gently rubbing it. Use restraint and don't handle silver too much. Don't use an instant dip, it might be slightly acid and harmful to the metal. If delamination of the plating has occurred and solution gets into that area, it can further destroy the plating and create corrosion. If a dip is used for some reason, wash the piece immediately afterward with distilled water and dry it thoroughly. Use a hair dryer on the lowest setting. Use the least abrasive silver cleaners. Baking soda or other abrasives can put tiny lines into the surface, which ultimately gives a buffed or satin finish rather than a shiny one.

When jewelry has a patina, it is an oxidation that means part of the surface has oxidized and if it is removed, part of the actual piece is being removed. The more often an oxidized piece is cleaned, the more surface metal is being removed.

If a piece shows some corrosion, use dental tools, a loupe, and either an eraser or a cotton swab to lightly brush the surface and knock off some grains. Next, with a slightly damp cotton swab, use distilled or filtered water or alcohol, and go over it again. Dry it at once with the other end of the swab. When using a cotton swab, keep one side dry and one side wet so the piece can be worked on with the wet side and dried immediately.

Major repairs may change aspects of a piece and therefore change the value. As collecting costume jewelry becomes more important and more highly regarded, the original marks of wear may add value rather than detract from it. In the future, as more superior and technically advanced ways are developed to repair and restore pieces, we may find that what we are doing today is irreversible. If someone buys a fabulous Forties pin to go with a new suit, it should be treated carefully. However, if a person is interested in establishing a collection for investment, or as a legacy for future generations *or* as a donation to the costume department of a museum, a different approach should be taken. At this moment costume jewelry is making the transition from use to value, so a different standard in the approach to preservation and restoration may have to be explored and adopted. Some pieces may transcend their functional or decorative use and be put away as collectibles.

Norman Crider, a well-respected dealer in Manhattan, says that he never re-enamels or regilds a piece of costume jewelry. He either doesn't buy a piece that's not in good condition or he leaves it in the state it's in. He doesn't think there's anything wrong in re-enameling if it makes the piece look nicer and the buyer wants to wear it. Crider says costume jewelry is to wear and enjoy. When it comes to reselling, it would be less valuable if it's been redone. He lets things keep their original patina, but he does replace stones, since they are constantly falling out. Again, your point of view on repair depends on your frame of reference for costume jewelry, adornment or investment.

NOTE: The following companies will repair their own jewelry. For other manufacturers, contact the customer service department to inquire about the repair policy. Most manufacturers are in Providence, Rhode Island; Attleboro, Massachusetts; and New York City.

Carolee
(203) 629-1139, ext. 238
Call before sending jewelry.

Chanel
Chanel jewelry that needs repair
should be taken to the closest Chanel
boutique for evaluation and repair.

Christian Dior
(800) 659-3269
The company will repair old and
new Christian Dior jewelry. Call
and a mailing label will be sent.

Ciner
Customer Service
20 West 37th Street
New York, NY 10018
(212) 947-3770
Call first for authorization.

Miriam Haskell Co.
(212) 764-3332
Call first to make arrangements to
either bring or send in the piece to
be repaired; an estimate will be
given, minimum charge is $50.

Monet
Customer Service
2 Lonsdale Avenue
Pawtucket, RI 02860
(401) 728-9800

Napier
Customer Service
230 Berlin Street
East Berlin, CT 06023
(800) 243-3106

Robert Lee Morris
409 West Broadway
New York, NY 10012
(212) 431-9405

Yves Saint Laurent
Return jewelry to the store
where it was purchased or
to any store that sells Yves
Saint Laurent jewelry. They will
contact the company. Pieces are
shipped to Paris for repair.

Designers and Manufacturers
We Know and Love

If we had all the time in the world, we're convinced we'd be able to research all the mystery companies that intrigue us. One of the best parts about writing this book is talking to all the people who've been involved in this industry. The owners, designers, manufacturers, managers, salespeople, and their relatives all have interesting stories to tell. We're discovered new information about old companies, researched companies we didn't know existed in the first edition, and laid the groundwork for the next edition. Manufacturers' marks are shown with each company's write-up.

In addition to the companies we've written about, the following designers and manufacturers are collectible now or have the potential to be (this is just a partial list, we are constantly discovering new and exciting designers):

ARPAD (Senior)   Coro
Fred A. Block   Lilly Daché
Cadoro   R. DeRosa
Calvaire   Dujay
Hattie Carnegie   Charles Elkaim
Oleg Cassini   Eugéne
Castlecliff   Fabiola
CIS (France)   Freirich
R. F. Clark/Wm. de Lillo   Florenza
Coppola e Toppo (Italy)   Jack Gilbert

Givenchy
Leo Glass
HAR
Hollycraft
House of Joy
Jonné
Korda
Lanvin
Line Vautrin (France)
Maison de Fou
Mazer/Mazer Bros./Jomaz
Ben Meltzer
Metalcraft
Mosell
Nucci
Pennino
Roger Jean Pierre

Rebajes
Regency
Réja
Renoir/Matisse
Richelieu
Nettie Rosenstein
Sandor/Sandor Goldberger
Roger Scemama (France)
Adele Simpson
Staret
Sterling Button Co.
Olga Tritt
Van S
Vêndome
Woloch (France)
Zentall

If any readers have any knowledge about companies we haven't written about, please contact the author in care of the publisher.

CAROLEE

Architect Carolee Friedlander got her start designing jewelry at her kitchen table, making necklaces and bracelets by hand for her friends and family. In 1973, she founded Carolee Designs, Inc., and went on to create a multimillion-dollar fashion jewelry company. In 1992, she celebrated her twentieth anniversary with a traveling retrospective exhibition and limited edition collection. Her styles ranged from classic pearls and Bulgari-style collars to themed charm bracelets and replicas of the Duchess of Windsor's collection. The limited edition collection consisted of ten designs, including a poodle chatelaine, a jaguar, a fountain pen, and an assortment of jeweled animals. Each design was produced in a limited edition of 1,500 pieces.

In 1989, in a protest against the slaughter of elephants, Carolee created a resin material that replicated the look and feel of authentic ivory. In special "Save the Elephant" promotions, 10% of all sales were donated to Wildlife Conservation International. In the spring of

Carolee Friedlander, founder of Carolee Designs, Inc.

1991, Carolee introduced pearls that coordinated with skin and hair tones, much as they did in the 1920s. In the spring of 1992, Carolee created dog pins, with a percentage of sales donated to the ASPCA.

On her fiftieth birthday, which was celebrated with a biking trip to France, Carolee was inspired to create pins of grape bunches and champagne bottles.

Carolee's tips for wearing jewelry:

• If your face is round, stick with shapes that are long, oval, and square. If your face is long, choose a big button earring. If you have a square face, stay away from anything angular. The oval face can comfortably wear any shape.

• Use your skin tone as a guide for makeup and accessories. Peachy or creamy white pearls are right for warm-toned skin. For tan or dark complexions, select gold dust and matte gold jewelry. Cool tones look best with black, white, and platinum jewelry.

CHANEL

Chanel

CHANEL

Gabrielle Chanel, known as "Mademoiselle" to her colleagues and "Coco" to her friends, was one of the most famous designers of all time. Long before fashion was the hot topic it is today, Mme. Chanel became an internationally known trendsetter.

According to Chanel, Inc., Mme. Chanel went to Paris in 1909 to escape from both her sad childhood and provincial boredom. There she designed hats for her friends. In 1912, she opened Chanel Modes on rue Cambon in Paris, where well-known actresses and fashionable women became her clients, quickly turning the shop into a success. In 1914, she introduced clothing made of jersey in her shop at Deauville. Previously, jersey material had been used only for men's work clothing. Her knitwear creations set off a design revolution. Later, in Biarritz, in the first couture house under the Chanel name, she presented her innovative collections of loosely fitting clothes, designed for ease of movement. The business soon grew to a staff of sixty seamstresses!

In 1921, Mme. Chanel opened a still-standing boutique at 31 rue Cambon in Paris, with salons decorated entirely in beige. Her simple decor remains a hallmark of the House of Chanel today. She also designed accessories and jewelry to go with her clothing. In the same year, Mme. Chanel launched Chanel No. 5 perfume. In 1929, she showed a brooch worn on her trademark beret and it became part of the Chanel look, along with the two-tone shoe and longer skirts that covered the knee. In the 1930s, *Vogue* magazine in the United States described the Chanel philosophy as a "total look"; everything could be bought at one boutique—a revolutionary concept.

In 1934, Chanel first introduced the combination of multicolored glass stones, chains, and pearls to be worn with daytime sportswear. Count Fulco di Verdura created jewelry for Chanel that incorporated hand-poured glass and designed distinctive plastic cuffs with Austrian glass in the shape of a Maltese cross.

In 1939, Mme. Chanel designed a handbag made of quilted jersey fabric that had a chain strap to be worn over the shoulder. Up until that time only handbags had been carried. Later in 1939, with the coming of World War II, Mme. Chanel retired to live in Switzerland.

Mme. Chanel was quite well-known in Paris and counted among her close friends millionaires as well as the best-known artists and poets of the 1920s and 1930s. Her private residences on the Faubourg St. Honore and "La Pausa" in Roquebrune were often the sites of stimulating gatherings of her friends, among whom were Colette, Max Jacob, Serge Lifar, Picasso, Dali, Georges Auric, Winston Churchill, and the Duke of Windsor. She designed costumes for Jean Cocteau's plays and the Diaghilev ballets. She was a patron of the arts, secretly supporting "The Group of Six," a musician's organization, Diaghilev, and Igor Stravinsky.

In 1954, at the age of seventy-one, Mme. Chanel returned to Paris and reopened the rue Cambon salon, creating the clothing and jewelry we associate with her name today. She continued to design suits with bordered jackets and gold buttons, simple silk blouses, quilted handbags with braided leather and gold chains, beige shoes with dark tips that lengthen the leg, and the wonderful classic costume jewelry that is so highly prized by today's collectors.

Mme. Chanel died in 1971, just days before her successful final collection. She had once said, "Luxury is not the opposite of poverty; it is the opposite of vulgarity."

In 1983, Karl Lagerfeld, who had been assistant to Pierre Balmain and artistic director of Jean Patou, became the designer for Chanel haute couture, ready-to-wear, and accessories. Under his aegis, Chanel designs are now available in more than fifty boutiques in major cities throughout the world. Chanel costume jewelry, particularly the couture pieces using *paté-de-verre* (also known as "poured glass") made by Gripoix are collected in both the United States and Europe.

> **NOTE:** Fulco Santostefano della Cerda, duc di Verdura, designed his first line of costume jewelry for Chanel in 1926. Large crosses, orders, and bead necklaces, done in Byzantine style, were set with a combination of semiprecious stones, simulated pearls, and glass. In 1938, he met Paul Flato and joined his company in Hollywood, where he designed precious jewelry. In 1939, Verdura opened his own shop in New York City, backed by Vincent Astor and Cole Porter.

CHRISTIAN DIOR

In 1947, Christian Dior revolutionized the fashion world with his "New Look." It was characterized by long flaring skirts, fitted waists, and softly rounded shoulders and hips. It heralded a return to femininity that was vastly different from the short, narrow skirts that were worn during the severe war years. In 1955, Dior signed a licensing agreement with the Grosse family to manufacture jewelry. Christian Dior costume jewelry was also manufactured by Kramer, Maer and Schreiner. Grosse pieces made for Christian Dior have a tag with the Christian Dior name and year of manufacture.

Collectors avidly seek out Dior pieces, particularly elaborate evening necklaces and earrings produced prior to the Seventies.

CINER

In 1892, Ciner was founded by Emanuel Ciner, the grandfather of current owner Pat Hill. Ciner's first location was on Maiden Lane in New York City. Up until the Thirties, the company worked only in gold and platinum, using precious stones. Then it switched to costume jewelry, using sterling silver and, later, white metal. The same approach to design and manufacturing was used in costume as in real jewelry. The Ciner look has always been that of "real" jewelry that could have come from any of the finest jewelry stores. Ciner ran the company until he was ninety-four years old and then turned it over to sons Irwin and Charles. In the late Seventies, Pat and David Hill took over the business, and now their two children work with them.

Everything is manufactured at the company's current location, which is midtown in the costume jewelry district in New York City. There the designing, modelmaking, casting, finishing, and selling take place. The Hills and their sales manager create new designs, along with a free-lance designer who renders the ideas so the modelmaker can work from them. Many of the original designs from Pat's father's time are still in the line. Some go back to the Forties and Fifties. If something is beautiful and classic, it stays in the line for as long as it sells. The styles range from very tailored to very elaborate pieces with glitter and rhinestone. Ciner puts a tremendous effort into maintaining the quality of the line. All the materials are the finest available, including Austrian rhinestones, European glass cabochons, and simulated pearls that are made to the company's specifications. Ciner uses no plastic. Every piece is signed "Ciner" with the same logo they've used since they started.

The Ciner customer is upscale and classic; not funky or trendy. Often it's the woman who owns precious jewelry but doesn't take it with her when she's traveling. The company sells to finer department stores and specialty stores. The story goes that Elizabeth Taylor once bought $20,000 worth of Ciner jewelry at one time!

EISENBERG

$\mathcal{E}$ Eisenberg
ORIGINAL

Eisenberg Ice   **EISENBERG ICE**

The Eisenberg Original dress company was founded in 1914 by current owner Karl Eisenberg's grandfather, Jonas Eisenberg. Large rhinestone dress clips were manufactured in New York to accessorize the dresses. The first year the dresses were shown, the chairman of Nordstrom's called and suggested the clips be sold separately since they were being stolen right off the dresses! The dresses were manufactured until 1958. Until that time, if a store had the Eisenberg dress franchise, it was able to get the Eisenberg jewelry franchise. There were about five hundred stores at that time that sold both the dresses and the jewelry. When Eisenberg went out of the dress business, all the stores who had wanted to carry the jewelry were now able to, and the number of stores carrying Eisenberg jewelry grew from five hundred to about two thousand in just a few years.

In 1973–1974, Eisenberg created and manufactured enameled artists' pieces, including Braque, Chagall, Miró, Calder, Vasarely, Picasso, and the clothing designer Pucci. The *Chicago Tribune* featured a story about the jewelry's being sold at the Art Institute and it sold out the first day it was exhibited.

Eisenberg Original clips and pins were produced from 1930 to 1945, and Eisenberg noted that they were compatible with the clothing of that time. Unfortunately, his mother and grandmother didn't save any of the old pieces and he had to buy Eisenberg Originals at an antiques shop for his daughters and daughter-in-law!

Eisenberg said that the big commercial pieces sold exceptionally well and many were made. The whimsical pieces such as the mermaid, the baskets, the angels, and various animals did not sell as well and fewer pieces were made. Of course, it is these pieces that today's collectors seek and pay the biggest prices for, in some cases up to $3,000. Eisenberg believes the next Eisenberg collectible is the 1992 Christmas pin.

Various trademarks have been used: the earliest pieces were not signed; from 1930 to the mid Forties "Eisenberg Original" was used; in the early Forties a script capital *E* was used alone or in conjunction with "Eisenberg Original"; "Eisenberg Ice" was used from the late Forties on, with most pieces rhodium plated; "Eisenberg" in block letters was used in the Seventies.

HOBÉ

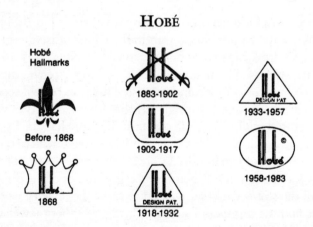

It was Paris in the late 1800s. The Eiffel Tower was completed and Jacques Hobé, a master craftsman and fine jewelrymaker, had a revolutionary new concept in jewelry. At that time, only the very rich owned precious jewelry. Jacques decided to manufacture fine jewelry at affordable prices using new manufacturing techniques.

His son William continued his tradition and brought his art and craftsmanship to America, where it was well received from New

York to Hollywood. Film stars and producers appreciated his creativity in both costume and jewelry design. The jewelry was designed by members of his family, except for one designer, Lou Vici, who was with the company from the Thirties through the early Seventies. Today, William's sons Donald and Robert and grandson James continue to produce fine Hobé jewelry.

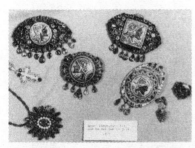 

The pins in this photograph are all Phoenician art, designed by William Hobé, who made the first pieces himself on the bench. This design line was begun in 1926 and ran through 1938. The back material is low-grade steel, which is soft enough to inlay the gold and silver wires that make up the design. The stones are French Soudais, all unfoiled. Since these stones are clear, the cuts had to be made finely to retain the light and not have it run from the back. The filigree is all sterling silver twisted wire. The gallery wire around the item was totally hand formed and made of silver or brass. The earring on the lower right is of the same period and workmanship as the lockets in the other photo. The earring on the upper right is unidentified. The necklace on the lower left, ca. 1968–1974, uses twisted silver wire, red and blue rhinestones, and a center stone of French *strass* surrounded by small, clear rhinestones. The garnet cross is from the Sixties. *Jewelry and photograph courtesy of Don Hobé, Hobé Cie Ltd.*

The lockets in this photograph, made in the Sixties, are brass with hard-fired enamel, cultured pearls, and garnets. They are part of a large collection created by Robert Hobé, who specialized in the firing of enamels, which were very much in the mode in the Sixties. The bracelets were manufactured from 1946 to the late 1950s. They illustrate the very careful soldering, twisting, and weaving done in the fine wire and mesh for which the Hobé company was famous. In its designs of this period, Hobé used, almost exclusively, semiprecious stones such as onyx, chrysoprase, garnet, lapis, malachite, jasper, cultured pearls, and labradorite. The bracelet at the top employs onyx with cultured pearls. The middle bracelet uses green chrysoprase, and the bracelet at the bottom uses enamels, cultured pearls, and garnets. Don Hobé, the designer of these pieces, emphasized the detail and labor-intensive winding of wire and mesh, which was unique in the industry at that time. *Jewelry and photograph courtesy of Don Hobé, Hobé Cie Ltd.*

Ann Miller wearing Hobé jewelry. *Photograph courtesy of Hobé Cie Ltd.*

Iradj Moini

Iradj Moini started out in the field of architecture and was slowly drawn to designing jewelry. He designed the runway jewelry for Oscar de la Renta's shows in the late Eighties and then began to make pieces for his own clients. When Oscar produced a special show for the five-hundredth anniversary of the Dominican Republic, Iradj created a tropical look with fantastic fruits and parrots. The pieces Iradj designs now for Oscar's shows, to accessorize the gowns, are quite dramatic and showy.

Iradj's jewelry is made of brass and copper, with glass stones from Austria and Czechoslovakia. No two pieces are exactly the same, because each piece is handmade. Even in a pair of earrings one is slightly different from the other. Each piece takes from one day to two weeks to make.

The jewelry is collected by some fabulous women, among them Maria Fleix and Marie-Helene Rothschild. Iradj designs for women who like an exotic look with a multidimensional feeling for fashion. His customers are women from many cultures and backgrounds. Iradj's unique jewelry has a universal appeal.

JOSEFF-HOLLYWOOD

JOSEFF HOLLYWOOD

In the early Thirties, Eugene Joseff worked in the advertising field and dabbled in jewelry design. He made his own models out of paste, and tried unsuccessfully to sell his ideas to the movie studios. It took a year and a half to make his first sale—a rhinestone bracelet and four buttons! By the end of the Thirties, Joseff's designs had become so sought after he could hardly keep up with the orders. Sometimes costume designers built entire costumes around his fabulous jewelry. He was known for doing extensive research on ancient jewelry designs in order to create accurate pieces for historical films.

Joseff used the best stones from Czechoslovakia and Austria. His skilled craftspeople worked with wood, glass, tin, platinum, gold, silver, and precious stones, as well as plastics. He formulated a special antiqued gold and silver plating that didn't reflect the movie lights. By using injection-molded acetate, he reproduced carved ebony and ivory antique jewelry. For the very ornate pieces, it was often necessary to use a plastic compound because metal would have been too heavy to wear. Virginia Bruce's fourteen-pound headdress in MGM's *The Great Ziegfeld* was made of pear-shaped jewels of cast transparent resin. In the same film a chorus girl wore a $2,000 costume, designed by Adrian, that consisted of a thousand pear-shaped transparent cast resin drops.

Joseff cleverly worked out a plan to rent, rather than sell, his jewelry to the movie studios, in order to maintain extensive archives. Mrs. Joseff has over three million pieces in the current rental library.

In 1937, Joseff developed a commercial line to be sold in retail stores, based partly on pieces he designed for the movies.

At his peak, Joseff was producing 90% of Hollywood's jewelry for motion pictures. He was influenced by forms that occurred in nature, as well as Renaissance designs. Seashells, flowers, and animals were recurring motifs in his jewelry.

Joseff's untimely death in 1948 did not end his imaginative line of costume jewelry. His wife, Joan Castle Joseff—or J.C., as she is known—continued to produce and sell pieces to fine department stores in the United States. In 1991, she began selling pieces to Harrod's in London, because her pieces had become very popular in England and Europe. Her business ability was such that *Fortune* singled her out as an outstanding woman executive, and in 1955, she received a lifetime membership in the Women of the Motion Picture Industry Association. Her citation read, in part: ". . . for the contribution she has made to the entire motion picture industry through her creative ability, conscientious research, and historical accuracy."

Eugene Joseff with jeweled armor he created for Douglas Fairbanks, Jr., in *Sinbad the Sailor*. *Photograph by Seawell, Paul A. Hesse Studios, courtesy of Joan Castle Joseff.*

Old designs using the original molds and stampings, as well as newer, often Renaissance-styled jewelry, are sold today. The pieces that were designed on a massive scale in order to be visible to movie audiences are appealing to today's collectors. Not only movies but television shows such as "Murder, She Wrote," "Dynasty," and "Mission: Impossible" used Joseff jewelry. Today, jewelry is just 5% of the Joseff company's business; the rest is in manufacturing precision parts for aircraft and missiles.

NOTE: According to Mrs. Joseff, the company stamped the jewelry "Joseff-Hollywood" in block letters through the Forties. Later, the jewelry was marked "Joseff" in script, either stamped into the piece or on a tag that was soldered on.

KENNETH JAY LANE

In 1993, Kenneth Jay Lane celebrated thirty years of being in the costume jewelry business. His name has always been synonymous with glamour and he summed up his philosophy like this:

> Elegance, luxury, and good taste never go out of style. I believe that every woman has the right to live up to her potential to be glamorous. I try to help her achieve that by creating affordable, beautiful jewelry that enhances her femininity.

Kenneth was born in Detroit and earned a degree in advertising design from the Rhode Island School of Design. He worked for Roger Vivier designing shoes, and occasionally embellished them with rhinestone ornaments. From these experimental beginnings, Kenneth's company grew to include twenty-two shops in the United States, England, and Europe. He has a reputation for designing jewelry for some of the most beautiful and well-known women in the

Kenneth Jay Lane. *Photograph courtesy of Kenneth Jay Lane.*

world, including the Duchess of Windsor, Jacqueline Onassis, Elizabeth Taylor, and Ivana Trump.

Lane talked about former First Lady Barbara Bush, who always wore her signature Kenneth Jay Lane three-strand pearls:

> Lots of women have always worn three strands of pearls. I don't think C. Z. Guest would take a bath without hers! When George Bush was vice president, Barbara called and asked if she could come to my showroom. Katy Aga Khan had given her some of my jewelry as a present. She was absolutely adorable—and that's when she started wearing my "poils"! She wore them with her Scaasi gown to the Inaugural Ball and now they're in the Smithsonian. She was the first First Lady to insist on having the designer's names featured. The day of the ceremony when she gave her inaugural costume to the Smithsonian, she gave a little lunch for Arnold Scaasi, Judith Lieber, whose bag she had carried, and me. Lunch was lovely.

Lane and this author are currently writing a book together about his work.

MARCEL BOUCHER

Sandra Boucher, well-known jewelry designer and teacher, related the history of the Marcel Boucher company:

In 1925, jeweler Marcel Boucher arrived in New York from Paris, and went to work for Cartier. When he left, he got a job designing shoe buckles. At that time, all jewelry was designed flat, without high modulation. Boucher started his own firm in the Thirties, with his first designs an extraordinary group of bird pins, made with colored rhinestones and bright enamels. Nothing like them had ever been done before. The pins were three-dimensional and included an ornate bird of paradise. With just six different designs, Saks Fifth Avenue gave him an order for $20,000 to $30,000!

Boucher kept his company small in order to maintain quality control, with about eighty employees. He did the designing and his partner was the modelmaker and salesperson.

In 1947, Sandra Boucher left France and moved to New York. Her background was also in fine jewelry. She was interested in learning about costume jewelry, so she joined the Marcel Boucher firm in 1949 and stayed with them until 1958, designing jewelry and selecting stones. In 1960, she left to become the head designer at Tiffany, later to return to Boucher and "marry the boss."

MIMI DI N

Mimi di Nascemi, originally from Palermo, Sicily, and from the same family as the famous jeweler Fulco di Verdura, was graduated from the Philadelphia Museum School with a degree in silversmithing and jewelry. While she was in school in the early Fifties, she studied ecclesiastical silversmithing with the renowned Dutch artist Rudolf Brom, who invited her to be his assistant when he taught at the Wichita Art Association.

In 1954, Mimi entered a competition for foreign art students who wanted to study in Paris and, along with a German student, won a scholarship to study for one year at L'Ecole National Superior des Arts Decoratifs, a well-known secondary art school. There she earned a diploma in silversmithing and jewelry and studied wrought iron, metalworking design, and rendering.

While still a student in Philadelphia, Mimi was hired to work for a manufacturer who had the license to produce Schiaparelli jewelry, where she learned the techniques of manipulation. When Mimi finished school and went to New York, she attracted the attention of Diana Vreeland, who introduced her to clothing designer Arnold Scaasi for the purpose of starting a jewelry company together. In the late Fifties, Mimi and Scaasi became partners in Jewels by Scaasi. Next Mimi worked for Brania, a New York bead house, and for a while there was a Brania/Mimi di N label. In 1962, Mimi started her own company, Mimi di N.

Mimi's concept was to start a company that would be run like a European concern by building a library of designs from which she could draw all the time. In her factory she had designs and molds and samples that accumulated year after year, in the same way that English or French or other continental companies functioned. The designs were not created for one season and then discarded. Mimi created a body of work, not "throwaway chic." She produced then and continues to produce what she calls "artisanal" designs.

Mimi di N talked about one of her favorite subjects—costume jewelry:

> An original design is not a novelty, it's worth infinitely more than that; it's a minor work of art. I adore costume jewelry but I do not enjoy a flashy novelty. The philosophy of transiency is a merchandising and advertising gimmick. It's not a true workshop or artisan's type of activity. Someone who really works at something seriously puts a tremendous amount of effort and love into it. It's like Tiffany glass or the work of a Swedish silversmith like Count Bernadotte. It doesn't matter if the material is precious or not, it's what the artisan does with the material that counts.

There's a healthy trend in fashion now in America. Some of the better sportswear designers have adopted a theme, which is to use good fabric in a simple way, producing "investment dressing." There is a cumulative and longer-lasting philosophy behind it rather than the flashy, trendy, instantaneous and then deader-than-a-doornail-in-five-minutes method. By producing something well made and beautiful, and intrinsically valuable in the way the materials are handled, and by using genuine fibers and fabrics, they have brought stability into the product and the market.

I aspire to achieve the same philosophy in making jewelry out of base metals. It is beautifully made and could just as easily be cast in sterling silver or gold. The material has no bearing on the workmanship. My jewelry is polished, enameled, finished, refined, and put together by hand after the molding process. It has an "investment" feel about it.

Costume jewelry is so indicative of the moment in time it is created. It evolves because, although the criteria for making the product remain the same, the interpretation of the product changes with the evolution of the era. Costume jewelry becomes a marvelous reflection of the time. Since glass, plastic, tin, and other materials are not as expensive as precious metal and real jewels, they allow the designer to exaggerate a bit and be more lavish without fear of exceeding the purchaser's budget. The designer can be more *au courant* and expressive of the period. Collectors enjoy jewelry from the past because it is truly a mirror of the moment.

Two distinct types of manufacturers are emerging. One is more distinctive and collectible because of the individual creator's own mark, vision, and type of design. The other is the skillful *copiste*, who makes copies and furnishes well-made imitations.

I predict more joyfulness in the future of costume jewelry! What was good about it in the past is even better now. It's always valid as a form and as an expression of the wearer. Humankind has always sought adornment, and costume jewelry is not as expensive as precious metals and stones and is an art form that will never die.

MIRIAM HASKELL

In 1924, petite, stylish Miriam Haskell created a new concept—fashion jewelry as an accessory to fashion and part of a woman's total appearance. At that time, most fashionable women wore real jewelry. Ms. Haskell was influenced by her friend Coco Chanel, who paved the way for costume jewelry to be accepted by well-dressed women in Paris. Her friends in the fashion world were impressed with her designs and encouraged her to open a small shop in the modish McAlpin Hotel in New York City. Some of New York's best-known and best-dressed women bought Miriam Haskell designs. The jewelry came in pretty boxes with her name inscribed in black in an Art Deco–style typeface. She also used silver labels with her distinctive logo printed in black. Her innovative and feminine designs were often inspired by natural motifs such as flowers and shells. Her success at the McAlpin led to a second shop and quite a large following among the chic women of New York.

By 1926, Ms. Haskell's creations were sought by retailers, and she established the Miriam Haskell company with a wholesale manufacturing division. From the first pieces, and even today, Miriam Haskell costume jewelry has always been made by hand, never mass-produced. Pieces made prior to the late Forties were unsigned but clearly recognizable by the fine quality workmanship and distinctive materials, as well as their look. Glass beads and tiny simulated seed pearls from Japan were manipulated on high-tensile brass wire to form delicate flowers and abstract designs. The finest cut rhinestones, beads, and findings were brought in from France and Italy. Ms. Haskell often used the patriotic colors red, white, and blue for her jewelry.

After 1953, Frank Hess, who was Ms. Haskell's protégé and assistant, continued to design the costume jewelry when she no longer could, due to illness. He and later successors adhered to Ms. Haskell's design concepts. In 1958, Sanford Moss joined Haskell Jewels, Ltd., as manager. In 1983, he became vice president and in 1984 purchased the company from Morris Kinsler, who had bought it from Ms. Haskell's brother, Joe. In 1990, Frank Fialkoff bought the company from Moss.

Haskell Jewels, Ltd., has introduced its Retro Collection, which is an interpretation of vintage pieces. In some instances, the pieces are reproductions using the original findings. This collection is the top of

The Miriam Haskell Boutique "Le Bijou de l'Heure" at the McAlpin Hotel, New York City, 1926. *Original photograph courtesy of Haskell Jewels, Ltd.*

the line, selling for up to $2,000. It is sold in the finest department and specialty stores. The rest of the collection is still "Haskell in feeling." The company still produces jewelry for *The Phantom of the Opera* and loans jewelry to the Sally Jessy Raphael show regularly. Miriam Haskell jewelry was worn at the Fashion Show Event at President Clinton's inauguration.

Miriam Haskell "Evening Star" necklace, tiara, and earrings, 1954. This crystal set was first designed for the exotic Russian-born wife of a famous British novelist. *Original photograph courtesy of Haskell Jewels, Ltd.*

MONET

MONET

Brothers Michael and Jay Chernow founded Monocraft in Providence, Rhode Island, in 1929. They manufactured metal Art Deco–style monograms that were individually set on handbags as they were purchased at the stores. They developed a reputation for quality manufacturing, and their initials often outlasted the merchandise to which they were attached. In 1937, encouraged by their success, the Chernows began to produce jewelry with the same fine gold plating as the monograms, and they called their new company Monet. Their goal was to make a collection of jewelry that gave fashionable women the look and feel of real jewelry at a reasonable price. Monet was the first jewelry house in the industry that had its trade name stamped on every piece of jewelry.

In the Forties, Monet jewelry, which was often made of gold-plated sterling silver, featured bold chain link bracelets, amusing enameled pins, and equestrian motifs. The styles mirrored popular designs made of precious metals. It was at this time that Monet developed its distinctive friction ear clip. The standard clip that was used by other manufacturers was like a mousetrap; it kept pressing on the ear, using a spring. The Monet clip could be adjusted to fit the ear, and it held in one position.

In the Fifties, when postwar Americans were again having fun, Monet's charm bracelets, poodle pins, and white jewelry perked up the young at heart. Monet's hoop earrings and bold drops looked great with the miniskirts and hip-huggers of the Sixties, and its adventurous pins, pendants, and bangles enhanced the brilliant colors, prints, and ethnic motifs that were in fashion. The biggest part of Monet's business in this decade was charms and charm bracelets. Its big innovation was to put a spring ring on each charm so that one could add, subtract, or change the charms just by opening the ring. Prior to that change, charms were put on with a jump ring that a jeweler had to open. Often there were movable elements in the charms such as ringing bells and turning parts. In 1968, General Mills acquired Monet as its first entry into the fashion business.

In the quality-conscious Seventies, Monet's chains, sculptural shapes, and designer styling accessorized the tailored designs women were wearing at the office. Until the Seventies, Monet did not manufacture pierced earrings because Michael Chernow did not want to put an uncomfortable earring on the market. At that time other manufacturers used a butterfly clutch, which was hard to hold and fit only one thickness of earlobe. Instead, he began using a barrel clutch, which gave adjustability to the wearer. He also changed the way posts were made. They had been chopped off with a rough edge; he pioneered the rounded, tapered, smooth tip that became standard within the industry. Up until Monet's pierced earrings, all the pierced earrings in the market were dainty balls and hoops. Monet produced a full range of fashion earrings.

In 1981, Monet launched a line of Yves Saint Laurent jewelry that was its introduction to the world of "frankly fake" costume jewelry. The Yves Saint Laurent line was a cooperative design effort, with all designs approved by the Yves Saint Laurent people in Paris.

Yves Saint Laurent by Monet

In an interview with the designer who created the Yves Saint Laurent line for Monet:

> In the early Eighties, there were about eight jewelers in Paris who worked with Yves Saint Laurent. I worked with Robert and Patrick Goosens and at Yves Saint Laurent with Lou Lou de la Falaise, who designed all the Yves Saint Laurent accessories. Monet did the pieces that were cast, other companies did the stone setting, and still others did the plastics. Europe is always further ahead than America. In the early Eighties, the pieces were fabulous, fashion pieces. I believe that Yves Saint Laurent started the whole look of big showy pieces in this country. Now the American woman has the same kind of sense of humor about costume jewelry that European women have always had. To keep both Yves Saint Laurent and Monet happy was quite a feat. Yves Saint Laurent in Paris approved every piece I designed. The couture pieces were done in Paris and sold at the Yves Saint Laurent boutique; they were wonderful and used all sorts of materials—glass and leather. The pieces made for the runway were not signed.

> The price range at the time was $25 to $250, with most pieces under $100. I designed the jewelry for about four years. There is a distinctive look to many of the pieces. The glass was cast into the setting. The pieces that look like "poured glass" are really built-up epoxy with foil backing. The "radiant back" of each piece was my design and became the Yves Saint Laurent signature. The earrings had the typical Monet friction ear clip. Some pieces were made in a limited edition—they were signed with a script Yves Saint Laurent signature and the number of the edition, for example, 38/500.

The founders of Monet established a very definite niche in the market, which was costume jewelry with the look of real. In an interview, Martin Krasner, the Chernows' nephew and president of Monet from the late Fifties until 1981, stated that Monet's look was always classic, not trendy or faddish. They were influenced by current fashions, but changes were subtle. Their jewelry never went out of style. There were long-term changes rather than seasonal shifts. The look was always classic, all metal, tailored, real-looking, and comfortable to wear. They became and remain the anchor of the jewelry department in stores.

Monet had a team of designers that changed over the years. In the Fifties and Sixties, the head designer was Edmund Granville. Michael Chernow and then Norman Gatof were the talents behind the merchandising concepts. There was a very distinctive advertising campaign in which the format remained the same for twenty years. Throughout the 1960s and 1970s the "lady in the hood" was the constant theme. One of the most elaborate high-fashion pieces was always selected for the ad, which was an innovation for the times. Most ads showed as many pieces of jewelry as could fit into the photograph. Monet had a few licenses over the years in addition to Yves Saint Laurent, including Shirley Temple and the Dionne quintuplets. In 1987, Monet became part of Crystal Brands, Inc.

NAPIER

NAPIER

Napier, the oldest fashion jewelry house in the United States, was founded in 1875 by Whitney & Rice in North Attleboro, Massachusetts. Its first products were watch chains, chatelaines, and silver-plate matchboxes. The company was purchased by its salesman, A. E. Bliss, and Mr. Carpenter, and they changed the name to Carpenter and Bliss.

By 1882, the company had become successful. Carpenter retired and the A. E. Bliss Company moved to its present home in Meriden, Connecticut. In 1883, the company opened a New York office. Ten years later, talented silversmith William R. Rettenmeyer joined the company as chief designer. He had apprenticed at Tiffany & Co. and studied design at Cooper Union. The company was the first to manufacture sterling silver products in Meriden, which became known as "the silver city." The Bliss Company was a pioneer in the new field of fashion jewelry. Bliss traveled extensively through Europe to research European fashions and to purchase stones and beads. At his death, his son William became the head of the company.

When Rettenmeyer retired in 1913, his son Frederick became the head designer. The following year James H. Napier became the general manager and director, setting off a tremendous period of growth.

During World War I, the company was one of the first in Meriden to turn over its plant to the war effort. Bayonet scabbards, gas masks, trench mirrors, and vane braces were manufactured. In World War II, the company had contracts from every branch of the service to manufacture such war materials as bronze silver-clad bushings, flying boat landing frames, belt buckles for officers, stainless steel moisture traps, radar panels, and ID tags.

In 1920, Napier became president and general manager and the company became Napier-Bliss, becoming The Napier Co. two years later. At Napier's death in 1960, Rettenmeyer became president and chairman of the board, and two years later, John A. Shulga became vice president. In 1964, Shulga became president when Rettenmeyer retired.

At that time, the Napier line consisted of more than 1,200 designs. Each spring and fall, more than 50% of the designs were new. The plant at Napier Park contained a press room where flatstock was blanked, drawn, formed, or swaged. In the wire-bending department, bending, shaping, adjusting, and cutting occurred. The soldering department performed both machine and hand soldering operations. Buffing and polishing were done by hand and by machine as well. The plating room plated copper, nickel, silver, gold, and rhodium. A lacquer room was where clear or colored lacquer was applied to the pieces. The tool room created and maintained tools, blanking forms, and embossing machines. Many inspection points between critical operations preserved the high quality standards.

Shulga retired in 1982, with Ronald J. Meoni appointed president and CEO in 1985. Napier is now the largest privately owned manufacturer of fashion jewelry in the United States.

PANETTA

Panetta was started right after World War II, in November of 1945, by Beneditto Panetta, who was originally a "platinum jeweler" from Naples, Italy. In Naples, Panetta had his own jewelry store. When he came to the United States, he continued to work as a platinum jeweler in New York City. During the Depression, he began making costume jewelry using white metal. His two sons, Amadeo and Armand, were born in New York and were always involved with jewelry—talking about it, handling it, examining it—so it was natural that when their father wanted them to learn a trade, they turned to jewelry manufacturing. Every day after high school they worked at learning to be jewelers.

From 1935, when he was graduated from high school, until 1941, Amadeo worked as a stone setter and modelmaker. His brother, Armand, set diamonds. After the war, they decided they knew more about making jewelry than anyone they worked for, so they started their own company.

At first, Panetta made sterling silver jewelry with hand-set stones. When sterling became too costly, the company used white metal but kept the same level of high-quality workmanship and design. The brothers found there was more freedom of expression in costume jewelry than in real.

Everything was manufactured by Panetta on its premises in New York City's jewelry district and sold to fine stores all over the world. The company made necklaces, pins, earrings, rings, and clasps for pearls. Many of its designs were original copyrighted designs; some were inspired by other pieces of jewelry the brothers saw in their research. The line always had a conservative but stylish "real" look. Every piece of jewelry was signed "Panetta" the same way it was done in the Forties, often on the catch. There were approximately ten thousand pieces in the line. If a style was successful it stayed in the line for up to thirty years.

The design was carved directly into the metal, as in sculpture. It was not made first in wax. It took about one week to finish a model, then castings were made from the original. When stones were set, Panetta took care to match and space the stones carefully in order to maintain quality and give the piece a "real" look. Each stone, which was always first quality, was hand-set individually in the same way diamonds were. They used very thick gold and rhodium plating and took great care in polishing each piece.

Both Panetta brothers could do every operation in the shop: modelmaking, casting, soldering, setting, and polishing. They set strict guidelines for quality for all of their workers. They said, "It had to look real or out it went!" In the late Eighties, they sold the company to one of their best customers in Japan.

ELSA SCHIAPARELLI

Schiaparelli

Elsa Schiaparelli was one of the most colorful figures in fashion history. Born in 1890 in Rome to a prominent family who encouraged intellectual pursuits, "Schiap" (as she was known to friends) attended an English boarding school until she was seventeen. She left there and moved to Greenwich Village in New York City. In the late Twenties, Mme. Schiaparelli moved to Paris and designed gold jewelry. She became a French citizen in 1927 and lived in Paris the rest of her life, except during the war, when she moved back to New York. A rebel against fashion and social convention, Mme. Schiaparelli became best known for introducing bright colors to haute couture in the Twenties. Popular colors at the time were shades of brown, blue, and black. "Shocking pink" became her trademark color.

Mme. Schiaparelli's designs always had a sense of fun and reflected her friendships with painters who led the Surrealist movement in Paris. Among her fashion innovations were halter necklines, formal sweaters, evening dresses with matching jackets, and furs in unusual colors. She had a long-standing rivalry with Chanel. Talking about her designs, she once said, "I like to amuse myself; if I didn't, I would die."

Mme. Schiaparelli was the first major designer to open a boutique of less expensive, ready-to-wear clothing. At her peak in the Forties, she had a ninety-eight-room establishment on the Place Vêndome and employed 350 seamstresses and young designers, among whom was Hubert Givenchy.

Starting in the late Thirties, Jean Schlumberger made unusual jeweled buttons for Mme. Schiaparelli and then a series of fanciful, artistically designed costume jewelry for her. Like her amusing hats, remarkable embroidered jackets, and unique perfume bottles, everything Mme. Schiaparelli designed had the touch of her genius.

Mme. Schiaparelli's autobiography, *Shocking Life*, was published in New York and London in 1954, when she ended her designing career. She continued to act as a consultant to companies that licensed her name for stockings, perfume, jewelry, and accessories.

SCHREINER

The interview with Terry Schreiner, the founder's daughter, was conducted at her farm. Instead of the usual form these interviews take, we talked in a kind of rambling way as she showed me the wonderful pieces in her private family collection. She saved many pieces that had been part of the line and pieces that she had worn. There were also many pieces her husband had made especially for her, often to match a particular dress. Ms. Schreiner's comments about the couturiers they designed jewelry for, the special stones they had made for them in Germany, and her personal recollections about the business were invaluable. We had a delightful lunch with her son, and as I was about to leave to drive back to Manhattan, a wild thunder-

and-lightning storm passed overhead. While the storm raged, we continued our talk about the jewelry and the way the business was in the Fifties and Sixties, when Schreiner designed for all the top American couturiers.

Henry Schreiner came to the United States in 1923 from Bavaria, Germany, where he had been a blacksmith. Since there weren't many horses left in New York City at that time, he took a job at Con Edison, then worked for a baker. In 1926 or 1927, Schreiner went to work for the Better shoe buckle company. Business was booming because, with dresses being worn shorter, decorative shoe buckles had become very popular. He was quite adept at soldering and very artistic. He was an opera buff and admired great painters. His first love was doing work for the couture designers. In 1951, Terry and

Schreiner rhinestone necklace and earrings set worn by Bette Davis, 1951. *Courtesy of the Schreiner family collection. Photograph of page by Kenneth Chen.*

her husband, Ambros Albert, joined the business. The designing of Schreiner jewelry was a family affair. When Schreiner died in 1954, Terry and Ambros continued the business until 1975.

Terry showed me tray after tray of fabulous Schreiner pieces—buttons, buckles, belts, early rhinestone pins, and elaborate necklaces and earrings. The buckles had been designed as closings on fur coats, particularly ones of Persian lamb. The rhinestone pins had been made for dress houses and the buttons for such designers as Pauline Trigère, Ben Reig, and George Halley in the Fifties and Sixties. The Schreiner buttons were made with jeweled settings that didn't have prongs, so they went through the coats without pulling the fabric.

The belts were made for the Midtown Belt company in the Fifties and Sixties. They made a special belt for Pauline Trigère that could also be used as a necklace because it was all hand linked and didn't turn. It was also used as a strap for handbags. All-jeweled belts were made by the Schreiner company in the Sixties. Terry noted that if she were to make the same belts today, they'd have to cost two to three thousand dollars, because the stones have gotten so expensive. She said they did a big business with belts for George Halley, whose wife, Claudia, was the model for Norman Norell. The Schreiner company produced all of Norell's jewelry, buttons, belts, and buckles. According to Terry, he usually wanted either all clear rhinestones or a combination of clear and emerald rhinestones, because he believed that diamonds were right twenty-four hours a day. Teal Traina used Schreiner pieces in his shows. They accessorized his designs and then sold the pieces to Bonwit Teller. They also designed pieces for Maurice Rentner and Originala coats. The Schreiner name tag never went on jewelry made for the dress designers. When they made pieces for the stores, they used the "Schreiner" or "Schreiner, N.Y." tags interchangeably—"whatever was in the drawer."

Schreiner pieces were made for Adele Simpson. The early ones were unsigned; the later pieces were marked "Adele Simpson." When Christian Dior came to New York in the late Forties and early Fifties, Schreiner designed original pieces for him. When they designed jewelry for couturiers, they would bring samples to their studios and often see famous women like Marilyn Monroe being fitted for clothing.

Schreiner rhinestone necklace and earrings set made
for Norman Norell, worn by Marilyn Monroe,
Harper's Bazaar, November 1, 1954. *Courtesy of the
Schreiner family collection. Photograph of page by
Kenneth Chen.*

In the 1970s, the Schreiner company made decorative stretch belts
for Saks Fifth Avenue using dome stones in topaz, coral, and chalk-
white plastic. Terry showed me a belt that had stones she called
"black iridescent," and she remarked that after 1941 or 1942 they
used only settings, not castings. They designed hair ornaments for
Elizabeth Arden and used a lot of "quivers" (*tremblants*) for their
couture ready-to-wear.

When Omar Khaim was the designer for Ben Reig after World
War II, he introduced gunmetal plating to the Schreiner company. It
was the only kind of plating that could be done in Paris, since there
was no gold, silver, or rhodium available because of the war. The flat-
looking gunmetal plating was done on the early pieces; shinier gun-

metal came later. He also persuaded Schreiner to use "flawed" emeralds because he liked the color—he encouraged them to have stones made with inclusions in them. When the jewelry containing the "flawed" emeralds was delivered to the stores, most of it was returned—the buyers thought the merchandise was imperfect!

Terry showed me a special stone she called the "paisley" stone. No two were made alike and they were used in belts and pins. They were made in shades of blue and wine in prewar Czechoslovakia. Most stones the Schreiner company used in the early years were made in Czechoslovakia, not Austria. In 1939, Schreiner had gone to Czechoslovakia to buy stones and they held them for him until after the war. The fine prewar stones from Czechoslovakia were full tens, like Waterford crystal, and came individually wrapped in tissue. Later they were made by Czechs who had fled from the Russians and settled in Kaufbayern, Germany. The "marble" stone came from Germany in the 1950s. It was an exclusive stone made for the Schreiner company. When Terry and her husband went to Germany, they designed the stone. Their signature "keystone" was made by Czechs in Germany. They used it in the "ruffle" pin Albert designed in 1957. There were many ruffle pins and ruffle crosses produced, all using the keystone. Terry and her husband brought in metallic stones from Germany. They had been popular at one time and then had a revival. They often used Lucite in combination with gunmetal plating. The pearls they used were handmade, from one special source.

Terry's favorite color is blue, and she showed me a necklace made of "iris" stones, which were a deep blue with dark pink centers, from the Fifties. There were many beautiful stones—"agate," barrel-shaped, "old mosaic," jade, and "nude." She explained that they often used unfoiled stones called "crushed ice," "brandy brown," and "black diamond" because they had a more subtle look.

In the Fifties, the Schreiner company produced thousands of flower pins: daisies, geraniums, sunflowers, cornflowers, and white margaritas. In the same years, they also made dragonflies, carrots, turnips, pineapples, peas in a pod, turtles, and acorns in different colors to match the tweeds in Originala coats. "Henry the Mouse" was originally done for a union in Cincinnati and became one of their most popular pieces. In 1962, the "quiver" bee was done in opaque colored stones.

Terry talked about a special piece they had produced: "We did a jeweled bra that Saks Fifth Avenue carried. They special-ordered one three inches longer in the back. About a month later, they special-ordered another one, also three inches larger in the back. It turned out it was for the same customer. Apparently she had gone to a party and lost it! She loved it so much, she wanted the same thing again."

The Schreiner company was known for its imaginative use of color, which Terry attributes to working for the couturiers and having the color swatches before anyone else. They often set the stones upside down, with the point at the top, in order to pick up the color of the material better. They used unfoiled stones for the same reason. If they put the "cracked ice" stones over a peachy color, it would pick up the peach tone and look like it was made for that garment.

The Schreiner company never produced a commercial type of jewelry; it did only fine hand work and never mass-produced pieces. It never paid for advertising, but always got wonderful editorial coverage in the magazines because the jewelry was right.

STANLEY HAGLER

In the early Fifties, Stanley Hagler designed a bracelet for the Duchess of Windsor on a whim. The staff at *Vogue* liked it so much they ordered pieces like it for themselves. Stan and the man who dared him to do the piece for the duchess formed a partnership, and they went "poking around the jewelry market" to see what was available.

On a cross-country trip, they went to see the jewelry buyer for the Joseph Magnin group. When they arrived, the buyer wasn't around but the assistant offered to look at their designs. While an annoyed Stan Hagler was showing the pieces, the assistant said good-morning to Mr. Magnin, who happened to be walking by. Mr. Magnin saw the jewelry and seemed interested. Stan's partner took the opportunity to

Award-winning designer Stanley Hagler wearing one of his own creations.
Original photograph courtesy of Stanley Hagler.

inform him it was the best jewelry in the country! Magnin asked him what he thought of the store's jewelry department and Stan's partner told him it was filled with junk. Surprisingly, Magnin agreed and gave them an opening order for several thousand dollars!

Each year, Swarovski gave out Great Designs in Jewelry awards for pieces that employed Swarovski crystals. Stan Hagler won eleven of them and was invited by Daniel Swarovski to go to Wattens, Austria, where the factories are, on a design consultation trip. In the course of Stan's career, he designed interesting pieces for Chase Metal, matching jewelry for Samsonite Luggage, jeweled swim fins for AMF Voit, obi belts for Seibu department stores in Japan, plastic jewelry for Celanese, aluminum and rhinestone clothing and wigs for Kennecott Copper, hosiery jewelry, cotton jewelry for the Cotton Council of America, and men's jewelry.

In the Fifties, Stan's designs were simpler. He was influenced by Fashion Press Week, which was held twice a year. He always designed pieces he believed were "just plain pretty." He believes it's important for designers to remember to work architecturally—earrings have to hang right and a necklace has to fit around a neck and lie in a particular way or it's not flattering.

Stan remembered a "very crazy rhinestone drop earring" *Vogue* wanted to photograph. They wanted to illustrate the trend toward long earrings. If the earrings he designed were three inches long, they wanted them eight inches long! They had the model jumping in the air and the drops were flying around in front of her face. Stan said it was a very wild shot, but they made their point.

Stan's pieces were often large in scale. He said the pieces varied according to the clothing fashions. In the Sixties, he used acrylic in cubic, squared-off shapes with seed pearls top and bottom. The name tags were smaller or larger depending on the size of the piece. A collector can't judge the decade in which a piece was made by the size of the tag.

Stan is still designing and producing costume jewelry in Florida, where he now resides. He has great enthusiasm about costume jewelry and said, "I've had a marvelous, speckled career. It's been really wonderful and I love the business. I thoroughly enjoy it!"

Stanley Hagler's rhinestone-studded swim fins for AMF Voit, a golden butterfly ring, and white sea serpent bracelet. *Original photograph courtesy of Stanley Hagler.*

SWAROVSKI

For over four generations, Swarovski has been the world's leading manufacturer of crystal stones. The finest manufacturers of costume jewelry in the United States and Europe have used Swarovski crystals. In 1892, Daniel Swarovski applied for a patent on his first invention—a machine capable of cutting crystal jewelry stones with perfect precision. Three years later he founded D. Swarovski & Co. in the Tyrolean mountain town of Wattens, Austria. Due to increased demand for crystal products, he enlarged his production facilities in 1900. Through experimentation, Swarovski created its own crystal, eliminating the need to import raw crystal. After 1914, Swarovski was forced to stop producing crystal and concentrate on the production of military equipment for the war effort. By 1920, there was again an increased demand for cut crystal resulting from the Roaring Twenties boom in the costume jewelry business.

The Great Depression of the early 1930s forced drastic cutbacks in crystal production, bringing about product diversification. Swarovski began to produce jewelry trimmings—stones processed into decorative bands and laces for application for garments or accessories. In the 1950s, aurora borealis stones were created by applying a thin layer of vaporized metal onto the cut and polished jewelry crystals.

In 1985, the Swarovski jewelry collection was launched in the United States, followed a year later by the Savvy collection. By then the fourth generation of the Swarovski family was running the company. In 1990, the Daniel Swarovski Corporation sponsored "Jewels of Fantasy—Fashion Jewellery of the Twentieth Century." It was the world's first traveling museum exhibit in the field and highlighted the impact of cultural and artistic movements on costume jewelry through the ages, validating jewelry design as an art form.

The Daniel Swarovski Corporation, now the world's largest crystal stone manufacturer, cuts up to 30 million stones daily and produces over 100,000 varieties of stones.

TRIFARI

KTF   TRIFARI

TRIFARI.

Trifari and Krussman was founded in 1918 by Gustavo Trifari, Sr., and Leo F. Krussman. Trifari had been in the business of manufacturing bar pins and hair ornaments made out of tortoiseshell and rhinestones. In the new company, Trifari made the jewelry and Krussman sold it. In 1925, Carl Fishel, a young hair ornament salesman, joined them and the company became Trifari, Krussman and Fishel (TKF).

In 1930, the well-known European designer Alfred Philippe joined the company as chief designer. His work had been sold in Cartier and in Van Cleef and Arpels in Paris. Through Philippe's use of multicolored Austrian crystals in wonderful new designs, Trifari, Krussman and Fishel became known as the "Rhinestone Kings." Stones were hand-set and pieces were made using the same workmanship as real jewelry, giving it the look of the finest precious jewelry.

Starting in the 1930s and continuing through the 1960s, Trifari created exclusive designs for Broadway productions, among them *The Great Waltz*, *Roberta*, and *Jubilee* with Ethel Merman. Sophie Tucker, Lena Horne, and Rosalind Russell wore specially designed jewelry by Trifari.

The famous "Crown Pin" was introduced in 1941. It was made of sterling silver and vermeil, with real-looking cabochons, rhinestones, and baguettes. It is highly collectible today.

During World War II, Trifari produced patriotic jewelry including pins depicting the American flag and the eagle, commemorating the American armed forces. From 1942 to 1945, Trifari used sterling silver in its jewelry collections because the metals that made up white metal were banned for use by private industry.

In 1953, Mamie Eisenhower commissioned Trifari to design her Inaugural Ball jewels. For the occasion Alfred Philippe designed a triple-strand pearl choker, matching bracelet, and earrings. Three sets were produced, one for Mrs. Eisenhower, one for the Smithsonian, and one for Trifari's archives. In 1957, Mrs. Eisenhower asked Trifari to design her jewels for her second Inaugural Ball. This time the set consisted of a triple strand of graduated pearls with small rhinestone rondelles, a matching bracelet, and cluster earrings. Pearl drops extended from the bottom strand of the necklace.

In 1954, in a landmark federal copyright case, Trifari was awarded a judgment that established fashion jewelry design as a work of art, therefore able to be copyrighted.

In 1964, sons Gustavo Trifari, Louis F. Krussman, and Carlton M. Fishel succeeded their fathers and witnessed a renewed interest in fashion inspired by the young, new First Lady, Jacqueline Kennedy.

Hallmark Cards, Inc., acquired Trifari in 1975, and in 1982, Trifari acquired Marvella, a company that specialized in simulated pearls. In 1988, Crystal Brands, Inc., acquired both companies, and in 1989 they joined Monet to form Crystal Brands Jewelry Group, a division of Crystal Brands, Inc.

Manufacturers' Marks

Manufacturers' marks and identification signatures are usually found on the back of a pin, the clasp of a necklace or bracelet, and on earring clips. Sometimes they're so small they have to be seen through a loupe. Often the mark is on a small tag that is soldered to the jewelry or it can be stamped right into the jewelry. Name tags can also hang from a place near the clasp of a necklace or bracelet. Occasionally, pieces can be identified by the design patent numbers that are imprinted into the jewelry. Small letters and numbers are often stamped into pieces of jewelry, usually those from the Thirties or Forties. These numbers are thought to be the stone setter's initials or number. Pieces should be examined thoroughly because often a mark can be partially worn away or in an unexpected location.

ART© $\mathcal{S}$ ATHENNIC ARTS ©

Barclay   BARTEK   bergere

CASTLECLIFF

cheneT

MADE IN ITALY BY
Coppolaē Toppo

Coro Craft

Corocraft

Sterling Coro·Craft

De NICOLA ©

R DeROSA STERLING

©EMMONS

EUGENE

FLORENZA©

FREDA. BLOCK

©HAR

Hattie Carnegie

HOLLYCRAFT COPR. 1955

JOMAZ

KRAMER.

Kreisler

LAGUNA

LISNER©

MARVELLA   *Matisse*   MAZER

McClelland Barclay   MOSELL

Nettie Rosenstein   PAULINE RADER   *Pennino*

Rebaje   REGENCY   REINAD   REJA

Renoir

© SANDOR CO..   SARAH © COV   STARET

Vendôme   VOGUE

WEISS   Wm deLillo

Collections

Collectors are as individual as their collections. Some look for names, some go for categories, and some collect anything that catches their eye. In this chapter, there are photographs of collections. Most of the photographs, because of space limitations, show just parts of collections. Some show composite collections from more than one collector just to illustrate what people collect. When collectors are asked why they collect what they do, they often have interesting reasons.

Rita Sacks is one of the best known dealers in New York City. In addition to the extensive inventory in her shop at the Manhattan Arts and Antiques Center, she has a vast and eclectic private collection. Rita has been collecting costume jewelry for twenty years. She used to wear costume jewelry for fun and in place of real jewelry when she went traveling. As a little private joke, she'd mix costume and real, with always a touch of the outrageous to complement the real. When she went to flea markets, she couldn't ignore all the wonderful pieces of costume jewelry, so she'd buy them. Then, because she couldn't bear to sell them, she'd save them. The pieces spoke to her in the same way a piece of fine art did. As she started collecting intriguing pieces, she'd put them away to preserve them.

Rita's art background and the way she was raised and educated led to an appreciation of fine workmanship and strong design. Rebajes's sculpture and jewelry have always been favorites of hers. Rita has collected copper in depth, and believes that Rebajes was a genius of design. She observed that his pieces have dimension and movement.

Rita likes to collect by subject. She began collecting outrageous pieces and went from flowers to creatures and faces. Her favorite flower is an old Hattie Carnegie flower pin, perhaps because at one time she worked for Hattie Carnegie. She also has a favorite Josephine Baker pin by Coro and an interesting collection of early dangle pins.

When Pierre Cardin came to Rita's shop and admired her jewelry, she knew she was on the right wavelength. At that time she was selling real jewelry as well as wonderful Forties costume jewelry. Cardin bought his first serious Trifari sterling pieces from her.

Rita has seen many changes over the years. Prices have gotten higher, which makes her feel bad because new collectors might be put off and miss out on something that was once affordable and fun. When she first started collecting, she had complete freedom because the prices were so reasonable. She would like people to be able to collect with complete abandon. She would enjoy sharing her collections if she had the means to do so, perhaps with students.

Rita said that if a person buys something from Tiffany's, he or she can be assured of the name and the price. Buyers are sometimes wary of buying antiques because there's no such assurance. Collectors, however, can buy anything, any place, because they put their own personal value on it. Rita always buys from dealers who are dependable. Rita's advice to collectors is, "Buy what you like;' if you are buying something to appreciate in price, you are buying for the wrong reason."

Royce Foster, an interior designer from California who has designed restaurants, a major country club, and both commercial and residential projects, collects Schreiner jewelry:

> I first saw Schreiner pieces when I went to a dealer's house to look at bracelets, which I had started to collect. Every time I saw a piece I liked, it was a Schreiner. I had never heard of the company before. At that time, which was about two years ago, I wasn't yet a jewelry collector. I approached it more from an artistic point of view.
>
> When I first started looking for Schreiner pieces, I went to every single show out here and talked to every single dealer. The dealers got to

their sources and pulled in what they could. Then I started spreading out my search. I flew back east and went to all the major shows. As a designer, I love to shop the shows, so it was perfect.

What I find interesting about Schreiner pieces is that each one is like a miniature piece of sculpture, so finely detailed and well thought out. Color is my favorite design element and the Schreiner color combinations caught me right away. They used odd combinations that were different and more fun than other companies'. Somebody who had a sense of humor and real creativity had designed these pieces and had a real good time doing it. The stones are interesting. I think that anyone who would turn a stone upside down has to be someone I'd like.

I like to look at Schreiner pins from the sides and the bottom. I always keep several on my desk because, for me, everything visual is an inspiration. It all gets stored and emerges in some form.

Another aspect of Schreiner jewelry I love is the endless variety. I'm still amazed when I get things in that I haven't seen before—and I now have between five and six hundred pieces in sets! When I first started collecting Schreiner it was purely about having an artistic collection. Then it became a quest. It was never about business or investment. I realized I might be the major Schreiner collector and it became important to me to find original drawings if possible, and to protect my pieces. I keep everything in plastic containers and trays, arranged by color. I know where everything is.

The fact that most people didn't know or particularly like Schreiner when I first started collecting didn't deter me. Now I'm convinced that most people hadn't seen the most fabulous pieces then. At first, I didn't even ask the dealers for their Schreiner pieces and I told my friends not to "help" me because I didn't want the word out. At that time, I felt that Schreiner was undervalued and I knew that no one else was collecting it the way I was. The major pieces were there for me to find, which was very exciting. When I started, I had no idea where it would lead.

I have a very definite connection with Schreiner jewelry. It's inspiring to me. I wear and look at my pieces all the time. They feed my soul and my creativity.

Animals

Animals. *Courtesy of Tania Santé's Classic Collectables, Miami, FL. Photograph by Phil Schlom.*

(clockwise from top)

Panetta Pin. Cat, faux sapphire eyes, gold plated with silver-plated bow tie, 1960s. *Courtesy of Tania Santé's Collectables.* $50–$125

Unsigned Pin. Seal, black enamel, round, clear rhinestones in collar, green glass ball, gold plated, 1960s. *Courtesy of Tania Santé's Collectables.* $75–$125

Unsigned Pin. Cat, white enameled body, green enameled spots, red enameled tongue, faux emerald eyes, 1960s. *Courtesy of Tania Santé's Collectables.* $25–$50

Unsigned Pin. Lion, white enamel, gold plated, 1960s. *Courtesy of Tania Santé's Collectables.* $30–$85

Trifari Pin. French poodle, white enamel with blue spots, red stone eyes, gold plated, 1960s. *Courtesy of Tania Santé's Collectables.* $30–$85

Jomaz Pin. Rooster: faux turquoises, rubies, and sapphires; blue-and-green enameled tail; red enameled cockscomb; gold plated: 1960s. *Courtesy of Tania Santé's Collectables.* $25–$65

Pauline Rader Pin (center). Butterfly with *tremblant* wings, simulated pearls and jet glass, gold plated, 1960s. *Courtesy of Tania Santé's Collectables.* $50–$125

Artists' Jewelry

Artists Jewelry. *Courtesy of Ilene Chazanof, Decorative Arts, New York, NY. Photograph by Kenneth Chen.*

Note: These pins designed by famous artists were given as gifts to individuals who made a substantial donation through the purchase of Israel Bonds during the 1960s through the 1970s. The prices range from $10 to $150 each. *Courtesy of Ilene Chazanof, Decorative Arts.*

(clockwise from top)

Salvador Dali Pin. Abstract winged figure, faux turquoise, gold plated.

Jacques Lipchitz pin. Menorah with Hebrew letters, gold plated, marked "Lipchitz."

Chaim Gross Pin. Doves of peace with faux emerald eyes, "Shalom" in Hebrew, gold plated, 3 inches wide.

Jacques Lipchitz Pin. Abstract menorah with an olive branch, faux turquoise, gold plated, marked "Lipchitz."

Jacques Lipchitz Pin (center). Doves of peace with a faux turquoise, "Shalom" in Hebrew, gold plated, marked "Lipchitz."

Baskets

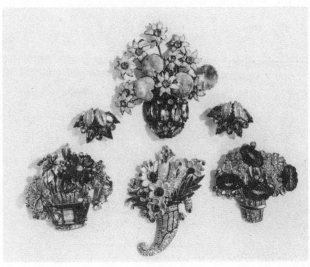

Baskets. *Courtesy of Rita Sacks, Limited Additions, New York, NY. Photograph by Kenneth Chen.*

(clockwise from top)

Sandor Pin and Earring Set. Basket, pink marquise and pear-shaped rhinestones, pale green round rhinestones, delicate pink and beige enamel petals, brass, 1930s. *Courtesy of Rita Sacks, Limited Additions.*

$900–$1200/set

Trifari Pin (unsigned). Basket; faux ruby, sapphire, and emerald blossoms; pavé rhinestone flowers and stems; gold plated; 1930s. *Courtesy of Rita Sacks, Limited Additions.* $900–$1200

Unsigned Clip. Cornucopia; faux emerald, ruby, and sapphire cabochon flower centers; pavé rhinestones; blue, pink, yellow, and white enameled petals; silver plated; 1930s. *Courtesy of Rita Sacks, Limited Additions.* $400–$500

R. DeRosa Clip. Large faux amethyst basket, faux topaz flower, pavé rhinestone petals and stems, clear teardrop-shaped rhinestone drops, gold plated, 1930s. *Courtesy of Rita Sacks, Limited Additions.* $1,200–$1,400

Birds

Birds. *Courtesy of Robin Feldman Collectibles, New York, NY, and E & J Rothstein Antiques, West Chester, PA. Photograph by Kenneth Chen.*

(clockwise from top)

Trifari Pin. Two birds on branches; faux citrine and amethyst bodies; faux ruby and sapphire domed cabochon heads; faux ruby, emerald, and sapphire baguettes in the tails; clear round rhinestone florets; green enameled buds; gold plated; Pat. No. 131365; marked "47"; 1930s. *Courtesy of Robin Feldman Collectibles.* $850–$1,200

Coro Craft Pin. Pelican, faux ruby eye, pear-shaped faux ruby feathers, pavé rhinestones on the neck and tail, sterling vermeil, 1940s.
Courtesy of E & J Rothstein Antiques. $400–$500

Trifari Clip. Pelican, triangular-cut faux topaz beak, clear round rhinestones around the eye and on the tail, rectangular-cut faux sapphire wing, sterling vermeil, 1940s. *Courtesy of E & J Rothstein Antiques.*
                                                                           $400–$500

Trifari Pin. Bird of paradise, oval, faux ruby belly (was also made with different color bellies), oval pink rhinestones, faux sapphire baguettes, round faux emeralds, pavé rhinestone head and clear round rhinestone accents, sterling vermeil, 1940s. *Courtesy of E & J Rothstein Antiques.*
                                                                           $400–$500

Bows

Bows. *Courtesy of Rita Sacks, Limited Additions, New York, NY, and Elayne Glotzer, New York, NY. Photograph by Kenneth Chen.*

(clockwise from top)

Unsigned Pin. Ornate ribbon bow, clear round rhinestones along the edges in a foliate design, gold plated, silver plated settings, 1930s.
Courtesy of Rita Sacks, Limited Additions. $600–$850

Ciner Pin. Retro-style bow, large central faux deep blue sapphire, channel-set square faux rubies, rhodium plated, ca. 1940s. *Courtesy of Elayne Glotzer.* $350–$450

Silson Pin. Ribbon bow, red enamel edges, clear round rhinestones, gold plated, 1930s. *Courtesy of Rita Sacks, Limited Additions.* $300–$350

Mazer Pin. Asymmetrical bow, oval faux citrines, trapezium-cut faux emeralds, small and medium clear round rhinestones, sterling vermeil, 1940s. *Courtesy of Rita Sacks, Limited Additions.* $900–$1,200

Big Bracelets

Big bracelets. *Courtesy of Rita Sacks, Limited Additions, New York, NY, and Joan Paley, Chicago, IL. Photograph by Kenneth Chen.*

(left to right)

Mazer Bracelet (unsigned). Hinged bangle, large, central faux topaz surrounded by clear round rhinestones, clear round rhinestone accents, gold plated, 1940s. *Courtesy of Rita Sacks, Limited Additions.* $1,000–$1,500

Unsigned Bracelet. Flexible bangle, large, square and octagon-cut faux light and dark blue sapphires, double snake chain band, gold plated, 1940s. *Courtesy of Joan Paley.* $700–$800

Calvaire Bracelet. Hinged oval bangle, large, rectangular and octagon-cut faux emeralds, gold plated, ca. 1940s. *Courtesy of Joan Paley.* $750–$850

Bracelets

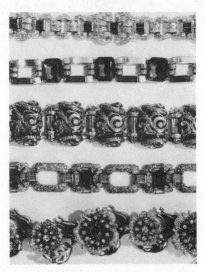

Bracelets. *Courtesy of the author and Rita Sacks, Limited Additions, New York, NY. Photograph by Kenneth Chen.*

(top to bottom)

Unsigned Bracelet. Links, Art Deco scroll and curved sections, faux rubies, clear round rhinestones, rhodium plated, 1930s. *Courtesy of the author.* $80–$140

Mazer Bracelet. Links, octagon-cut faux emeralds, clear round rhinestones, gold plated, 1940s. *Courtesy of the author.* $75–$125

R. DeRosa Bracelet. Rare, scroll design links, navy blue enamel and clear round rhinestones, sterling vermeil, 1940s. *Courtesy of Rita Sacks, Limited Additions.* $1,200–$1,500

TKF Bracelet. Links, faux sapphires, pavé rhinestones, white metal, marked "19," 1930s. *Courtesy of the author.* $125–$175

R. DeRosa Bracelet (unsigned). Floral links, alternating round faux ruby and clear round rhinestone centers, surrounded by clear round rhinestones and pavé rhinestones, gold plated, 1940s. *Courtesy of Rita Sacks, Limited Additions.* $900–$1,200

Ceramic Faces

Ceramic faces. *Courtesy of Carol Moskowitz, New York, NY; Rita Sacks, Limited Additions, New York, NY; and Joan Paley, Chicago, IL. Photograph by Kenneth Chen.*

(clockwise from top)

Unsigned Pin. Ceramic face, wooden backing, headdress made of gold fabric, beige feather and heart-shaped faux emeralds, costume made of rose-and-gold fabric. The beige enameled face has black enameled brows and lashes and red lips, a paper label on the back is marked "MADE IN CALIFORNIA," 1940s. *Courtesy of Carol Moskowitz.*

$175–$200

Unsigned Pin. Ceramic face, wooden backing, beige fabric and red wooden hat, multicolored tassel. The tan enameled face has blue enameled eye shadow, black enameled lashes, and red enameled lips, 1940s. *Courtesy of Carol Moskowitz.* $125–$150

Unsigned Pin. Ceramic face, wooden backing, braids made of stiffened gold threads over yarn, pink-and-mauve iridescent mother-of-pearl feather, simulated pearl ornament. The beige enamel face has aqua and violet eye shadow, black enameled brows and lashes, and red enameled lips, 3¾ inches high, 1940s. *Courtesy of Joan Paley.* $175–$200

Unsigned Pin. Ceramic face, purple Lucite hat, gold ribbon, red stone, faux topaz cabochon center. The beige enameled face has pink-and-blue enameled eye shadow, black enameled brows and lashes, and red enameled lips, 1940s. *Courtesy of Rita Sacks, Limited Additions.* $150–$200

NOTE: Apparently these pins were made in California, possibly in one studio or workshop. They were probably done in the Forties, during the war, and decorated with bits and pieces of fabric, leather, Lucite, ribbons, upholstery material, pom-poms, and so forth. No precious materials were used. The faces are all of different ethnic groups—Native American, African-American, and Asian. Some have patent numbers, some are marked "Made in California." The California manufacturers used two trademarks, Elzac and Black Magic. The faces are ceramic glazed and painted.

Chanel

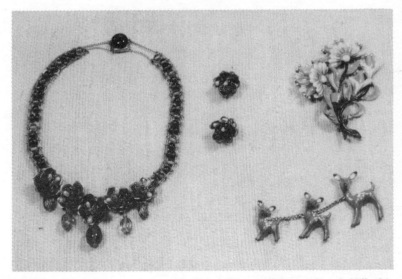

Chanel. *Jewelry and photograph courtesy of Maria Domont Collection, Beverly Hills, CA.*

Chanel Necklace and Earrings Set (unsigned). Choker; red, blue, and green glass beads; simulated pearls; silver plated; made by Madame Gripoix; ca. 1950s. *Courtesy of Maria Domont Collection.* $850–$1,200/set

Chanel Pin. Flower, pale pink and blue enameled flowers, brown enameled stem, white metal, script signature, 1930s. *Courtesy of Maria Domont Collection.* $500–$600

Chanel Chatelaine. Three deer pins; beige, white, and black enameled bodies; graduated in size; white metal; script signature; 1930s. *Courtesy of Maria Domont Collection.* $800–$900

Chatelaines

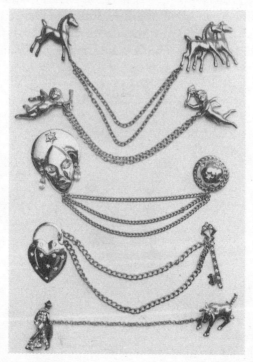

Chatelaines. *Courtesy of Only Yesterday, Hudson, NY. Photograph by Kenneth Chen.*

Unsigned Chatelaines. Figural pins connected by chains, clear round rhinestone accents, silver, gold and rose gold plated, 1940s. *Courtesy of Only Yesterday.* $30–$50

Christmas Pins

Christmas pins. *Courtesy of the author and Rita Sacks, Limited Additions, New York, NY. Photograph by Kenneth Chen.*

(clockwise from top)

Unsigned Pin. Two ringing bells, two-tone green enameled holly leaves, red simulated pearl berry, gold plated, 1950s. *Courtesy of the author.* $25–$40

Gerry's Pin. Candle, red and green enameled poinsettia and holly, red and white enameled flame, gold plated, 1950s. *Courtesy of the author.*
$25–$40

Unsigned Pin. Wreath, red plastic berry clusters, faux marquise ruby flame, white enameled candle and green enameled leaves, gold plated, 1950s. *Courtesy of the author.* $25–$40

Unsigned Pin. Reindeer, faux ruby eye, enameled green holly with red berries, gold plated, 1950s. *Courtesy of the author.* $25–$40

Hattie Carnegie Pin. Christmas tree, faux round ruby, emerald and sapphire lights, pavé rhinestone star at the top, gold plated, marked "Lic. Pat. No. 3119564," 1960s. When the base is pressed, a concealed battery lights up the tree. *Courtesy of the author.* $30–$50

Robert Pin. Red and black enameled boot, green and red enameled holly, gold plated, marked "Original by Robert," 1960s. *Courtesy of Rita Sacks, Limited Additions.* $50–$75

Vogue Pin (center). Metallic red, green, blue, silver, gunmetal, and copper sparkly glass domes arched over a metal circle; clear round rhinestone accents; gold plated; 2¾-inch diameter; 1960s. *Courtesy of Rita Sacks, Limited Additions.* $300–$350

Cini

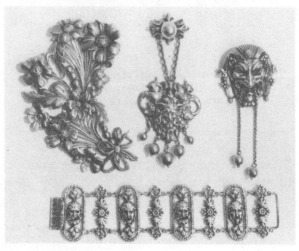

Cini. *Courtesy of E & J Rothstein Antiques, West Chester, PA. Photograph by Kenneth Chen.*

(left to right)

Cini Pin. Large flower bouquet, sterling silver, 1940s. *Courtesy of E & J Rothstein Antiques.* $400–$450

Cini Pin. Dangle, Renaissance design, face and fantasy creatures, ball dangles, marked "Sterling by Cini," 4½ inches high, 1940s. *Courtesy of E & J Rothstein Antiques.* $200–$300

Cini Pin. Devil mask, ball dangles, marked "Sterling by Cini," 1940s. *Courtesy of E & J Rothstein Antiques.* $350–$450

Cini Bracelet. Renaissance-design links, alternating masks and flowers, sterling silver, 1940s. *Courtesy of E & J Rothstein Antiques.* $300–$500

Coro Craft Animals

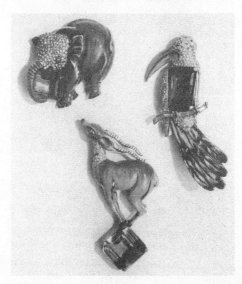

Coro craft animals. *Courtesy of Rita Sacks, Limited Additions, New York, NY. Photograph by Kenneth Chen.*

Coro Craft Pin. Elephant holding a large, square-cut faux sapphire in its trunk; gray enameled body and trunk; red enameled mouth; pavé rhinestone head; faux citrine eye; sterling vermeil; 1940s. *Courtesy of Rita Sacks, Limited Additions.* $1,200–$1,800

Coro Craft Pin. Gazelle standing atop a large, square-cut faux topaz, gray-and-brown enameled body and head, black-and-ivory horns, pavé rhinestone neck, sterling vermeil, 1940s. *Courtesy of Rita Sacks, Limited Additions.* $1,200–$1,800

Coro Craft Pin. Toucan; yellow-and-red enameled beak; black, blue, and ivory enameled tail; pavé rhinestone head, wing, and body; large, rectangular faux emerald belly; sterling vermeil; 1940s; 3¾ inches high. *Courtesy of Rita Sacks, Limited Additions.* $1,200–$1,800

Coro Duettes

Coro Duettes. *Courtesy of Charles France, Divine Idea, New York, NY. Photograph by Kenneth Chen.*

(top to bottom)

Coro Craft Duette Pin/Clips and Earrings Set. Acorns, square-cut invisibly set faux rubies, pavé rhinestones on the caps, clear baguettes on the leaves, matching earrings, gold plated, 1930s. *Courtesy of Charles France, Divine Idea.* $200–$300/set

Coro Craft Duette Pin/Clips. Triplet owls, faux ruby bodies, faux emerald eyes, pavé rhinestone accents, sterling vermeil, 1930s. *Courtesy of Charles France, Divine Idea.* $325–$425

Coro Duette Pin/Clips. Monkeys, faux amethyst bodies and ears, glass bead eyes, pavé rhinestone accents, rose gold sterling vermeil, 1930s. *Courtesy of Charles France, Divine Idea.* $400–$500

Coro Duette Pin/Clips. Rare, carved ivory Asian man and woman, faux turquoises and corals, simulated pearls, gold plated, 1930s. *Courtesy of Charles France, Divine Idea.* $900–$1,200

Coro Craft Duette Pin/Clips. Large birds; enameled red, green, yellow, and black; pavé rhinestone accents; sterling silver; 1930s. *Courtesy of Charles France, Divine Idea.* $150–$200

Coro Duette Pin/Clips. Rare, lovebirds on a heart, pavé rhinestones, opalescent pink unfoiled rhinestone bodies, blue-and-green enameled tails, dark pink enameled wings, black enameled beaks, faux ruby eyes, sterling silver. *Courtesy of Charles France, Divine Idea.* $700–$1,200

> **NOTE:** Coro Duettes are twin clips attached to a pin back, so they can be worn together as a pin or separately as dress clips. They range in price depending on how rare and how popular the individual designs are. Other companies, such as Trifari, Mazer, and Hattie Carnegie, also made double pin/clips under different patented names.

R. DeRosa

R. DeRosa. *Courtesy of Charles France, Divine Idea,
New York, NY; and Rita Sacks, Limited Additions,
New York, NY. Photograph by Kenneth Chen.*

(left to right from top)

R. DeRosa Clip. Retro-style spray, oval, faux sapphire in the center, oval faux rubies, clear round rhinestones and simulated pearls, gold plated, 1930s. *Courtesy of Charles France, Divine Idea.* $350–$475

R. DeRosa Pin. Unusual design; bow with suspended fan-shaped sections in graduated sizes, the smallest one having a pin fastening, each with clear round rhinestones and simulated pearls; sterling vermeil; 1940s. *Courtesy of Rita Sacks, Limited Additions.* $1,500–$2,500

R. DeRosa Clip. Flower, large, oval faux emerald center, square-cut faux rubies at the edges, clear round rhinestone accents, tiny enameled lavender flowers, clear round rhinestone centers, gold plated, 1930s. *Courtesy of Rita Sacks, Limited Additions.* $900–$1,100

R. DeRosa Clip. Bouquet of flowers, faux ruby bead centers surrounded by simulated pearls, pavé rhinestone and green enameled leaves, gold plated, 1930s. *Courtesy of Charles France, Divine Idea.* $400–$600

Eisenberg Figurals

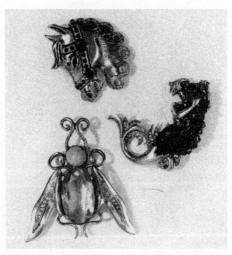

Eisenberg figurals. *Courtesy of Robin Feldman Collectibles, New York, NY. Photograph by Kenneth Chen.*

Eisenberg Pin. Horse's head, oval and round faux rubies, clear round rhinestones, gold plated, 1930s. *Courtesy of Robin Feldman Collectibles.*
$1,500–$2,000

Eisenberg Original Clip (unsigned). Rare, fly, pale blue oval rhinestone belly, opaque faux turquoise head, clear round rhinestones on wings, gold plated, marked "34," 1930s. *Courtesy of Robin Feldman Collectibles.*

$1,800–$2,300

Eisenberg Pin. Rare, mermaid, faux emerald belly, emerald glass beads, clear round rhinestones on head and tail, sterling vermeil, marked "M," 1930s (also made in blue, pink, and amber). *Courtesy of Robin Feldman Collectibles.*

$1,800–$2,500

Eisenberg (1940s)

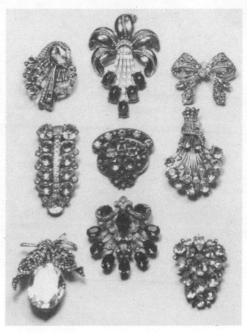

Eisenberg (1940s). *Courtesy of Alexandra Vangel. Photograph by John Merowski.*

Eisenberg Pin and Clips. Various designs; some with all clear rhinestones, faux emeralds, or sapphires; sterling silver; ca. 1940s. *Courtesy of Alexandra Vangel.*

$200–$650

Eisenberg (1950s–1960s)

Eisenberg (1950s–1960s). *Courtesy of Alexandra Vangel. Photograph by John Merowski.*

Eisenberg Pins. Various designs; some with clear or pink rhinestones, faux rubies, amethysts, or sapphires; rhodium plated; ca. late 1940s–1960s. *Courtesy of Alexandra Vangel.* $150–$225

Eisenberg Enamels

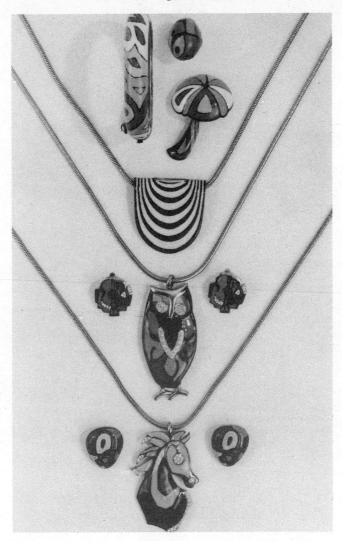

Eisenberg enamels. *Courtesy of the author. Photograph by Kenneth Chen.*

Eisenberg Necklaces, Bracelets, Earrings, and a Ring. Multicolored enamels, part of the artists' series, marked "Eisenberg" in block letters, gold plated, 1973–1974. *Courtesy of the author.* $50–$125/each

Faces

Faces. *Courtesy of Rita Sacks, Limited Additions, New York, NY; Prudence Huang, New York, NY; and Elayne Glotzer, New York, NY. Photograph by Kenneth Chen.*

(clockwise from top)

Coro Pin. "Josephine Baker"; enameled hair ornaments in yellow, red, and green; black enameled hair; beige enameled face with black, red, and white accents; gold plated; 1930s. *Courtesy of Rita Sacks, Limited Additions.* $300–$400

Cecil B. DeMille Pin. Native American head, multicolored enameled feather headdress, copper plated face, marked "North West Mounted Police Cecil B. DeMille." *Courtesy of Rita Sacks, Limited Additions.* $300–$400

Trifari Pin. Smiling Buddha head suspended from three oval rings, silver plated, designed by Diane Love, 1969–1970. *Courtesy of Prudence Huang*. $150–$200

R. DeRosa Pin. Exotic woman; pink crystal face; pale blue, pink, faux amethyst, and citrine feather headdress; clear round rhinestones at bottoms of braids; gold plated; 1930s. *Courtesy of Elayne Glotzer*. $500–$600

Joseph Weinstein Pin (center). Art Nouveau face on an Art Deco geometric background, enameled green-and-white flowers and leaves, brass, marked "Joseph Weinstein, N.Y.C.," ca. 1920s. *Courtesy of Rita Sacks, Limited Additions*. $150–$200

Flowers

Flowers. *Courtesy of Carol Moskowitz, New York, NY, and Rita Sacks, Limited Additions, New York, NY. Photograph by Kenneth Chen.*

(left to right)

B. Blumenthal Pin and Unsigned Clip. Flower pin, silvery peach and ivory metallic closed petals (made of composition celluloid or plastic), gold-plated stem; three-leaf clip, antique finished brass, ca. 1930s. *Courtesy of Carol Moskowitz*. $275–$350/pin and clip

Unsigned Pin. Dogwood blossoms; pink, yellow, and white ceramic; green celluloid stems; brown wooden branches; 5¼ inches high; 1930s. *Courtesy of Rita Sacks, Limited Additions.* $450–550

Unsigned Clip. Flowers, pink "poured glass," faux aquamarine centers, gold plated, 5½ inches high, 1930s. *Courtesy of Rita Sacks, Limited Additions.* $750–$850

Hattie Carnegie (HC)

Hattie Carnegie (HC). *Jewelry and photograph courtesy of Maria Domont Collection, Beverly Hills, CA.*

Hattie Carnegie Pin. Flower, Venetian glass blossoms, simulated pearls, marked "HC," ca. 1940s. *Courtesy of Maria Domont Collection.* $350–$450

Hattie Carnegie Pin. Flower, faux turquoise beads, clear rhinestones, faux rubies, marked "HC," ca. 1940s. *Courtesy of Maria Domont Collection.*
                    $350–$450

Hattie Carnegie Pin. Figure, light blue enamel, clear round rhinestones. *Courtesy of Maria Domont.* $450–$550

Jelly Bellies

Jelly bellies. *Courtesy of Susan Kelner Freeman, New York, NY. Photograph by Kenneth Chen.*

Trifari Pins and Clips. Rare; "jelly belly" poodle clip, Pekingese pin, Airedale clip, elephant clip; Lucite bellies; pavé rhinestone heads, tails, and legs; black enameled accents; faux ruby cabochon eyes; rhodium plated; 1930s. *Courtesy of Susan Kelner Freeman.*

$2,400–$2,800/each

Leo Glass

Leo Glass. *Courtesy of Joan Paley, Chicago, IL; Rita Sacks, Limited Additions, New York, NY; and Charles France, Divine Idea, New York, NY. Photograph by Kenneth Chen.*

Leo Glass Pin. Abstract flower, large, oval faux aquamarine belly, triangular-cut faux sapphires, large clear round rhinestones, gold plated, ca. 1940s. *Courtesy of Joan Paley.* $600–$700

Leo Glass Clip. Circle design, large, central square-cut faux aquamarine, movable circle dangles, gold plated, ca. 1940s. *Courtesy of Rita Sacks, Limited Additions.* $350–$450

Leo Glass Pin. Turtle, large, oval faux sapphire back, faux ruby cabochon eyes, red-and-green enameled flower, green enameled feet, gold plated, ca. 1940s. *Courtesy of Charles France, Divine Idea.* $300–$425

Lucite and Wood Figurals

Lucite and wood figurals. *Courtesy of Joan Orlen, Joan's Jewels, Lynbrook, NY. Photograph by Kenneth Chen.*

Unsigned Pins. Figurals, wood, Lucite, brass accents, 1930s. *Courtesy of Joan Orlen, Joan's Jewels.* $75–$125/each

Maltese Crosses

Maltese crosses. *Courtesy of Muriel Karasik, Westhampton Beach, NY. Photograph by Kenneth Chen.*

(left to right from top)

Jomaz Pin. Maltese cross, pink faux opals, faux rubies, clear round rhinestones, gold plated, 1960s. *Courtesy of Muriel Karasik.* $300–$500

Jomaz Pin. Maltese cross, central faux rubies, faux emerald cabochon, pavé rhinestones, gold plated, 1960s. *Courtesy of Muriel Karasik.*

$250–$400

Mimi di N Pin/Pendant. Double Maltese cross, faux turquoise beads, faux sapphire cabochons, large central faux aquamarine, clear round rhinestones, gold plated, 1960s. *Courtesy of Muriel Karasik.* $250–$400

Jomaz Pin. Maltese cross, faux ruby cabochons, clear round rhinestones, gold plated, 1960s. *Courtesy of Muriel Karasik.* $300–$500

Trifari Pin. Maltese cross, faux emerald cabochons, pavé rhinestones, gold plated, 1960s. *Courtesy of Muriel Karasik.* $300–$400

Jomaz Pin. Maltese cross, faux turquoises and lapis lazulis, pavé rhinestones, gold plated, 1960s. *Courtesy of Muriel Karasik.* $300–$500

Marcel Boucher

Marcel Boucher. *Courtesy of Carol Moskowitz, New York, NY, and Robin Feldman Collectibles, New York, NY. Photograph by Kenneth Chen.*

(left to right)

Marcel Boucher Pin. Flower, round faux topaz petals, faux aquamarine centers, pavé rhinestones on the pale yellow enameled stems, gold plated on the front, rhodium plated on the back, marked "L," ca. 1930s. *Courtesy of Carol Moskowitz.* $150–$250

Marcel Boucher Pin. Flower, round faux amethysts and pink rhinestone petals, clear round rhinestones on the pale green and gold enameled stems, rhodium plated, marked "MB." *Courtesy of Robin Feldman Collectibles.* $350–$400

Marcel Boucher Pin (unsigned). Double flower, round faux citrine petals, pale green rhinestone centers, pale green enameled leaves, red accents, clear round rhinestones on the stems, rhodium plated, marked "H," ca. 1930s. *Courtesy of Robin Feldman Collectibles.* $150–$300

My Fair Lady

My Fair Lady. *Courtesy of Charles France, Divine Idea, New York, NY. Photograph by Kenneth Chen.*

B.S.K. Pins. My Fair Lady pins, manufactured in conjunction with the Broadway show, all enameled, some with faux rubies and clear round rhinestones, gold plated, marked "MY FAIR LADY," the largest is 2½ inches high, 1950s. *Courtesy of Charles France.*

$300–$350/collection, $25–$50/each

Nettie Rosenstein (1930s–1940s)

Nettie Rosentein (1930s–1940s). *Courtesy of Alexandra Vangel. Photograph by John Merowski.*

(left to right from top)

Nettie Rosenstein Pin. Shield, crossed swords, faux coral cameo, simulated pearls, faux turquoise cabochons in crown, ca. 1940s. *Courtesy of Alexandra Vangel.* $150–$300

Nettie Rosenstein Clip. Pansy, white enameled petals, pink enameled center, pink rhinestones, clear round rhinestone edges, ca. 1930s. *Courtesy of Alexandra Vangel.* $75–$125

Nettie Rosenstein Pin. Hand-painted pastel floral center, clear round rhinestones, ca. 1940s. *Courtesy of Alexandra Vangel.* $90–$140

Nettie Rosenstein Clip. King of Hearts, simulated pearls in crown, pavé rhinestones, rose gold sterling vermeil, 1940s. *Courtesy of Alexandra Vangel.* $175–$280

Nettie Rosenstein Clip. Octopus, opal, sterling silver, 1940s. *Courtesy of Alexandra Vangel.* $400–$500

Nettie Rosenstein Pin. Pansy, yellow enameled petals, faux topaz center, sterling silver, 1940s. *Courtesy of Alexandra Vangel.* $50–$85

Nettie Rosenstein Pin. Bug, faux turquoise body, sterling silver, 1940s. *Courtesy of Alexandra Vangel.* $75–$125

Nettie Rosenstein (1940s–1960s)

Nettie Rosentein (1940s and 1960s–1970s). *Courtesy of Dr. Raymond Carol and Rita Sacks, Limited Additions, New York, NY. Photograph by Kenneth Chen.*

(left to right)

Nettie Rosenstein Pin. Hand-painted miniature portrait of a woman, ornate crown design frame, pavé rhinestones, simulated pearls, gold plated, 2½ inches high, ca. 1960s. *Courtesy of Dr. Raymond Carol.* $200–$300

Nettie Rosenstein Pendant. Hand-painted miniature French Directoire portrait, simulated pearls in a bow-and-foliate frame, clear round rhinestones, sterling vermeil, 1940s. *Courtesy of Rita Sacks, Limited Additions.* $1,500–$1,800

Nettie Rosenstein Pin. Watch fob design, hand-painted miniature portrait of a blackamoor, pavé rhinestones, gold plated, ca. 1960s. *Courtesy of Dr. Raymond Carol.* $200–$300

|| NOTE: Portrait jewelry was called "souvenir jewelry" in the || nineteenth century.

Patriotic

Patriotic. *Courtesy of Rita Sacks, Limited Additions, New York, NY. Photograph by Kenneth Chen.*

Unsigned Pin. Red, white, and blue enameled eagle in flight; eagle holds a locket in its mouth; gold plated; 1940s. *Courtesy of Rita Sacks, Limited Additions.* $150–$200

Unsigned Pin. "Uncle Sam" hat; red, white, and blue enameled crown; gold plated; 1940s. *Courtesy of Rita Sacks, Limited Additions.*
$150–$200

Unsigned Pin. A pair of drums suspended from an eagle; red, white, and blue braided leather trim on the drums; white enameled drums; gold plated; 1940s. *Courtesy of Rita Sacks, Limited Additions.* $150–$200

Rebajes

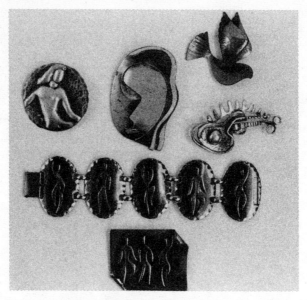

Rebajes. *Courtesy of Ilene Chazanof, Decorative Arts, New York, NY. Photograph by Kenneth Chen.*

(left to right from top)

Rebajes pin. Woman in a circle, sterling silver, 2-inch diameter, ca. 1940s. *Courtesy of Ilene Chazanof, Decorative Arts.* $100–$200

Rebajes Pin. Rare piece, "Veronica Lake," sterling silver, 3 inches high, ca. 1940s. *Courtesy of Ilene Chazanof, Decorative Arts.* $250–$350

Rebajes Pin. Dove in flight, shadowed copper, 2¼ inches high and wide, ca. 1950s. *Courtesy of Ilene Chazanof, Decorative Arts.* $35–$75

Rebajes Pin. Abstract guitar, silver plated, 2¹³⁄₁₆ inches wide, ca. 1950s. *Courtesy of Ilene Chazanof, Decorative Arts.* $100–$150

Rebajes Bracelet and Pin. Dancers, shadowed copper, ca. 1950s.
Courtesy of Ilene Chazanof, Decorative Arts. $100–$150/set

Retro

Retro. *Courtesy of Charles France, Divine Idea, New York, NY, and Robin
Feldman Collectibles, New York, NY. Photograph by Kenneth Chen.*

R. DeRosa Clip. Retro style, large round faux sapphire in the center,
stretched-cut faux rubies, clear round rhinestones at the top, simulated pearls at the base, gold plated, early 1940s. *Courtesy of Charles
France, Divine Idea.* $450–$650

Mazer Pin. Retro style, large rectangular faux topaz center, faux topaz baguettes, unusually cut hexagon faux amethysts, clear round rhinestones, sterling vermeil, 3 inches high, 1940s. *Courtesy of Robin Feldman Collectibles.* $475–$650

Unsigned Pin. Unusual double hoop, lozenge-cut faux aquamarines, pavé rhinestones, sterling vermeil, 3⅜ inches high, 1940s. *Courtesy of Charles France, Divine Idea.* $400–$600

Eisenberg Original Pin. Bow, large faux emerald center (also made with faux sapphire, ruby, and amethyst centers), sterling vermeil, 1940s. *Courtesy of Charles France, Divine Idea.* $400–$500

Rings

Rings. *Courtesy of Joan Paley, Chicago, IL. Photograph by Kenneth Chen.*

(clockwise from top)

Ciner Ring. Octagon-cut faux ruby flanked by trapezium-cut faux sapphires, sterling silver, 1940s. *Courtesy of Joan Paley.* $275–$400

Unsigned Ring. Large, antique square-cut faux sapphire, ringed with clear round rhinestones and faux lapis lazuli beads, gold plated, 1960s. *Courtesy of Joan Paley.* $150–$250

Kenneth Jay Lane Ring. Large, oval faux emerald cabochon, pavé rhinestones, gold plated, marked "KJL," 1960s. *Courtesy of Joan Paley.* $200–$350

Jomaz Ring. Large, round faux emerald, green-and-ivory enameled geometric pattern, pavé rhinestones, gold plated, 1960s. *Courtesy of Joan Paley.* $150–$250

Ciro Ring (center). Large octagon-cut faux diamond and aquamarine, oval faux diamond, sterling silver, 1940s. *Courtesy of Joan Paley.* $350–$500

Roses

Roses. *Courtesy of Rita Sacks, Limited Additions, Lorraine Wohl Collection, and Elayne Glotzer, all of New York, NY. Photograph by Kenneth Chen.*

(left to right)

Nettie Rosenstein Clip. Rose, pink enameled petals, green enameled leaves, clear round rhinestones on the petal edges, rose gold sterling vermeil, 1940s. *Courtesy of Rita Sacks, Limited Additions.* $900–$1,000

Unsigned Clip. Rose, prong-set clear round rhinestones, simulated teardrop-shaped pearls, silver plated, marked "Deposé," ca. 1930s. *Courtesy of Lorraine Wohl Collection.* $600–$750

Unsigned Pin. Rose, pavé rhinestones, green-and-brown enameled leaves, silver plated, 1930s. *Courtesy of Elayne Glotzer.* $400–$500

Scenes

Scenes. *Courtesy of Rita Sacks, Limited Additions, New York, NY. Photograph by Kenneth Chen.*

Unsigned Pins. Four framed three-dimensional scenes: circus, ballet, nautical, and western; multicolored enameled objects; gold plated; 2 inches wide by 1½ inches high, 1930s. *Courtesy of Rita Sacks, Limited Additions.* $150–$250/each

Thief of Bagdad

Thief of Bagdad. Courtesy of Rita Sacks, Limited Additions, New York, NY. Photograph by Kenneth Chen.

(from left top)

Thief of Bagdad *Pin*. Scimitar, multicolored rhinestones and simulated pearls, gold plated, silver plated, marked "Thief of Bagdad Korda J13 6," 4¼ inches wide, 1940. *Courtesy of Rita Sacks, Limited Additions.* $150–$200

Alexander Korda Pin. Tiger, black enameled stripes, gold plated, marked "Alexander Korda," 3 inches high, 1940. *Courtesy of Rita Sacks, Limited Additions.* $200–$300

Thief of Bagdad *Pin*. Flying dragon, silver plated, marked "Thief of Bagdad Korda J13 61," 3½ inches high, 1940. *Courtesy of Rita Sacks, Limited Additions.* $250–$300

Thief of Bagdad *Pin*. Ship, silver plated, marked "Thief of Bagdad Korda J13 61," 2½ inches high, 1940. *Courtesy of Rita Sacks, Limited Additions.* $150–$250

NOTE: The story is that producer Alexander Korda had the jewelry manufactured during the filming of the 1940 movie *Thief of Bagdad* and presented it as gifts to members of the cast and crew.

Tigers

Tigers. *Courtesy of Craig Smith and Pamela D. Smith, Ridgewood, NJ, and the author. Photograph by Kenneth Chen.*

(from left top)

LG Pin. Tiger, black enameled stripes on an orange-and-ivory background, faux emerald eyes, gold plated, 1950s. *Courtesy of Craig Smith.*

$35–$55

Jomaz Pin (unsigned). Leopard, black enameled spots, clear round rhinestone eyes, gold plated, 1950s. *Courtesy of Pamela D. Smith.*

$65–$100

Unsigned Pin. Tiger, black enameled stripes, red enameled toes and tongue, faux emerald cabochon eyes, clear round rhinestones, gold plated, 3½ inches wide, 1950s. *Courtesy of the author.* $60–$85

Tremblers

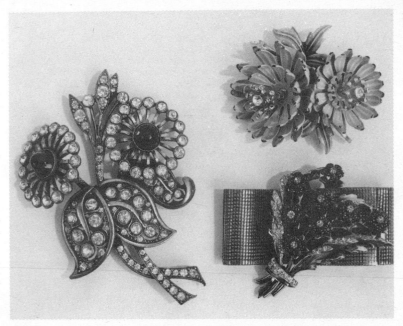

Tremblers. *Courtesy of Norman Crider Antiques, New York, NY; Rennie Myers, Rochester, NY; and Joan Paley, Chicago, IL. Photograph by Kenneth Chen.*

(clockwise from left)

Unsigned Pin. Double *tremblant* flower; faux ruby domed cabochon centers; clear round rhinestones on the flowers, leaves, and stems; gold plated; 4 inches high; 1930s. *Courtesy of Norman Crider Antiques.*
$1,200–$1,500

Unsigned Pin. Double flowers, *tremblant* centers, lilac enameled petals, green enameled leaves, gold plated, 1950s. *Courtesy of Rennie Myers.*
$85–$125

Unsigned Bracelet. Flower spray, *tremblant* blossoms, round faux ruby petals, clear round rhinestone centers, pavé rhinestone stems and band near base, wide flexible band, gold plated, 1¼ inches wide, 1940s. *Courtesy of Joan Paley.*
$600–$800

More Tremblers

More tremblers. *Courtesy of Rita Sacks, Limited Additions, and Robin Feldman Collectibles, both of New York, NY. Photograph by Kenneth Chen.*

Unsigned Pin. Cobweb, *tremblant* spider and fly, gold-plated web, silver-plated spider and fly, 1950s. *Courtesy of Rita Sacks, Limited Additions.*

$125–$150

Unsigned Pin. Dragonfly; *tremblant* wings; teal, mauve, and white enameled wings and body; clear round rhinestones on body and wings; white metal; 1930s. *Courtesy of Robin Feldman Collectibles.*

$100–$150

Unsigned Pin. Birds on a branch, the lower bird *tremblant*, clear round rhinestones on the wings, faux ruby eyes, blue-and-black enameled birds, green-and-brown enameled leaves and stems, 1940s. *Courtesy of Rita Sacks, Limited Additions.*

$150–$250

Whimsy Figures

Whimsy figures. *Courtesy of Rita Sacks, Limited Additions, New York, NY. Photograph by Kenneth Chen.*

Unsigned Pin. Woman walking a dog; red, black, white, and green enameled trim; gold plated; 1930s. *Courtesy of Rita Sacks, Limited Additions.*

$100–$200

Unsigned Pin. Man smoking a cigar; red, black, and white enameled trim; gold plated; 1930s. *Courtesy of Rita Sacks, Limited Additions.*

$100–$200

Whimsy Pins

Whimsy pins. *Courtesy of Joan Orlen, Joan's Jewels, Lynbrook, NY. Photograph by Kenneth Chen.*

Signed and Unsigned Pins. Figural pins; leather; enamel; simulated pearls; faux sapphires, emeralds, and rubies; gold plated; 1940s and 1950s. *Courtesy of Joan Orlen, Joan's Jewels.* $35–$45/each

A Century of
Costume Jewelry
(Almost)

The Twenties

The Twenties—when the nation came alive after a devastating war and women hiked up their skirts, bobbed their hair, and smoked in public. In Paris, Paul Poiret banned corsets and and petticoats. Chanel showed sailors' jackets and men's pullovers for women in her shop at Deauville. The "new silhouette" was long and flat, without feminine curves.

Androgynous dressing was quite the rage. Women wore men's smoking jackets and affected short, short haircuts. They even wore men's blazers, shirts, ties, and cuff links with their pleated skirts. It was seen as the ultimate statement of independence by the newly emancipated woman.

Art Deco was launched in 1925 at the Paris Exposition Internationale des Arts Decoratifs et Industriels Modernes. The "wild years," the Jazz Age, had officially begun. The geometric shapes and brilliant colors of Art Deco permeated art, fashion, furniture, and industrial design. Skyscrapers reflected Babylonian ziggurats and stepped Mayan and Aztec temples. Jewelry designers had a heyday with the materials of Indian art—obsidian, onyx, rock crystal, and jade. In Paris, Cartier's Indian-inspired jewelry used carved cabochon rubies, emeralds, and sapphires that were later copied by fine costume jewelers in the United States. Jewelry designers experimented with German silver, marcasites, pewter, and rhinestones. Noted designer Auguste Bonaz introduced a galalith necklace in 1923, and newly inexpensive chrome was used in combination with

Bakelite and other new plastics for jewelry. Jewelry took on the shapes of the Art Deco motifs of simple geometric forms that overlapped and repeated.

In fine art, the Twenties spawned avant-garde movements in every European country. Picasso's Cubism, the Italian poet Marinetti's "Futurist Manifesto," and Holland's Piet Mondrian and his Neo-Plasticism paintings all echoed the "modernistic" style. The emphasis was on the "new." The Fokine ballet, Hunt Diederich's sculptures, Leon Bakst's costume sketch exhibit, the Gish sisters of Hollywood, Edna St. Vincent Millay's romantic poetry, and Ziegfeld and his Follies had far-reaching global effects. Fashion designers were inspired by dancer Martha Graham, Paul Manship's *Salomé*, Isadora Duncan's dance troupes in Paris and Greece, and Pavlova, who was pictured in a Gypsy costume. King Tut's tomb was opened in 1922 and it inspired Egyptian designs in jewelry for the rest of the decade. In 1925, Josephine Baker's *Revue Negre* not only galvanized Parisian audiences but inspired costume jewelry designers in America to create jewelry in her image that is highly prized by today's collectors.

In Paris, Chanel's to-be-legendary jersey suits and dresses were easy to wear for women who now had freer, more active lives. Women were depicted in advertisements wearing tennis and golf outfits and driving cars. Pearl chokers, pearl-and-coral bracelets, and long necklaces were suggested for "sports costume and evening wear" in a 1920s magazine advertisement. Chanel accessorized pleated skirts and sweaters with triangle scarves and chunky glass bead necklaces. Vionnet showed supple fashions worn without undergarments. In 1926, short skirts and beaded sheaths were worn for evening, as were evening gowns made of gold-and-silver embroidery with sequins over lace and chiffon. Designer Louiseboulanger created an elegant chiffon dress, short in front and gracefully long in back. Shoes were made of black satin with cut steel buckles. Longer skirts and the slim profile encouraged women to wear long strings of beads that often ended in fringes and tassels. Turbans and cloches were adorned with diamond-and-paste clips or brooches.

Before Chanel boldly mixed imitation stones with real gems, jewelry worn by the fashionable 1920s' woman consisted mostly of strings of pearls in every variety of size and length, bracelets with links made of precious stones, and brooches, brooches everywhere. For evening, loose strands of pearls were worn, with pearl-studded medallions that stopped above the elbow. Long, dangling necklaces filled in plunging necklines and decorated bare backs. The demand for pearls was so great that Japan accelerated production of cultured pearls for export.

After World War I, women's traditional role had changed drastically. They had taken over men's jobs and often stayed in the work force when the war ended. Heavy fabrics were needed at the front, so women got used to wearing lighter weight rayon and muslin. Lighter fabrics took lighter jewelry. Women no longer wore gloves for every occasion, and rings became more important. They were made of large pearls, combinations of materials in geometric patterns, and had machine-inspired designs. By the end of the Twenties, jewelry evolved into daring, large motifs with distinct outlines.

Bracelets were wide and earrings long. In 1923, hat pins decorated cloches. Women cut their hair short and exposed their ears, hence the popularity of long, dangly earrings. In the late Twenties, earrings were so long they touched the shoulders. Sautoirs were made of strings of beads in every material from wood to semiprecious stones. No longer were they worn just in the front; they hung down over the back, across one shoulder, or wrapped around one leg. The long necklaces that complemented flappers' short tunic dresses had pendants and tassels that hung down to the stomach or even to the knees. The ups and downs of the hemlines in the Twenties created a constant need for new jewelry. The spirit of the day encouraged everyone to look for excitement in something new and daring.

Brooches sparkled on hats, shoulders, dress straps, belts, and buckles. Sleeveless dresses stimulated great interest in bracelets. They were worn in ways that ranged from four or five flat, flexible, narrow bands decorated with flowers and geometric shapes worn at the wrist, to bangles or slave bracelets worn several at a time on the upper arm. The elongated, sleek silhouette required new-looking jewelry with simple lines, minimal design, and bright colors. Advertisements in fashion magazines showed plastic cameos; rhinestone bar pins; bracelets in white metal, ivory, plastic, and elephant hair; artificial pearls of all lengths; and reproductions of Victorian jewelry.

From 1925 to 1929, chic style was short skirts, short hair, cloche hats, fox furs, vivid colors, jazzy patterns, simplicity in evening wear, and sparkly rhinestone buckles.

Everything changed by the end of the Twenties. Skirts were long again with a narrow silhouette and harder lines. Colors were navy, brown, black, and gray with fur-trimmed suits and coats. Hats were small and worn at an angle; handbags were envelopes or *pochettes* with gold metal clasps. Women were wearing Art Deco jewelry, precious jewelry pendants, and diamond clips at each side of the décolletage. In 1929, Schiaparelli opened her salon in Paris and introduced "shocking," a bright magenta pink.

The outstanding motifs of the Twenties were roses; baskets; cornucopia; flowers; bouquets; leaping animals; Asian symbols such as pagodas, urns, Buddhas, and dragons; and Egyptian designs such as scarabs and sphinxes, which were often made of early plastics. Materials frequently used were rock crystal, faux jade and ivory, simulated pearls, mother-of-pearl, and *paté-de-verre* (glass paste).

Costume jewelry made in the Twenties is not as collectible today as that of the Thirties through the Fifties. In England and Europe, however, it is very popular, particularly Art Deco paste bracelets. What is collected here in the United States are the rigid and flexible sterling silver bangles set with colored rhinestones—usually white, blue, green, and red. There are many collectors here and abroad who seek out Art Deco designs in necklaces, bracelets, pins, and earrings that are made of combinations of plastic and chrome. René Lalique designed costume jewelry made of glass that was often frosted or etched and is quite collectible today. Most costume jewelry made in the 1920s is unsigned.

Hobé chessman pin. *Original advertisement courtesy of Hobé Cie Ltd.*

Hobé Pin. Thibetan (*sic*), bezel-set dentelles, foliate setting, sterling silver, 1920s. *Original advertisement courtesy of Hobé Cie Ltd.* $500–$700

Miriam Haskell wrap bracelets. *Courtesy of Haskell Jewels, Ltd. Photograph by Kenneth Chen.*

(left to right)

Miriam Haskell Bracelet (unsigned). Wrap style, floral motif, simulated seed pearls, filigree center, clear round rhinestones, elongated simulated seed pearls on the wristband, gold plated, ca. 1920s. *Courtesy of Haskell Jewels, Ltd.* $250–$350

Miriam Haskell Bracelet (unsigned). Wrap style, floral motif, faux turquoise beads, simulated pearls, brass wire, gold plated leaves, ca. 1920s. *Courtesy of Haskell Jewels, Ltd.* $200–$300

Miriam Haskell Bracelet (unsigned). Wrap style, end domes of clear round rhinestone florets, metallic gold wrapped material wristband, ca. 1920s. *Courtesy of Haskell Jewels, Ltd.* $175–$250

Miriam Haskell wrap bracelets. *Courtesy of Haskell Jewels, Ltd. Photograph by Kenneth Chen.*

Miriam Haskell Bracelet (unsigned). Wrap style, cobalt marbleized glass center, faux coral beads and simulated pearl separators on the wristband, brass star-shaped leaves, ca. 1920s. *Courtesy of Haskell Jewels, Ltd.* $200–$300

Miriam Haskell Bracelet (unsigned). Wrap style; red, white, and blue Bakelite stars; Bakelite ball centers on a blue elastic wristband; ca. 1920s. *Courtesy of Haskell Jewels, Ltd.* $200–$300

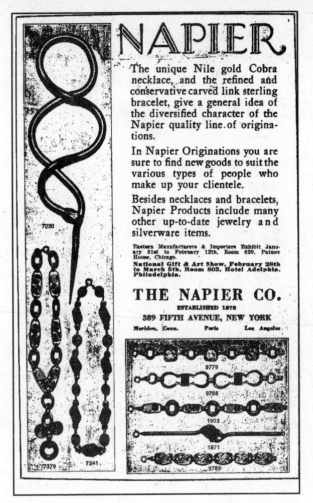

Napier necklaces and bracelets. *Original advertisement for* Giftwares *courtesy of The Napier Co.*

Napier Necklaces. "Gold cobra necklace," amulet necklace, Egyptian-style beads, 1920s. *Courtesy of The Napier Co.* $175–$250/each

Napier Bracelets. Art Deco links, snake chain, sterling silver, 1920s. *Courtesy of The Napier Co.* $125–$250/each

Unsigned Egyptian revival pins and necklace. *Courtesy of Ilene Chazanof, Decorative Arts, New York, NY. Photograph by Kenneth Chen.*

(top to bottom)

Unsigned Pin. Egyptian revival bird with outstretched wings, carrying an ankh, amethyst enamel and amethyst and iridescent green *plique-a-jour*, silver, marked "800," 1920s. *Courtesy of Ilene Chazanof, Decorative Arts.* $350–$500

Unsigned Pin. Egyptian revival faux jade scarab holding faux lapis balls, turquoise enameled wings, dark red and white, silver vermeil, marked "Silver 800," 1 inch wide, 1920s. *Courtesy of Ilene Chazanof, Decorative Arts.* $65–$125

Unsigned Pin. Egyptian revival vulture; outstretched wings; *plique-a-jour* enameled wings in turquoise, lapis, copper, green, and yellow; silver vermeil; marked "800," 3⅜ inches wide; 1920s. *Courtesy of Ilene Chazanof, Decorative Arts.* $150–$250

Unsigned Necklace. Rare Egyptian revival charm necklace with scarabs, ankhs, and figures; enameled sections of turquoise, dark red, lapis, coppery red, and white; silver vermeil; marked "800," 1920s. *Courtesy of Ilene Chazanof, Decorative Arts.* $350–$500

Unsigned "Machine Age" necklaces. *Courtesy of Muriel Karasik, Westhampton Beach, NY. Photograph by Kenneth Chen.*

Unsigned Necklaces. "Machine Age" designs, chrome and colored enamel, 1920s. *Courtesy of Muriel Karasik.* $250–$400/each

Unsigned Art Deco necklace and clip. *Necklace courtesy of Pamela D. Smith, Ridgewood, NJ; clip courtesy of Joan Paley, Chicago, IL. Photograph by Kenneth Chen.*

Unsigned Necklace. Art Deco geometric design, blue glass, geometric design on the chain links, silver plated, 1920s. *Courtesy of Pamela D. Smith.* $100–$140

Unsigned Clip. Art Deco circle pin, black Bakelite, red Bakelite sphere, pavé rhinestones, chrome plated, marked "CZECHOSLOV," ca. 1920s. *Courtesy of Joan Paley.* $200–$350

‖ **NOTE:** This circle pin has an unusual post fastening that allows ‖
‖ the pin to be attached to a sleeve or hat. Cartier and Van Cleef ‖
‖ used the same design for hats and purses.

Unsigned celluloid bracelets. *Courtesy of Dullsville, New York, NY. Photograph by Kenneth Chen.*

Unsigned Celluloid Bracelets. Assortment of white and translucent celluloid, red and white rhinestones in geometric designs, 1920s. *Courtesy of Dullsville.* $125–$250/each

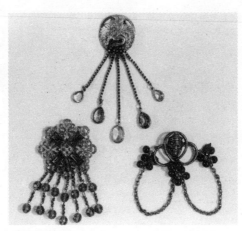

Unsigned dangle pins. *Courtesy of Rita Sacks, Limited Additions, New York, NY. Photograph by Kenneth Chen.*

(top to bottom)

Unsigned Pin. Peacock with spread wings, pale blue and dark pink oval and pear-shaped unfoiled rhinestone dangles, white metal, 1920s. *Courtesy of Rita Sacks, Limited Additions.* $350–$450

Unsigned Pin. Rectangular faux topazes, topaz-colored glass bead dangles, clear round rhinestones, white metal, 1920s. *Courtesy of Rita Sacks, Limited Additions.* $150–$250

Unsigned Pin. "Confucius" face centered in twisted loops; ruby, sapphire, amethyst, and topaz glass ball dangles; gold plated; 1920s. *Courtesy of Rita Sacks, Limited Additions.* $300–$400

Unsigned glass necklaces. *Leaf necklace courtesy of Elayne Glotzer, New York, NY; others courtesy of Amy Smith. Photograph by Kenneth Chen.*

(left to right)

Unsigned Necklace. Sautoir, green glass beads, brass, 1920s. *Courtesy of Amy Smith.* $30–$65

Unsigned Necklace. Tassel, green glass beads, paste rondelles, brass, 1920s. *Courtesy of Amy Smith.* $40–$60

Unsigned Necklace. Choker; green glass leaves; blue, green, and garnet-colored glass grape clusters; brass chain; ca. 1920s. *Courtesy of Elayne Glotzer.* $200–$300

Unsigned Necklace. Choker, green and clear crystal beads, brass spacers, 1920s. *Courtesy of Amy Smith.* $40–$60

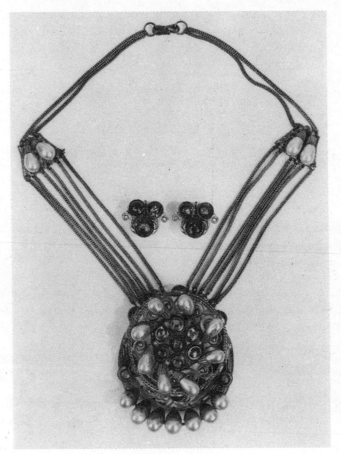

Unsigned necklace and Freirich earrings. *Courtesy of Charles France, Divine Idea, New York, NY. Photograph by Kenneth Chen.*

Unsigned Necklace and Freirich Earrings. Pendant necklace on six strands of chain, unusual blue and green "peacock" glass stones, round faux rubies and teardrop simulated baroque pearls, gold plated, ca. 1920s. The newer-looking matching earrings have the same "peacock" stones, marked "Freirich." *Courtesy of Charles France, Divine Idea.* $600–$800/set

Unsigned Art Deco clip and pins. *Courtesy of Terry Rodgers, New York, NY. Photograph by Kenneth Chen.*

(top to bottom)

Unsigned Clips. Art Deco, triangular shape, clear round rhinestones and baguettes, jet glass beads in a geometric design, white metal, 1920s. *Courtesy of Terry Rodgers.* $60–$85

Unsigned Pin. Large bird, pavé rhinestones, faux emerald eye, faux emeralds and amethysts in the tail, white metal, 1920s. *Courtesy of Terry Rodgers.* $75–$100

Unsigned Pin. Arrow, large clear rhinestones, marked "sterling 935," Austria, 1920s. *Courtesy of Terry Rodgers.* $150–$200

Unsigned Pin. Art Deco, frosted glass, faux sapphires, clear round rhinestones, white metal, 1920s. *Courtesy of Terry Rodgers.* $75–$125

. . . More Twenties

Unsigned Clip. Shield-shaped clip with central melon-cut faux ruby, accents of triangular and square-cut faux emeralds, clear round rhinestones and baguettes, rhodium plated, 1¹³⁄₁₆ inches. *Courtesy of Ilene Chazanof, Decorative Arts.* $50–$100

Unsigned Pin. Bar-shaped with a large central faux emerald cabochon, three oval faux emerald cabochons at each side, clear round rhinestones on an embossed frame, sterling silver, 2½ inches wide, 1920s. *Courtesy of Ilene Chazanof, Decorative Arts.* $75–$125

The Thirties

The Thirties glittered with glamour. Sinuous, bare-backed, body-clinging satin evening gowns were worn seductively by Hollywood's most captivating women. In Paris, Vionnet created the figure-flattering bias cut and became known as the "architect among dressmakers."

Schiaparelli, the rebel, showed padded, squared-off shoulders in *Vogue* magazine in 1933. In Hollywood she dressed Anita Loos, Marlene Dietrich, Gloria Swanson, and Lauren Bacall. Designer Adrian created fashions for many of the most glamorous stars. Clara Bow had "it" in 1930 and everyone else tried to get it. Ginger Rogers, Joan Crawford, Greta Garbo, Vivien Leigh, and Bette Davis were filmdom's leading women. In Hollywood, Greta Garbo's slouch hat, Katharine Hepburn's loose trousers, Joan Crawford's ankle strap shoes, and Marlene Dietrich's men's attire influenced women all over the world. Marlene Dietrich shocked haute couture when she wore a man's trouser suit on a film set. Fox-trimmed coats, halters, hip wraps, dramatic hats, and showy jewelry were the hallmarks of Hollywood style.

In New York, people flocked to Broadway to see Ethel Merman in *Anything Goes*. In Paris, Josephine Baker and Colette gathered avid followers, and First Lady Eleanor Roosevelt inspired women everywhere. The eyes of the world were on Joe Louis's and Jesse Owens's triumphs. Salvador Dali jolted the art world with his dreamscapes and Fred Astaire was the quintessential debonair gentleman. Chain letters circled the globe, African art was the rage, and dinner at the Rainbow Room in New York City was $3.50 plus $1.50 *couvert*.

Sports clothes for women appeared in shops, reflecting women's active lives. Schiaparelli designed knitted T-shirts and blouses to wear with tailored skirts. She launched culottes, showed tweeds for evening, and her hand-knitted jumpers had African, Cubist, and Surrealist art motifs. In New York, women were wearing denim wrap skirts. Nautical motifs appeared on everything. Fabrics were lively with Art Deco designs.

For fashionable women the flapper silhouette was finished. The style of the Chrysler tower, built in 1930, was called "zigzag moderne." Art Deco jewelry was seen mostly as brooches and clips. "Mad little hats" and hats with brims folded back were worn everywhere. In 1933, Patou showed a collection with zebra stripes that echoed the infamous El Morocco's decor.

By the mid Thirties skirts flared out gracefully from a slim waist and narrow hips. Alice Marble wore shorts while playing tennis at Wimbledon in 1936 and the public was aghast. From 1935 to 1939, women showed their defiance by their choices of clothing. In 1938, the fitted silhouette was popular, with wider shoulders, a more definite waistline, and a higher hemline that brushed the knees. Colors were darker and hair was worn either coiled at the nape or swept up. Hats were perched atop the head and snoods were the fashionable way to hold one's hair back.

By the end of the 1930s, Balenciaga in Spain was showing broader shoulders, shorter skirts, eccentric hats with veils, and elbow-length gloves. Vionnet retired in 1939 and her pupil Mad Carpentier took over her couture house, showing smooth satin and crepe de chine dresses without fastenings. French fashion designers were still the world's leaders, but American designers were emerging as an important force.

Costume jewelry became even more popular during the Depression. Established designers of precious metal jewelry turned to costume jewelry out of economic necessity. They experimented with metals, plastics, glass, imitation stones, ceramics, enamels, shells, wood, and leather. Women were buying Miriam Haskell's ultrafeminine designs and Schiaparelli's whimsical creations as well as rhinestone-and-plastic jewelry from the five-and-ten. Large rhinestone pins and clips were created to accessorize Eisenberg & Sons dresses, and women found them more appealing than the dresses themselves. Hobé used semiprecious stones and sterling silver in floral and Asian motifs. The well-known European jewelry designer Alfred Philippe joined Trifari and created real-looking costume jewelry. Eugene Joseff was creating fabulous, historically accurate pieces for most of the movies made in Hollywood, and in 1937 began producing a commercial line to be sold in fine stores. Marcel Boucher left Cartier and a successful career designing precious jewelry to start his own company in New York designing costume jewelry.

Beads of all kinds were worn as long strings, often with combinations of colored rhinestones and pearls, à la Chanel. Black-and-white evening gowns were worn with matching crystal-and-pearl sets. Earrings were buttons and studs instead of long drops. Curves and flowers were favored over the harder geometric lines of the 1920s. Every woman had to have an enameled flower pin for her favorite jacket lapel. Clips were worn on hats, at the end of the V in a V neckline, and at each corner of a square neckline. These clips were often triangles set with clear or colored rhinestones in geometric designs.

The "chunky" look was popular, rather than the delicate designs of the 1920s. Art Deco and Art Moderne still had a strong influence on costume jewelry. Loretta Young was shown wearing jewelry in a new way—a four-strand pearl choker with the clasp in the front. Schiaparelli designed necklaces, bracelets, and earrings of "silver latticework studded with exotic dark woods" and necklaces of ivy leaves with pearls.

There was great interest in African and Cubist jewelry in gold and silver plate, enamel and tortoiseshell. Pearl chokers, Coro "Duettes," Machine Age metal creations, bulkier pins, East Indian influences, and even Gypsy coin necklaces were part of the "look" of the Thirties.

Today, the costume jewelry made in the Thirties is extraordinarily popular among collectors. There's a great appreciation for the design and workmanship—skillfully applied paint and enamel, whimsical figurals, and the elegance of Art Deco–styled evening jewelry. Manufacturers had begun to sign their jewelry, and TKF (early Trifari, when the company was known as Trifari, Krussman and

Fishel), Eisenberg Original figurals and large Art Deco clips and pins, Coro Duettes, script and unsigned Chanel pieces, Marcel Boucher enamels (marked "MB" with a bird), Trifari "fruit salad" pieces, Josephine Baker likenesses made by various manufacturers, Pennino, and R. DeRosa are some of the important collectible pieces. Unsigned enameled pot metal floral pins, showy wide rhinestone bracelets, and large pins are among the unsigned collectible pieces.

Athennic Arts statue necklace;
Style Metal Specialty key dangle
pin; Fred A. Block starburst pin.
*Courtesy of Rita Sacks, Limited
Additions, New York, NY.
Photograph by Kenneth Chen.*

(*top to bottom*)

Athennic Arts Necklace. Ornate chain, Greek statue pendant in a niche, faux emerald and ruby in the base, pearl and faux ruby and emerald dangles, gold plated, 1930s. *Courtesy of Rita Sacks, Limited Additions.* $500–$600

Style Metal Specialty Co. Pin. Ornate key, dangling charms, brass, early 1930s. *Courtesy of Rita Sacks, Limited Additions.* $300–$350

Fred A. Block Pin. Floral cluster; starburst design; round faux aquamarines, topazes, and amethysts; clear round rhinestones; pear-shaped alternating jet and pink rhinestones; black enameled tips; clear round rhinestones on the spokes; sterling vermeil; ca. late 1930s. *Courtesy of Rita Sacks, Limited Additions.* $750–$950

Chanel "Puss in Boots" and pierced-heart pins.
Courtesy of Robin Feldman Collectibles,
New York, NY. Photograph by Kenneth Chen.

Chanel Pin. Rare, "Puss in Boots," red enameled suit and mouth, black enameled *tremblant* legs and head, pavé faux citrines on the violin and faux emerald eyes, white metal, script signature, 1930s. *Courtesy of Robin Feldman Collectibles.* $1,100–$1,500

Chanel Pin. Red enameled heart pierced by an arrow, white metal, script signature, 1930s. *Courtesy of Robin Feldman Collectibles.* $900–$1,200

Chanel Egyptian-style bib. *Courtesy of Joan Paley, Chicago, IL. Photograph by Kenneth Chen.*

Chanel Necklace. Egyptian-style triangular dangles with round faux moonstone centers, silver plated, script signature, 1930s. *Courtesy of Joan Paley.* $750–$1,000

Chanel dangle pin and earrings set. *Courtesy of Joan Paley, Chicago, IL. Photograph by Kenneth Chen.*

Chanel Pin and Earrings Set (unsigned). Dangle pin; carved faux rubies, emeralds, and sapphires; rectangular faux rubies, emeralds, and sapphires; melon-cut faux rubies, emeralds, and sapphires; simulated pearls; gold plated; pin 3½ inches high; ca. 1930s. *Courtesy of Joan Paley.* $800–$1,000/set

Coro Craft Josephine Baker pin and earrings set. *Courtesy of Charles France, Divine Idea, New York, NY. Photograph by Kenneth Chen.*

Coro Craft Pin and Earrings Set. Josephine Baker, brown enameled face, red-and-green enameled feathers, green enameled necklace, pavé rhinestone accents, matching earrings, sterling vermeil, ca. 1930s. *Courtesy of Charles France, Divine Idea.* $1,200–$1,600/set

R. DeRosa thistle pin, Nettie Rosenstein rose clip, unsigned lily of the valley pin, Reja cucumber pin. *Courtesy of Rita Sacks, Limited Additions, New York, NY. Photograph by Kenneth Chen.*

(clockwise from right)

R. DeRosa Pin (unsigned). Thistle flower and bud, pavé rhinestones, faux amethysts, iridescent ivory enameled head, translucent green enameled stems and leaves, gold plated, 1930s. *Courtesy of Rita Sacks, Limited Additions.* $1,200–$1,300

Nettie Rosenstein Clip. Rose, pink enameled petals, green enameled leaves, clear round rhinestones on the petal edges, rose gold sterling vermeil, ca. late 1930s. *Courtesy of Rita Sacks, Limited Additions.* $1,200–$1,400

Unsigned Pin. Lily of the valley stalk, pearly celluloid bells, translucent white and clear pale green bead dangles, brass, 4½ inches high, 1930s. *Courtesy of Rita Sacks, Limited Additions.* $200–$300

Reja Pin. Cucumber, green enameled, clear round rhinestone accents, gold plated, 1930s. *Courtesy of Rita Sacks, Limited Additions.* $400–$500

R. DeRosa floral and rose clips, Sandor rose pin. *Courtesy of Rita Sacks, Limited Additions, New York, NY. Photograph by Kenneth Chen.*

(left to right from top)

R. DeRosa Clip. Abstract floral design, large oval, central faux ruby and pavé rhinestone accents, simulated pearl centers in a pair of flowers, green enameled leaves, gold plated, 3¼ inches high, 1930s. *Courtesy of Rita Sacks, Limited Additions.* $1,500–$1,800

R. DeRosa Clip. Red enameled rose with buds, green enameled leaves, gold plated, 4¼ inches high, 1930s. *Courtesy of Rita Sacks, Limited Additions.*
$1,200–$1,500

Sandor Pin. Three red enameled roses in a bouquet, light green round rhinestones, red-and-brown enameled berries, bright yellow enameled ribbon, gold plated pin back, 1930s. *Courtesy of Rita Sacks, Limited Additions.*
$500–$700

Eisenberg Original necklace. *Courtesy of Norman Crider Antiques, New York, NY. Photograph by Kenneth Chen.*

Eisenberg Original Necklace. Rare, oval and round faux topazes, clear round rhinestone spacers, gold plated. *Courtesy of Norman Crider Antiques.*
$1,250–$1,500

Eisenberg basket clip. *Courtesy of Susan Kelner Freeman, New York, NY. Photograph by Kenneth Chen.*

Eisenberg Clip. Rare; pearlized basket; clear marquise, round, and teardrop-shaped rhinestone flowers; clear round rhinestone florets at the base; 3¼ inches high; 1930s. *Courtesy of Susan Kelner Freeman.*

$1,400–$1,800

Eisenberg Original angel clip and duck pin. *Courtesy of Robin Feldman Collectibles, New York, NY. Photograph by Kenneth Chen.*

Eisenberg Original Clip. Rare, angel, pavé rhinestone wings, white metal wings, gold plated body, marked "22" in a circle, 1930s. *Courtesy of Robin Feldman Collectibles.*

$1,900–$2,400

Eisenberg Original Pin. Rare, duck, large clear oval rhinestones, traces of red enamel on eye and beak, marked "L" in a circle, white metal, 1930s. *Courtesy of Robin Feldman Collectibles.* $1,800–$2,200

Fashionart crown chatelaine, B. Blumenthal sword pin, Kandell & Marcus chatelaine. *Courtesy of Rita Sacks, Limited Additions, New York, NY. Photograph by Kenneth Chen.*

(top to bottom)

Fashionart Chatelaine. Large and medium-sized crowns; faux topazes, amethysts, rubies, sapphires, and emeralds; white metal; marked "PE-6-3878" (the company's telephone number); 1930s. *Courtesy of Rita Sacks, Limited Additions.* $400–$500

B. Blumenthal Pin. Asian-design sword; carved green jade glass; red-and-navy enameled hat; blue, red, and aqua carved glass; jade glass dangles; white metal; marked "B. Blumenthal & Co. Inc.," 5¼ inches wide; 1930s. *Courtesy of Rita Sacks, Limited Additions.* $400–$500

Kandell & Marcus Chatelaine. Filigree Renaissance design, two shades of blue rhinestones, white metal, marked "Kandell & Marcus N.Y.," 1930s. *Courtesy of Rita Sacks, Limited Additions.* $350–$450

Joseff floral pin shown in an advertisement for Bullock's, 1930. *Original advertisement courtesy of Joan Castle Joseff.*

Marcel Boucher bird pins. *Jewelry and photograph courtesy of Maria Domont Collection, Beverly Hills, CA.*

Marcel Boucher Pins. Birds, pavé rhinestones, gold plated, marked "MB," ca. 1930s. *Courtesy of Maria Domont Collection.* $950–$1,100/each

Marcel Boucher cuff bracelet. *Courtesy of
Susan Kelner Freeman, New York, NY.
Photograph by Kenneth Chen.*

Marcel Boucher Bracelet. Cuff, "ruffled" design, clear round rhinestones
and baguettes in an unusual peaked design, rhodium plated, marked
"MB," ca. 1930s. *Courtesy of Susan Kelner Freeman.* $1,600–$2,000

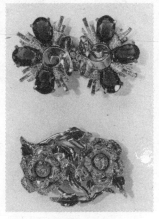

Mazer double clip/pin, Coro
Duette clip/pin. *Mazer pin courtesy
of Beverly Austrian, Tarrytown, NY;
Coro Duette courtesy of Charles
France, Divine Idea, New York, NY.
Photograph by Kenneth Chen.*

(top to bottom)

Mazer Double Clip/Pin. Rare, abstract shape, large oval faux amethysts,
clear round rhinestones and baguettes, pavé rhinestones, gold plated,
3½ inches wide, ca. 1930s. *Courtesy of Beverly Austrian.* $300–$450

Coco Duette Pin. Two roses, lavender-and-purple enameled petals, green enameled leaves, pavé rhinestone edges, rhodium plated, marked "Pat. No.1798867," 3¼ inches wide, 1930s. *Courtesy of Charles France, Divine Idea.* $300–$450

McClelland Barclay grapes and bird pins, McClelland Barclay coils pin. *Grapes and bird pins courtesy of Prudence Huang, New York, NY; coils pin courtesy of Carol Moskowitz, New York, NY. Photograph by Kenneth Chen.*

(top to bottom)

McClelland Barclay Pins. Rare pieces; grape and vine motif, 2¼ inches wide; hummingbird and flower motif, 2½ inches wide; sterling silver; 1930s. *Courtesy of Prudence Huang.* $200–$300/each

McClelland Barclay Pin. Unusual loose coils design, silver plated, 1930s. *Courtesy of Carol Moskowitz.* $300–$350

Miriam Haskell glass leaf necklace. *Jewelry and photography courtesy of Maria Domont Collection, Beverly Hills, CA.*

Miriam Haskell Necklace (unsigned). Rare, four strands of green glass beads, varying shades of green glass leaf clusters, gold plated, ca. 1930s. *Courtesy of Maria Domont Collection.* $600–$850

Mosell devil and carousel pins. *Devil pin courtesy of Carol Moskowitz, New York, NY; carousel pin courtesy of Susan Kelner Freeman, New York, NY. Photograph by Kenneth Chen.*

Mosell Pin. Devil playing a jeweled harp, oval and clear round rhinestones, gold plated, 3¾ inches high, 1930s. *Courtesy of Carol Moskowitz.* $750–$950

Mosell Pin. Carousel, *tremblant* figures, movable working bells, enameled flag, gold plated, 2½ inches high, 1930s. *Courtesy of Susan Kelner Freeman.* $550–$750

Sandor snowman "jelly belly" clip, R. DeRosa Lucite basket clip, Sandor Lucite face pin, Coro Craft Lucite basket clip. *Snowman courtesy of Rita Sacks, Limited Additions, New York, NY; baskets and face courtesy of Robin Feldman Collectibles, New York, NY. Photograph by Kenneth Chen.*

(clockwise from top)

Sandor Clip. Snowman "jelly belly," blue ceramic face, pavé rhinestone body, faux sapphire cabochons on arms, gold plated, 3 inches high, 1930s. *Courtesy of Rita Sacks, Limited Additions.* $2,500–$2,800

R. DeRosa Clip. Lucite basket shape, square-cut faux rubies at the tops of abstract stems, amethyst-and-violet enameled florets, yellow dots and green leaves, clear round rhinestone accents and a single simulated pearl at the base, gold plated, 1930s. *Courtesy of Robin Feldman Collectibles.* $1,200–$1,800

Sandor Pin. Rare, Lucite face, gold-plated metal hair, headband made of lozenge-cut faux rubies, clear round rhinestones, rhinestone accents in the bottom curl, 3⅜ inches high, 1930s. *Courtesy of Robin Feldman Collectibles.* $900–$1,500

Coro Craft Clip. Lucite basket holding multicolored enameled fruit, channel-set faux rubies, clear round rhinestones in the base, sterling vermeil, ca. 1930s. *Courtesy of Robin Feldman Collectibles.* $800–$1,400

Staret rooster, Staret fish, Staret wishing well. *Rooster and wishing well courtesy of Rita Sacks, Limited Additions, New York, NY; fish courtesy of Robin Feldman Collectibles, New York, NY. Photograph by Kenneth Chen.*

(top to bottom)

Staret Pin. Rare; rooster; red, blue, and green enameled feathers; red enameled cockscomb; orange enameled feet; faux ruby eye; gold plated; 1930s. *Courtesy of Rita Sacks, Limited Additions.* $2,500–$2,600

Staret Pin. Smiling fish, large faux ruby belly, pavé rhinestone body, green-and-yellow speckled enameled eyes, pink-and-green enameled mouth, faux ruby eye, white metal, 1930s. *Courtesy of Robin Feldman Collectibles.* $500–$800

Staret Pin. Wishing well hanging from a pavé rhinestone bow, pavé rhinestone roof, base and key and lock charm dangles, pink-and-blue enameled bricks, red enameled trim, gold plated, 1930s. *Courtesy of Robin Feldman Collectibles.* $1,800–$2,500

Trifari branch spray pin. *Courtesy of Susan Kelner Freeman, New York, NY. Photograph by Kenneth Chen.*

Trifari Pin. Abstract branch spray, pavé rhinestone balls, pale pink enameled finish, gold plated, 4⅛ inches wide, 1930s. *Courtesy of Susan Kelner Freeman.* $1,500–$2,500

Trifari "fruit salad" fan clip, Trifari "fruit salad" wheelbarrow pin and earrings set, unsigned "fruit salad" bouquet pin. *Fan courtesy of Rita Sacks, Limited Additions, New York, NY; wheelbarrow set and bouquet courtesy of Robin Feldman Collectibles, New York, NY. Photograph by Kenneth Chen.*

(top to bottom)

Trifari Clip. An Alfred Philippe design; Cartier-inspired "fruit salad" fan; "carved" faux rubies, sapphires, and emeralds; tiny faux ruby cabochons; clear round rhinestones and baguettes; rhodium plated; marked "Des. Pat. No. 125164," 1930s. *Courtesy of Rita Sacks, Limited Additions.* $1,800–$2,200

Trifari Pin and Earrings Set. "Fruit salad" flower cart; faux rubies, emeralds, and sapphires; pavé rhinestones and baguettes on the cart; faux sapphire cabochon in the center of the wheel and matching small round earrings; rhodium plated; marked "J4 + 10 Pat. Pend." on the pin; "22" on one earring; 1930s. *Courtesy of Robin Feldman Collectibles.* $1,000–$1,500 (sold for $1,500 in early 1993)

Unsigned Pin. "Fruit salad" bouquet; faux rubies, emeralds, and sapphires; multicolored rhinestone accents; pavé rhinestone rose, leaves, and ribbons; rhodium plated; marked "4"; 1930s. *Courtesy of Robin Feldman Collectibles.* $2,000–$2,500 (sold for $2,500 in early 1993)

Trifari "fruit salad" bouquet clip, unsigned "fruit salad" floral clip. *Courtesy of Norman Crider Antiques, New York, NY. Photograph by Kenneth Chen.*

(left to right)

Trifari Clip. Bouquet; Cartier-inspired "fruit salad" design; "carved" faux rubies, sapphires, and emeralds; clear round rhinestones and baguettes; rhodium plated; 1930s. *Courtesy of Norman Crider Antiques.*
$850–$1,100

Unsigned Clip. Floral; Cartier-inspired "fruit salad" design; "carved" faux rubies, sapphires, and emeralds; clear round rhinestones; rhodium plated; marked "Pat. Pend."; 1930s. *Courtesy of Norman Crider Antiques.*
$800–$950

Trifari frog clip. *Courtesy of Robin Feldman Collectibles, New York, NY. Photograph by Kenneth Chen.*

Trifari Clip. Rare, large frog, lozenge-cut faux topaz back, pavé rhinestone body and legs, round faux ruby cabochons on the feet, gold plated, marked "Des. Pat. No. 125849," 1930s. *Courtesy of Robin Feldman Collectibles.* $2,700–$3,200 (sold for $3,200 in early 1993)

Trifari harlequin clip. *Courtesy of Beverly Austrian, Tarrytown, NY. Photograph by Kenneth Chen.*

Trifari Clip. Rare, harlequin, black-and-white enameled ruff, blue enameled eyes, red enameled lips and folds of ruff, pavé rhinestones, rhodium plated, 2¼ inches high, 1930s. *Courtesy of Beverly Austrian.* $975–$1,200

Trifari swan pin. *Courtesy of Susan Kelner Freeman, New York, NY. Photograph by Kenneth Chen.*

Trifari Pin. Rare, "pearl belly" swan, design probably inspired by "The Ugly Duckling," pavé rhinestone wings edged in clear baguettes, faux ruby baguette underwing, pavé rhinestone tail and crown, faux emerald cabochon tips, faux ruby cabochon eye, gold plated, marked "Des. No. Pat. 1299535," 4¾ inches high, 1930s. *Courtesy of Susan Kelner Freeman.*

$3,500–$4,500

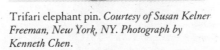

Trifari elephant pin. *Courtesy of Susan Kelner Freeman, New York, NY. Photograph by Kenneth Chen.*

Trifari Pin. Elephant; black enameled body; pavé rhinestone howdah; simulated baroque pearl top; faux emerald, sapphire, and ruby baguettes; faux ruby and emerald cabochons on head; simulated pearl held in trunk; gold plated; marked "Pat. Pend."; 2⅝ inches wide; 1930s. *Courtesy of Susan Kelner Freeman.* $1,200–$1,400

Unsigned floral pin. *Courtesy of Ilene Chazanof, Decorative Arts, New York, NY. Photograph by Kenneth Chen.*

Unsigned Pin. Flower, Cartier design, faux coral beads, black enameled leaves, pavé rhinestone edges, 3½ inches wide, backed with clear celluloid, silver plated, 1930s. *Courtesy of Ilene Chazanof, Decorative Arts.* $65–$100

NOTE: A photograph of the original Cartier pin, which was designed in December 1937, appeared in the Cartier publication *1976 Retrospective—Louis Cartier, One Hundred & One Years of the Jeweler's Art,* page 27, plate 37.

Unsigned butterfly and flower pins. *Butterfly courtesy of Charles France, Divine Idea, New York, NY; flower courtesy of Carol Moskowitz, New York, NY. Photograph by Kenneth Chen.*

Unsigned Pin. Large butterfly with marquise and pear-shaped faux aquamarines, topazes, sapphires, rubies, emeralds, citrines, and peridots; gold plated; 3¼-inch wingspan; ca. 1930s. *Courtesy of Charles France, Divine Idea.* $600–$750

Unsigned Pin. Large flower; marquise faux rubies, sapphires, aquamarines, citrines, emeralds, and pink rhinestones; oval faux emeralds and clear round rhinestones; gold plated; ca. 1930s. *Courtesy of Charles France, Divine Idea.* $600–$750

Unsigned parrot clip. *Courtesy of Susan Kelner Freeman, New York, NY. Photograph by Kenneth Chen.*

Unsigned Clip. Parrot, pavé rhinestone wings and tail, faux ruby cabochons in the chest, pink enameled eye, rhodium and rose gold plated, 3¾ inches high, 1930s. *Courtesy of Susan Kelner Freeman.* $2,500–$3,500

Unsigned fish pins. *Courtesy of Pauline Ginnane-Gasbarro, New York, NY. Photograph by Kenneth Chen.*

(top to bottom)

Unsigned Pin. Sailfish; light green enameled body; aqua enameled fins and tail; pink, black, and white enameled eyes; pink mouth with a white center; pavé rhinestone head, fin, and tail; white metal. *Courtesy of Pauline Ginnane-Gasbarro.* $115–$140

Unsigned Pin. Goldfish; light blue enameled body; red and yellow dots; green, black, and white enameled eyes; green mouth with a pink center; pavé rhinestone head, fin, and tail; white metal. *Courtesy of Pauline Ginnane-Gasbarro.* $85–$125

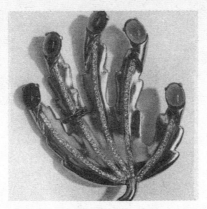

Unsigned hand pin. *Courtesy of Susan Kelner Freeman, New York, NY. Photograph by Kenneth Chen.*

Unsigned Pin. Surrealistic hand/leaf, faux emerald cabochon fingernails, ring made of faux emerald baguettes, pavé rhinestone "veins," gold plated, 4 inches high, 1930s. *Courtesy of Susan Kelner Freeman.* $950–$1,200

Unsigned fringe bib. *Courtesy of Elayne Glotzer, New York, NY. Photograph by Kenneth Chen.*

Unsigned Necklace. Bib, simulated pearl dangles ending in metal leaves, ornate stamped clasp, silver plated, ca. 1930s. *Courtesy of Elayne Glotzer.* $200–$300

Unsigned animal bracelet. *Courtesy of Joan Orlen, Joan's Jewels, Lynbrook, NY. Photograph by Steven D. Freeman.*

Unsigned Bracelet. Unusual, each link a different animal, silver plated, ca. 1930s. *Courtesy of Joan Orlen, Joan's Jewels.* $95–$125

Unsigned rhinestone necklace. *Courtesy of Charles France, Divine Idea, New York, NY. Photograph by Kenneth Chen.*

Unsigned Necklace. Graduated leaf cluster pendants; clear oval, round, and triangular-shaped rhinestones; white metal; belonged to Carole Lombard; 1930s. *Courtesy of Charles France, Divine Idea.*

$1,000–$1,500

Unsigned Art Deco sets. *Top necklace and earrings set courtesy of Joia, New York, NY; bottom necklace, bracelet, and earrings set courtesy of Muriel Karasik, Westhampton Beach, NY. Photograph by Kenneth Chen.*

(top to bottom)

Unsigned Necklace and Earrings Set. Art Deco upside-down ziggurat pendants, clear rectangular rhinestones, matching drop earrings, white metal, 1930s. *Courtesy of Joia.* $350–$450/set

Unsigned Necklace, Bracelet, and Earrings Set. Necklace, Art Deco, square faux aquamarines, clear rhinestones in a stepped pattern, matching link bracelet and drop earrings, white metal, 1930s. *Courtesy of Muriel Karasik.* $500–$750/set

Unsigned rhinestone chatelaines. *Courtesy of Norman Crider Antiques, New York, NY. Photograph by Kenneth Chen.*

Unsigned Chatelaine. Man with a large, oval, faux sapphire body and clear round, marquise, and square-cut rhinestones; dog with a large, oval, faux ruby body and round, pear-shaped, and marquise rhinestones; silver plated; 1930s. *Courtesy of Norman Crider Antiques.*

$150–$195

Unsigned Chatelaine. Stork with a smaller stork, clear round rhinestones, white metal, 1930s. *Courtesy of Norman Crider Antiques.* $110–$150

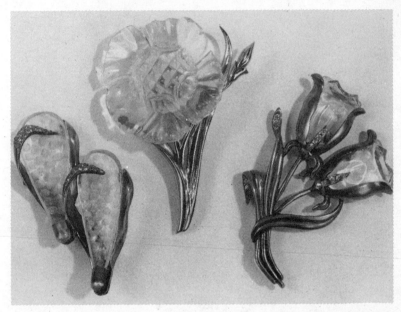

Unsigned Lucite pins. *Eggplant courtesy of Rita Sacks, Limited Additions, New York, NY; single flower courtesy of Rennie Myers, Rochester, NY; double flower courtesy of Robin Feldman Collectibles, New York, NY. Photograph by Kenneth Chen.*

(left to right)

Unsigned Pin. Etched Lucite eggplants, pavé rhinestone and green enameled leaves, gold plated, 1930s. *Courtesy of Rita Sacks, Limited Additions.* $900–$1,200

Unsigned Pin. Large Lucite flower, gold-plated stems, 4 inches high, 1930s. *Courtesy of Rennie Myers.* $400–$700

Unsigned Pin. Double Lucite flower, clear round rhinestones on the stems, light and dark green enameled leaves, gold plated, 4½ inches high, 1930s. *Courtesy of Robin Feldman.* $800–$1,200

Unsigned bubbles necklace. *Courtesy of Carol Moskowitz,
New York, NY. Photograph by Kenneth Chen.*

Unsigned Necklace. Pearlized bubbles (possibly a special plastic developed by Du Pont), celluloid chain, 1930s. *Courtesy of Carol Moskowitz.*

$150–$175

Unsigned clear Bakelite bracelets. *Bangle courtesy of Robin Feldman
Collectibles, New York, NY; links courtesy of Marene Weinraub,
Teaneck, NJ. Photograph by Kenneth Chen.*

Unsigned Bracelet. Hinged oval bangle of clear Bakelite, square-cut faux rubies and round clear rhinestones, 1930s. *Courtesy of Robin Feldman Collectibles.*

$200–$250

Unsigned Bracelet. Rare; clear and black Bakelite links with a hidden clasp; each clear link is 1⅞ inches long, ¾ inches wide; 1930s. *Courtesy of Marene Weinraub.*

$350–$500

Unsigned celluloid couple. *Courtesy of Rita Sacks, Limited Additions, New York, NY. Photograph by Kenneth Chen.*

Unsigned Pins. Pearlized celluloid Russian couple; the man in a pale green tunic, pink face and hands, pale yellow trousers, brown boots and hat, with black painting; the woman is wearing a white dress with an orange apron, pink face and hands, dark pink scarf, and black boots with green-and-brown painted decorations; 1930s. *Courtesy of Rita Sacks, Limited Additions.* $950–$1,100/pair

Unsigned Bakelite bangles. *Courtesy of Dullsville, New York, NY. Photograph by Kenneth Chen.*

Unsigned Bracelets. Bakelite, geometric designs, cream-colored and black, 1930s. *Courtesy of Dullsville.* $125–$275/each

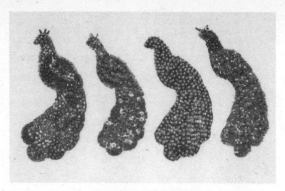

Unsigned sequined peacocks. *Courtesy of Flashy Trash, Chicago, IL. Photograph by A Big Production.*

Unsigned Pins. Peacocks, multicolored sequins, handmade "Depression jewelry," cloth bodies, 1930s. *Courtesy of Flashy Trash.*

$25–$125/each

Unsigned sequined horses' heads. *Courtesy of Flashy Trash, Chicago, IL. Photograph by A Big Production.*

Unsigned Pins. Horses' heads, black-and-white sequins, handmade "Depression jewelry," cloth bodies, 1930s. *Courtesy of Flashy Trash.*

$25–$125/each

. . . More Thirties

Coro Pin. Rose, pink, red, and black enameled petals outlined with pavé rhinestones; green-and-brown enameled stems; rhodium plated; 4 inches high; 1930s. *Courtesy of the author.* $300–$450

Coro Pin. Three pansies enameled in pale yellow with purple edges, red and yellow centers, and three tiny clear round rhinestones in each center; clear round rhinestones on the stem; gold plated, 3¼ inches high; 1930s. *Courtesy of Charles France, Divine Idea.* $150–$200

Coro Pin. Double flower, *tremblant* centers, faux emerald baguettes, pavé rhinestone blossoms, green enameled stems, gold plated, 1930s. *Courtesy of Prudence Huang.* $125–$175

R. DeRosa Clip. Rare, gauntlet holding a torch, faux sapphire domed cabochon at the top, allover embossed design, gold plated, 3 inches high, 1930s. *Courtesy of Rita Sacks, Limited Additions.* $500–$750

R. DeRosa Clip. Double flower, navy blue glass beads, clear round rhinestone accents, bright green enameled leaves and ribbon at the base, brown enameled stems, gold plated, 1930s. *Courtesy of Rita Sacks, Limited Additions.* $400–$650

R. DeRosa Pin (unsigned). Three yellow-and-white enameled flowers, clear yellow glass beads, clear round rhinestones on the stems, gold plated, 4 inches high, 1930s. *Courtesy of Rita Sacks, Limited Additions.*
                                $400–$600

R. DeRosa Pin (unsigned). Three abstract flowers, unusual triple stepped faux citrines on movable bases, clear round rhinestones at the tips and bases of each flower and accents on the stems, gold plated, 4 inches wide, 1930s. *Courtesy of Rita Sacks, Limited Additions.* $500–$750

Hattie Carnegie Clip. Unicorn, marquise faux emerald eye, simulated pearl mane and accents at the neck, clear round rhinestones, gold plated, marked "HC," 3½ inches high, ca. 1930s. *Courtesy of Rita Sacks, Limited Additions.* $600–$900

Hattie Carnegie Clip. Flower; marquise, oval, and pear-shaped faux aquamarines; two clear round rhinestones; pink marquise rhinestone; white metal; marked "HC"; 3 inches high and wide; ca. 1930s. *Courtesy of Rita Sacks, Limited Additions.* $500–$750

Hattie Carnegie Clip. Rare, squirrel on a corn stalk, oval faux emerald corn, white metal with some traces of gold plating, marked "HC," ca. 1930s. *Courtesy of Rita Sacks, Limited Additions.* $500–$750

Staret Pin. Rare; rooster; red, blue, and green enameled feathers; red enameled cockscomb; orange enameled feet; faux ruby eye; gold plated; 1930s. *Courtesy of Rita Sacks, Limited Additions.* $600–$750

Staret Clips (unsigned). A pair of wishing wells; marquise faux rubies, sapphires, and emeralds on the base; green enameled roofs; red enameled pails; clear round rhinestones outlining the roofs and bases; dark plated metal; 1930s. *Courtesy of Rita Sacks, Limited Additions.* $400–$650

Trifari Clip. Apple, baroque pearl and pavé rhinestone leaves, gold plated, 1⁹⁄16 inches high, 1930s. *Courtesy of Rita Sacks, Limited Additions.*

$275–$325

Walt Disney Productions Pin. Giraffe in a cage on wheels; gold-plated giraffe; silver-plated cage; marked "W.D.P." on the cage, "Coro" on the giraffe; 1¾ inches wide; ca. 1930s. *Courtesy of Charles France, Divine Idea.*

$250–$350

Walt Disney Productions Pin. Dumbo with a ringmaster in red, white, and blue enamel; gold plated; marked "W.D.P."; ca. 1930s. *Courtesy of Rita Sacks, Limited Additions.* $150–$250

Unsigned Pin. Marlene Dietrich; painted features and headdress in gold, teal, and red; ceramic; 1930s. *Courtesy of Rita Sacks, Limited Additions.*

$150–$250

Unsigned Pin. Sea creature, amber Lucite belly, etched scales, faux ruby eye, clear round rhinestones at the neck, white metal, 1930s. *Courtesy of Rita Sacks, Limited Additions.* $200–$300

Unsigned Pin. Three pink-and-white enameled flowers, clear round rhinestone centers, green enameled leaves, gold plated, 3 inches high, 1930s. *Courtesy of Rita Sacks, Limited Additions.* $400–$650

Unsigned Pin. Sailboat; red, white, and blue enameling; clear round rhinestone waves; white metal; 2½ inches high; 1930s. *Courtesy of Rita Sacks, Limited Additions.* $100–$200

The Forties

The Forties—the time when people's minds were on war, not fashion. Women working in industry were wearing pants, and snoods kept their hair out of their eyes and away from dangerous machinery. Practical shoulder bags, short "Eisenhower" jackets, tie-belted coats, and shorter skirts were popular. The typical wartime look was a square-shouldered, severely tailored jacket worn with a narrow, short skirt. The look wasn't just a fashion whim, it was a necessity due to severe rationing of material.

In the war years of 1939 to 1947, women's fashions were static. Hats were the only interesting expression of individuality and the only item of clothing that wasn't rationed. Women were working in defense and the masculine, "no nonsense" look prevailed, partly out of necessity, partly due to an emotional identification with the war effort. Turbans mirrored the head coverings factory workers wore. Shoes were usually a version of practical lace-up oxfords with open toes or sling backs.

Some brave designers such as Charles James, with his sculptured looks and elegant ball gowns, Norman Norell, and Mainbocher continued to introduce new American styles. Pauline Trigère from Paris showed her first New York collection in 1942. American Claire McCardell introduced the "ballerina look" and in 1946 showed the "baby dress" with a Napoleonic Empire line. She used double stitching, a tubelike top, and presented a wraparound coverall dress.

American designers were supported by the brilliant publicist

Eleanor Lambert and her famous Press Weeks. She was the first person to coordinate the leading American fashion designers with members of the press. *Vogue* magazine featured American designers Nettie Rosenstein, Hattie Carnegie, and Maurice Rentner in its editorials.

In 1947, Dior launched his "New Look," which paved the way for truly feminine elegance—unpadded, rounded shoulders; a defined bust line; and a waistline accentuated by slightly padded hips and a full billowing skirt that fell below the calves. It was worn with wide, flounced petticoats. In 1948, Lana Turner was "The Sweater Girl," and everyone watched Dorothy Lamour's and Veronica Lake's newest movies. Flattering looks were coming back. Once again shoes had sexier high heels, platform soles, and ankle straps. Hats were small pillboxes.

In the early Forties there were no imports from France, and imitation stones from Czechoslovakia and Austria were rationed or cut off completely. By then 85% to 90% of the total jewelry manufacturing was done in Providence, Rhode Island, where workers were known for fine metalwork. Brass and copper were outlawed for use in the jewelry industry in order to be made into bullet casings, so sterling silver was used instead for stampings and stone settings.

Peter DiCristofaro of Providence noted that virtually no jewelry was produced in the early Forties. When manufacturers got their allotment of metal, it was sterling silver and was used to make figural sterling pins—dogs, horses, palm trees, sailboats, swordfish, owls, and penguins, and heavy, bold pins for coats and suits. Women wore what they had saved from the Thirties. Factories in Providence were practically shut down because there were no men available to work in them. When the men returned from the war, Coro, Lisner, Monet, and others went back into production.

Sterling link bracelets, sterling pins with Lucite "bellies," two- or three-toned gold plating on sterling, snake chains, mesh, and chunky chrome bracelets appealed to the Forties woman.

Tailored clothing called for something elaborate like a showy brooch with matching earrings, bold sunburst and "atomic" designs, and heavy bracelets worn in groups. Oversized bows, flower pins, and clips had a single large real or imitation aquamarine, topaz, or amethyst because the smaller stones weren't available. Novelty jewelry made of leather, shells, and wood—and little Disney character pins—showed up on sweaters. War-related jewelry such as flags, airplanes, and other patriotic objects reflected the nation's sentiment. By the end of the Forties, dressy jewelry came back to accessorize the "New Look" and pearls reappeared in necklaces of all lengths with matching bracelets. There was a Victorian revival in evening jewelry.

Some of the most collectible jewelry was made in the Forties. Bold pins, chunky link bracelets, and amusing enameled figural designs, as well as Cartier-inspired "real-looking" jewelry, are all sought after. Trifari, Hobé, Staret, Hattie Carnegie, Joseff-Hollywood, Ciner, Coro, Coro Craft, Eisenberg Original, Pennino, Reja, Marcel Boucher, R. DeRosa, Miriam Haskell, Mazer, Monet, Napier, and Nettie Rosenstein are some of the most important designers and manufacturers of the Forties. Leo Glass, Fred A. Block, Joseph Morton, Ben Meltzer, and Sterling Button Co. were lesser known but equally interesting designers of that period.

Christian Dior floral necklace. *Courtesy of Charles France, Divine Idea, New York, NY. Photograph by Kenneth Chen.*

Christian Dior Necklace. Domed flowers, clear round rhinestones, silver plated, marked "Christian Dior France," ca. 1940s. *Courtesy of Charles France, Divine Idea.* $900–$1,200

Ciner retro bracelet and pin set. *Courtesy of Norman Crider Antiques, New York, NY. Photograph by Kenneth Chen.*

Ciner Bracelet and Pin Set. Retro-style bracelet, mesh band in a brickwork pattern, central motif of oval faux citrines and rubies, pavé rhinestone scroll designs, matching pin marked "343," gold plated, 1940s. *Courtesy of Norman Crider Antiques.*　　　$2,500–$3,000/set

Coro swirl pin, Coro bouquet pin, unsigned floral pin, unsigned retro pin, (center) unsigned bouquet pin. *Courtesy of Tania Santé's Classic Collectables, Miami, FL. Photograph by Phil Schlom.*

(clockwise from top right)

Coro Pin. Retro swirl design, large central rectangular faux aquamarine, sterling vermeil, 1940s. *Courtesy of Tania Santé's Classic Collectables.*

$50–$85

Coro Pin. Abstract floral bouquet design with retro swirls, square faux amethysts, gold plated, 1940s. *Courtesy of Tania Santé's Classic Antiques.*
$60–$100

Unsigned Pin. Floral design, round bezel-set faux amethysts, sterling vermeil, 1940s. *Courtesy of Tania Santé's Classic Antiques.* $40–$75

Unsigned Pin. Retro floral design, large central rectangular faux aquamarine, small round faux aquamarines, sterling vermeil, 1940s. *Courtesy of Tania Santé's Classic Antiques.* $60–$125

Unsigned Pin (center). Flower bouquet, round faux amethysts, gold plated, 1940s. *Courtesy of Tania Santé's Classic Antiques.* $40–$85

Dewees spray pin and earrings set, Pennino bouquet pin. *Courtesy of Rita Sacks, Limited Additions, New York, NY. Photograph by Kenneth Chen.*

(top to bottom)

Dewees Pin and Earrings Set. Spray, marquise faux aquamarines and clear round rhinestones, sterling vermeil, 1940s. *Courtesy of Rita Sacks, Limited Additions.* $900–$1,200

Pennino Pin. Bouquet, three flowers, oval faux aquamarines in a setting that is typical of Pennino pieces, faux ruby cabochon centers, clear round rhinestones, gold plated, 1940s. *Courtesy of Rita Sacks, Limited Additions.* $900–$1,100

Hattie Carnegie figural clips. *Courtesy of Robin Feldman Collectibles, New York, NY. Photograph by Kenneth Chen.*

Hattie Carnegie Clips. Male and female figures, pavé rhinestone breastplate and ruff, simulated pearl chests, clear rhinestone baguettes at the waists, faux ruby in the female's crown, white metal, marked "HC," ca. 1940s. *Courtesy of Robin Feldman Collectibles.*

$1,000–$2,000/pair (a pair sold for $2,000 in early 1993)

Joseff sun god necklace and earrings set. *Courtesy of the author. Photograph by Kenneth Chen.*

Joseff Necklace and Earrings Set. Sun gods suspended from Art Deco links, clear round rhinestone eyes, matching drop earrings, antique gold plated, marked "Joseff" in script, ca. 1940s. *Courtesy of the author.*

$1,500–$2,000/set

Joseff moon god necklace and earrings set. *Courtesy of the author. Photograph by Kenneth Chen.*

Joseff Necklace and Earrings Set. Moon gods suspended from links with Art Deco concentric circle design, clear round rhinestone eyes, matching drop earrings, antique gold plated, marked "Joseff" in script, ca. 1940s. *Courtesy of the author.* $600–$900/set

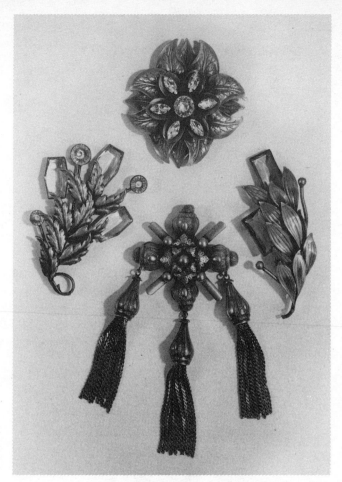

Joseff pins. *Courtesy of the author. Photograph by Kenneth Chen.*

(clockwise from the top)

Joseff pins. Calla lily, marquise and round faux topazes; leaves, rectangular-cut faux amethysts; Victorian-style tassel pin; leaves, stretched hexagon-cut and round clear rhinestones; antique gold plated; marked "Joseff" in script; ca. 1940s. *Courtesy of the author.*

Calla lily $300–$400; leaves $500–$700;
tassel pin $500–$700; leaves $500–$750

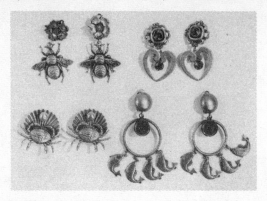

Joseff earrings. *Courtesy of the author. Photograph by Kenneth Chen.*

(left to right from top)

Joseff Earrings. Bees and flower drops; heart drops, round faux amethysts; crabs and shells, simulated pearls; fish drops, faux topaz cabochon; antique gold plated; marked "Joseff" in script; ca. 1940s. *Courtesy of the author.*　　Bees $125–$150; hearts $150–$200; crabs $125–$150; fish $150–$200

Joseff rooster necklace and earrings set. *Courtesy of the author. Photograph by Kenneth Chen.*

Joseff Necklace and Earrings Set. Roosters, filigree dangles, matching drop earrings, antique gold plated, marked "Joseff" in script, ca. 1940s. *Courtesy of the author.*　　$700–$1,000/set

Joseff lotus necklace and earrings set, Joseff scarab necklace and earrings set. *Lotus set courtesy of the author; scarab set courtesy of Prudence Huang, New York, NY. Photograph by Kenneth Chen.*

(top to bottom)

Joseff Necklace and Earrings Set. Egyptian-inspired lotus motif, matching drop earrings, antique gold plated, marked "Joseff" in script, ca. 1940s. *Courtesy of the author.* $600–$900/set

Joseff Necklace and Earrings Set. Art Deco links, faux turquoise scarabs, matching earrings, marked "Joseff" in script, antique gold plated. *Courtesy of Prudence Huang.* $500–$750

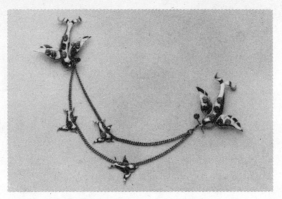

Leo Glass bird chatelaine. *Courtesy of Joan Orlen, Joan's Jewels, Lynbrook, NY. Photograph by Steven D. Freeman.*

Leo Glass Chatelaine. Rare, pair of birds holding the chains, three smaller birds on the chains, multicolored rhinestones, sterling vermeil, 1940s. *Courtesy of Joan Orlen, Joan's Jewels.* $125–$175

Leo Glass bracelet, earrings, and clip. *Courtesy of the author. Photograph by Kenneth Chen.*

Leo Glass Bracelet, Clip, and Earrings Set. Flower links, translucent frosted glass petals, pink enameled centers, simulated pearls, matching clip and earrings, gold plated, ca. 1940s. *Courtesy of the author.*
                                                            $750–$950

Miriam Haskell parure *(unsigned)*. Rare; early example of Haskell's use of French glass beads, ca. 1920s. $1,500–2,000.
Courtesy of Susan Hirsch; photo by Kenneth Chen.

Unsigned pin/pendant. Bisque doll face, coral, garnets, rhinestones, 1920s, 3" high. $1,700–2,000.
Courtesy of Susan Kelner Freeman; photo by Kenneth Chen.

Eisenberg dangle clip *(unsigned)*. Molded glass central stone, 4 ⅜" high, ca. 1930s. $1,400–1,800.
Courtesy of Susan Kelner Freeman; photo by Kenneth Chen.

Blumenthal pin *(ctr)*. $275–350.
Calvaire pin *(l)*. $550-650.
Unsigned pin *(r)*. Glass/celluloid. All 1930s. $1,200–1,500.
Courtesy of Carol Moskowitz and Rita Sacks; photo by Kenneth Chen.

Hattie Carnegie bracelet *(unsigned)*. Babylon design, sterling vermeil, 1939. $1,400–1,800.
Courtesy of Susan Kelner Freeman; photo by Kenneth Chen.

Chanel pins. Double flower *(unsigned)*, Frog, flower with buds, and rose (all script signatures), 1930s. $900–1,800/each.
Courtesy of Robin Feldman, Rita Sacks, Ira Scheck; photo by Kenneth Chen.

Leo Glass pin. Rare; plastic body, enameled branches, head and accents, 3⅜ " high, ca. 1930s. $1,600-2,200.
Courtesy of Susan Kelner Freeman; photo by Kenneth Chen.

Marcel Boucher pin. Rare; enameled pelican, *tremblant* fish inside mouth that opens and closes when the chain is pulled, 1930s. $3,500–4,000.
Courtesy of Susan Kelner Freeman; photo by Kenneth Chen.

Marcel Boucher pin. Enameled octopus,
marked MB, 1930s. $2,500–3,500.
*Courtesy of Susan Kelner Freeman;
photo by Kenneth Chen.*

Marcel Boucher pin. Flower, enameled
petals, 4" high, 1930s. $1,500–1,800.
*Courtesy of Susan Kelner Freeman;
photo by Kenneth Chen.*

Unsigned clip. Female blackamoor,
plique-a-jour enameled headdress and
vest, 3" high, 1930s. $2,200–2,800.
*Courtesy of Susan Kelner Freeman;
photo by Kenneth Chen.*

Staret pins. Rare; enameled parrot on a roost,
3 ½" high, $4,500–4,800. Enameled
floral swirl, 1930s. $1,200-1,400.
Courtesy of Rita Sacks; photo by Kenneth Chen.

Trifari pin. Alfred Philippe "fruit salad"
design, 3⅞" high, ca. 1930s. $3,500-3,800.
Courtesy of Susan Kelner Freeman;
photo by Kenneth Chen.

Trifari pin. Enameled Japanese cherry
tree, 3¼ " high, ca. 1930s. $2,000–2,500.
Courtesy of Susan Kelner Freeman;
photo by Kenneth Chen.

Unsigned pin. Bouquet, 4½" high,
1930s. $2,400–2,800.
Courtesy of Susan Kelner Freeman;
photo by Kenneth Chen.

Unsigned Bakelite bracelets/pins. Oval
bracelet $800–1,200; D-shaped bracelet
$1,400-1,800; boy $1,500-1,800; wheelbarrow
$1,500–1,800.
Courtesy of Susan Kelner Freeman;
photo by Kenneth Chen.

Chanel bracelet. Bangle, marked CHANEL in block print and J. Hugo in script, 1940s. $3,500–4,000.
Courtesy of Susan Kelner Freeman; photo by Kenneth Chen.

Eisenberg pin. Patriotic eagle design, 1940s. $1,200–1,800.
Courtesy of Robin Feldman; photo by Kenneth Chen.

Unsigned bracelet. Articulated bangle, retro design, 1940s. $3,000–3,500. *Note:* This bracelet is "Cartier Bijoux" from the Folies Bergere auction held in Paris.
Courtesy of Susan Kelner Freeman; photo by Kenneth Chen.

Chanel necklace *(unsigned)*. Classic style, ca. 1950s. $4,000–6,000.
Courtesy of the author; photo by Marcelo Maia.

Jomaz parure.
Foliate design, 1950s.
$800–1,000.
*Courtesy of Charles France;
photo by Kenneth Chen.*

Miriam Haskell parure.
Glass beads, 1950s. $1,000–1,500.
Jewelry and photo courtesy of Maria Domont.

Miriam Haskell necklace. Ornate collar in fan-shaped sections, 1950s. $1,000–1,300.
*Courtesy of the author and Robin Feldman;
photo by Kenneth Chen.*

Schreiner necklace. Elaborate bib collar
made for Teal Traina, 1960s. $750–950.
*Courtesy of Schreiner family collection;
photo by Kenneth Chen.*

Kenneth Jay Lane pins. Maltese crosses,
the lower piece is an unsigned pin/pen-
dant, 1960s. $250–400/each.
*Courtesy of Kenneth Jay Lane Vintage Collection;
photo by Kenneth Chen.*

Vendome pins. Rare; designed in
the style of Georges Braque.
$225–425/each.
*Courtesy of Carol Moskowitz;
photo by Kenneth Chen.*

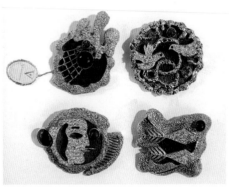

R. F. Clark pin and earrings.
"Discotheque," hand constructed,
marked de Lillo, 4" square, 1970s.
$2,500–2,700.
*Courtesy of Rita Sacks;
photo by Kenneth Chen.*

Jay Strongwater necklaces. Cameo choker, Spring, 1993. $175. Multi-strand beads, Spring, 1993, $500.
Jewelry and photo courtesy of Jay Strongwater.

Yves Saint Laurent necklaces *(unsigned)*. Pendant style and cross, early 1980s. $750–950/each.
Courtesy of the author and Sloane Miller; photo by Kenneth Chen.

Iradj Moini pin and earrings *(unsigned)*. Large parrot pin 13 ½" high, 1992. $750. Parrot on swing earrings, 1992. $750.
Courtesy of Iradj Moini; photo by Kenneth Chen.

Gerard Yosca bracelets. Enameled cuff, sunburst design, 1991, $225. Enameled biker cuff, 1990s. $175.
Courtesy of Gerard Yosca; photo by Kenneth Chen.

Marcel Boucher retro floral clip, Hattie Carnegie retro flower clip. *Courtesy of Robin Feldman Collectibles, New York, NY. Photograph by Kenneth Chen.*

(left to right)

Marcel Boucher Clip (unsigned). Retro-style flower, pink center rhinestone surrounded by clear baguettes, pavé rhinestone petals and stem accents, gold plated, 4¼ inches high, 1940s. *Courtesy of Robin Feldman Collectibles.* $1,500–$2,000

Hattie Carnegie Clip. Retro-style abstract flower, large central faux amethyst, clear round and rectangular-cut rhinestones, rose gold plated, marked "HC," 1940s. *Courtesy of Robin Feldman Collectibles.* $800–$1,000

Marcel Boucher bracelet and earrings set. *Courtesy of Charles France, Divine Idea, New York, NY. Photograph by Kenneth Chen.*

Marcel Boucher Bracelet and Earrings Set. Engine-turned leaves, round faux rubies, clear round rhinestones, gold plated, marked "6290" on the bracelet and "U.S. Pat. 2668341," ca. late 1940s. *Courtesy of Charles France, Divine Idea.* $350–$550/set

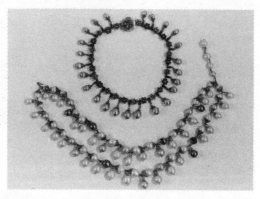

Miriam Haskell simulated pearl dangle choker, Chanel simulated pearl necklace. *Courtesy of Lorraine Wohl Collection, New York, NY. Photograph by Kenneth Chen.*

(top to bottom)

Miriam Haskell Necklace (unsigned). Choker; simulated pearl dangles; clear rhinestone florets; pale yellow, light and dark blue, pink, fuchsia, and chartreuse baguettes in between the dangles; floral clasp; simulated pearls; gold plated; 1940s. *Courtesy of Lorraine Wohl Collection.*

$1,400–$1,600

Chanel Necklace. Two strands, simulated ivory, gray and pink pearls, gold-plated brass caps, rhinestone rondelles, clear crystals on each bead, gold plated, ca. 1940s (reputed to be a copy of the gift given to Mme. Chanel by her Russian lover, Count Dmitri). *Courtesy of Lorraine Wohl Collection.* $2,000–$2,500

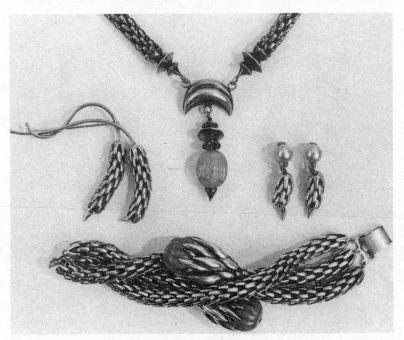

Napier necklace, bracelet, pin, and earrings. *Courtesy of Joan Paley, Chicago, IL. Photograph by Kenneth Chen.*

(top to bottom)

Napier Necklace (unsigned). Thick linked chain, barrel clasp, ending in a green glass melon-cut bead, silver plated, ca. 1940s. $300–$500

Napier Pin and Earrings Set. Wheat design, silver plated, 1940s.
                                                                 $250–$350/set

Napier Bracelet. Triple thick strand, wheat design linked chain, two melon-cut faux coral beads, silver plated, 1940s. $300–$500

Napier necklace, bracelet, and earrings set. *Courtesy of Tania Santé's Classic Collectables, Miami, FL.*

Napier Necklace, Bracelet, and Earrings Set. Multistrand necklace and bracelet, various types of chain links, matching dangle earrings, brass, 1940s. *Courtesy of Tania Santé's Classic Collectables.* $300–$550/set

Nettie Rosenstein fly pin and frog chatelaine. *Courtesy of Charles France, Divine Idea, New York, NY. Photograph by Kenneth Chen.*

Nettie Rosenstein Pin. Fly on a double bar, pear-shaped faux emerald belly, faux ruby eyes, pavé rhinestone wings and clear round rhinestones on the legs, simulated pearl head, sterling vermeil, 4 inches wide, 1940s. *Courtesy of Charles France, Divine Idea.* $500–$650

Nettie Rosenstein Chatelaine. Large frog connected by a chain to a smaller frog, clear round rhinestone eyes, green enamel accents, sterling vermeil, 1940s. *Courtesy of Charles France, Divine Idea.* $350–$450

Nettie Rosenstein umbrella and scissors pins. *Courtesy of Norman Crider Antiques, New York, NY. Photograph by Kenneth Chen.*

Nettie Rosenstein Pins. Umbrella with bird handle, clear round rhinestone accents, small simulated pearls; scissors with lion handles, clear round rhinestone accents; both sterling vermeil; 1940s. *Courtesy of Norman Crider Antiques.*   Umbrella $200–$250; scissors $300–$380

Reja king and queen pins. *Courtesy of Frances Cavaricci, New York, NY. Photograph by Kenneth Chen.*

Reja Pins. Rare, king and queen, triangular-cut faux emeralds in the tiaras, round faux emerald eyes, clear round rhinestones and two faux rubies in his tiara, clear round rhinestones in her tiara and earrings, black enameled hair, red enameled lips on both faces, sterling vermeil, king 2⅝ inches high, 1940s. *Courtesy of Frances Cavaricci.*

$1,200–$1,500/pair

Reja sea horse pins. *Courtesy of Robin Feldman Collectibles, New York, NY. Photograph by Kenneth Chen.*

Reja Pins. Rare, pair of sea horses, faux moonstone cabochons in the bodies, pavé rhinestone heads and tails, faux ruby eyes, sterling vermeil, 2¾ inches high, 1940s. *Courtesy of Robin Feldman Collectibles.*

$1,600–$2,000/pair

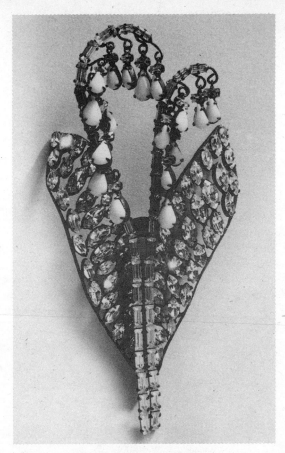

Schreiner lily of the valley pin. *Courtesy of the Schreiner family collection. Photograph by Kenneth Chen.*

Schreiner Pin/Clip. Lily of the valley, clear marquise and baguette rhinestones, white opaque marquise dangles, gunmetal plated, 1940s.
Courtesy of the Schreiner family collection. $250–$400

NOTE: In Europe during World War II, rhodium and gold could not be used for plating jewelry. This pin shows the first use by Schreiner of the black or gunmetal plating that was used in Paris in the Forties, as brought to the United States by Omar Khaim of Ben Reig.

Schreiner floral pin. *Courtesy of the Schreiner family collection. Photograph by Kenneth Chen.*

Schreiner Pin. Large floral "quiver" pin, jet and clear marquise and round rhinestones, gunmetal plated, 1940s. *Courtesy of the Schreiner family collection.* $250–$400

Trifari star necklace, bracelet, and earrings set. *Courtesy of Marene Weinraub, Teaneck, NJ. Photograph by Kenneth Chen.*

Trifari Necklace, Bracelet, and Earrings Set. Stars, graduated dangles, clear round rhinestone centers, matching link bracelet and dangle earrings, gold plated, 1940s. *Courtesy of Marene Weinraub.* $200–$300/set

Unsigned ballet dancer pins. *Courtesy of Norman Crider Antiques, New York, NY. Photograph by Kenneth Chen.*

Unsigned Pins. Three Surrealistic ballet dancer scatter pins, each with a large pear-shaped faux aquamarine body, pavé rhinestone leaflike heads and arms, sterling silver, 2½ inches high, 1940s. *Courtesy of Norman Crider Antiques.* $150–$200/each

Unsigned Romeo and Juliet pins. *Courtesy of Pauline Ginnane-Gasbarro, New York, NY. Photograph by Kenneth Chen.*

Unsigned Pins. Romeo and Juliet, oval, marquise and round faux sapphires, clear round rhinestones, red-and-green translucent enameled costumes, sterling vermeil, 2¼ inches high, 1940s. *Courtesy of Pauline Ginnane-Gasbarro.* $800–$1,000/pair

Unsigned branch pin and earrings. *Courtesy of Charles France, Divine Idea, New York, NY. Photograph by Kenneth Chen.*

Unsigned Pin and Earrings Set. Large branch with blossoms, leaves of graduated clear marquise rhinestones, blossoms of clear round rhinestones, marked "Made in Austria," gunmetal plated, ca. 1940s. *Courtesy of Charles France, Divine Idea.* $400–$600/set

Unsigned fountain retro pin, Irving Silverman retro pin. *Fountain pin courtesy of the author; Irving Silverman pin courtesy of Rita Sacks, Limited Additions, New York, NY. Photograph by Kenneth Chen.*

(left to right)

Unsigned Pin. Retro fountain spray design, gold plated, 1940s. *Courtesy of the author.* $125–$175

Irving Silverman Pin. Retro style, top design of concentric circles, flat snake chain loops, gold plated, marked "Irving Silverman NY," 1940s. *Courtesy of Rita Sacks, Limited Additions.* $200–$275

Unsigned African mask pins. *Courtesy of Flashy Trash, Chicago, IL.*
Photograph by A Big Production.

Unsigned Pins. African masks; hand-carved wood with brass, plastic, and felt trim; ca. 1940s. *Courtesy of Flashy Trash.* $35–$85/each

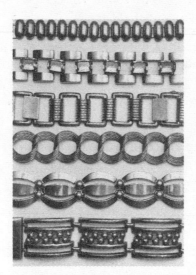

Unsigned link bracelets. *Courtesy of*
Terry Rodgers, New York, NY.
Photograph by Kenneth Chen.

Unsigned Bracelets. Links, one with faux topazes, brass, gold plated and gold filled, 1940s. *Courtesy of Terry Rodgers.* $75–$125/each

. . . More Forties

A.B. Pin. Starburst shape, large faux emerald domed cabochon with inclusions, surrounded by simulated baroque pearls topped by clear round rhinestones, clear round rhinestone rays, silver plated, marked "France," ca. 1940s. *Courtesy of Prudence Huang.* $200–$300

Adele Simpson Pin. Starburst design; large, central, round faux sapphire; surrounded by oval faux rubies and clear, small and medium, round rhinestones; black enameled tips; sterling vermeil; 1940s. *Courtesy of Rita Sacks, Limited Additions.* $200–$300

Amourelle Earrings. Drop hoops, simulated seed pearls, gold plated, ca. 1940s. *Courtesy of Metropolis.* $40–$75

Amourelle Earrings. Drops, simulated seed pearls and central faux sapphires, ca. 1940s. *Courtesy of Metropolis.* $40–$75

Coro Pin. Three enameled pansies in yellow, blue, and mauve atop a large, lozenge-cut faux topaz; sterling vermeil; marked "STERLING CRAFT by Coro"; 1940s. *Courtesy of Charles France, Divine Idea.* $250–$400

Coro Craft Clip. Horse's head, mane of faux ruby baguettes, marquise faux sapphire eye, red and green enameled flowers and leaves at the base, clear round rhinestone centers, sterling vermeil, 1940s. *Courtesy of Rita Sacks, Limited Additions.* $150–$250

Coro Craft Pin. Calla lily, round faux rubies and clear round rhinestones, pavé rhinestones on the stem and near the base, gold plated. *Courtesy of Rita Sacks, Limited Additions.* $350–$450

Hobé Bracelet and Pin Set. Bow-shaped pin, floral cascade, large oval and round faux emeralds and topazes, 3 inches; bracelet of rectangular links, bow/floral design, alternating large round faux emeralds and topazes; both pieces sterling $\frac{1}{20}$, 14K vermeil; 1940s. *Courtesy of Prudence Huang.* $400–$500/set

Joan Castle Joseff Pin. Shield-shaped, three teardrop filigree ball pendants, central oval faux sapphire, ca. 1940s. *Courtesy of Ginger Moro.*

$350–$500

Joseff-Hollywood Pin. Rare, floral design, large, unusually shaped rectangular faux citrines, antique gold-plated brass, 5½ inches wide, ca. 1940s. *Courtesy of Ginger Moro.*

$500–$700

Alexander Korda Pin. Lion atop faux ivory horn, round and marquise faux turquoises, silver plated, early 1940s. *Courtesy of Waltzman's Old Place.*

$75–$100

Kreisler Bracelet. Mesh band, 9/16 of an inch wide, central floral motif, large faux aquamarine center, pavé rhinestone accents, adjustable clip clasp, gold plated, marked "Kreisler-Quality U.S.A.," 1940s. *Courtesy of Prudence Huang.*

$150–$250

Leo Glass Necklace, Bracelet, and Clip. Four large chains in the front, a pair of matching antique rectangular-cut faux topazes at either side, narrowing to two chains back to the clasp, matching bracelet with three faux topazes, clip with a single faux topaz in a circle with five rings suspended and a single large ring suspended from them, gold plated, 1940s. *Courtesy of the author.*

$1,500–$1,800/set

Marslieu Pin. Stylized Cleopatra profile, simulated pearls and pavé rhinestones in the headdress and earrings, simulated pearl necklace, red enameled lips, sterling vermeil, 1940s. *Courtesy of Prudence Huang.*

$175–$275

Mazer Pin and Earrings Set. Abstract flower/bow pin, pavé rhinestones and baguettes, faux blue moonstones, coordinated earrings, sterling vermeil, 1940s. *Courtesy of Prudence Huang.*

$250–$325

Monet Pin. A pair of greyhounds, sterling vermeil, one yellow gold, one rose gold, 1940s. *Courtesy of Rita Sacks, Limited Additions.*

$200–$350

Nettie Rosenstein Clip and Earrings Set. Snowflake design with stars, central round clear rhinestones, sterling vermeil, 1940s. *Courtesy of Metropolis.*

$150–$250

Pennino Pin. Floral swirl design, pavé rhinestone center and alternating petals, spray of round faux ruby florets, clear round rhinestone centers, gold plated, 3 inches high, 1940s. *Courtesy of Prudence Huang.*

$300–$425

Pennino Pin. Classic design; round flower made of clear baguettes; a round, pink, multirhinestone center; clear round rhinestone florets; alternating metal leaves; metal interlocking swirls at the base; 3 inches high, sterling silver; 1940s. *Courtesy of Prudence Huang.*

$400–$600

Robert Pin. Reindeer head, large antlers, floral spray sprouting from behind the head, pink oval rhinestones, pear-shaped faux emeralds and clear round rhinestones, gold plated, marked "FASHION CRAFT robert," 4⅝ inches wide, 1940s. *Courtesy of Charles France, Divine Idea.*

$400–$750

Unsigned Pin. Large dragonfly, marquise faux light and dark blue sapphires on the wing tips, a stretched hexagon-cut pink central rhinestone, openwork wings, gold plated, 1940s. *Courtesy of Rita Sacks, Limited Additions.*

$600–$800

The Fifties

The fabulous Fifties! While teenagers were wearing dungarees and their father's shirts and dancing to the new craze, rock and roll, their mothers were trying out the chemise, the unfitted look, and Yves Saint Laurent's "trapeze." Coats looked like cocoons, suits were unstructured, and the *bateau* (boat) neckline was featured on everything.

Skirts were slimmer, everyone was wearing casual dresses with push-up sleeves, and Balenciaga was showing the "semi-fit," which was close to the body in front and easy and straight in the back. The sheath dress was topped with a high Empire-line bolero, and for a different look, several bouffant crinolines were worn under short, full skirts that paired up with man-tailored shirts and wide, wide cinch belts. Crinolines were kept stiff with a bath of sugar and water. Some high schools put a limit on the number of crinolines worn to classes due to congestion in narrow hallways.

The trendy "beatniks" were wearing black leotard tights under black sweaters and skirts or tweed jumpers. Large overshirts were worn over tapered pants that stopped mid-calf as "toreadors" or ended just at the ankle. Little round-toed flat "ballerinas" completed the look.

The chemise dress was a natural to pair up with ropes up to 120 inches long, bibs, and lariats. Scatter pins in twos or threes dressed up the simple lines and were worn everywhere, even on the hemline. Dog collars sparkled on bare necks. Matching pin and earrings sets were bold; some had moving parts. Pins were noticeably bigger, more vibrantly set with multicolor stones, and worn high on the bodice to accent the rising waist and hemline. Colorful bracelets were worn in multiples with push-up sleeves. Rings of all types were popular. Beads ranged from the monochromatic in 1957 to vivid shades in 1958 that came in all textures, including faceted baroque pearls and brushed gold.

Round necklines took huge, bulky, light necklaces worn on bare necks. Some necklaces dropped down to an Empire waistline and ended with a huge, showy pendant that was often a detachable pin. Bib necklaces looked best with the bateau neckline. Earrings were designed to continue the upswept look. Some fanciful ones looked like wings poised for flight. Large rhinestone earrings were popular for evening. Giant button earrings went well with chokers; string bean or shower styles complemented longer necklaces or chains. Peacock, jet, and chalk white were used in combination or alone.

Watches had shapes inspired by space exploration. Some looked like flying saucers and featured asymmetrical cases. Shorter sleeves encouraged manufacturers to produce fashion watchbands and wide silver- and gold-plated mesh bracelets.

There was a scarab revival, and in 1957 Angelo del Sesto of the Van Dell Company of Providence, Rhode Island, presented First Lady Mamie Eisenhower with a scarab belt, matching bracelet, and two matching pairs of earrings.

By 1955 plastics were molded, compressed, extruded, combined with rhinestones, pearlized, made into chains, and popped apart to form different length beads, as desired by the wearer. Lucite, polystyrene, acetate, nylon, vinyl, and catalin were used for various effects that ranged from iridescence to chalky opaqueness. Plastics imitated faceted and cabochon jewels or were made to look like metal and pearls. Jewelry made out of plastic was inexpensive to manufacture and easy to assemble using glue.

Metals used for costume jewelry were primarily brass, copper, copper-zinc alloys, bronze, tin, tin-base alloys, aluminum, nickel, and stainless steel. Gold, silver, rhodium, nickel, and chromium were electroplated onto the base metals for various effects. Costume jewelry manufacturing became a successful union of craftsmanship, mass production techniques, and innovative materials.

In 1958, during the Korean "emergency," aluminum was used extensively in the jewelry trade, taking the place of traditional jewelry materials that were in short supply. "Alumilite" by Alcoa was featured in an exhibit at Macy's in New York, showing gold-finished bracelets that accessorized the newest sleeveless fashions. A thirty-five-strand aluminum necklace was pictured in an advertisement.

In the fall of 1958, an article in *American Jewelry Manufacturers* suggested that all shades of amethyst would be important in jewelry that emphasized the bust, neck, and head, newly prominent because of the high-waisted look in dresses. The author of the article suggested shorter, more ornate necklaces, pins in the center of the dress, large *Directoire* pieces, groups of smaller pins, and important earrings. Chokers, beads, and pearls looked smart on suits that were once again in style.

In France, innovative costume jewelry designers were using bamboo, seashells, melon pits, nuts, tortoiseshell, ivory, and plastic. Half of their output was exported to the United States. Costume jewelry was still not being mass-produced in Europe and was closely connected to the high-fashion dressmaking industry. Each year the collections were shown in the spring and in the fall. Costume jewelry was not considered "cheap" but luxurious, integrated with the costumes of the great French couturiers.

In Paris, shorter skirts, suits with longer jackets, the barrel silhouette, dolman and three-quarter sleeves, and hats that covered the ears all needed a new look in jewelry. For evening wear, hemlines were moving downward, low necklines and strapless backs were shown. Ropes and sautoirs ninety inches long were caught at the hip with a large brooch. In Italy, earrings 4 to 6 inches long balanced the short skirts and showed out from under the new hats. Pins often had dangles and were worn vertically on hats.

In the United States, the fashion focus shifted from the Twenties to the Thirties in feeling. The sheath dress became the slim-hemmed, tapered look, similar to the chemise. Waistlines came back, with feminine peplums, tucking and draping at the hipline. Softer fabrics cut on the bias, standaway collars, capes, and capelets were shown in restrained colors such as black, gray, beige, plum, and cranberry. Colorful pins were used to brighten suits and capes. Rope necklaces were draped over tapered sheaths and open collars. Chokers in varied materials sat high on the neck. Rhinestone necklaces and jeweled bibs complemented elegant evening wear.

Everyone loved "character" jewelry. Two weeks after Sputnik was launched, Coro had a Sputnik bracelet on store counters. Mano also created a Sputnik bracelet, and another company quickly manufactured a satellite charm bracelet. Disney characters and Zorro bracelets were made by Dexter, Coro put out a *Ten Commandments* bracelet, Mano created Liberace's piano and candelabra earrings, and for Leru, Barclay produced an *Around the World in Eighty Days* bracelet. The movies had a very strong influence on fashion, as always.

At the U.S. World Trade Fair in 1958, Switzerland, Italy, and Israel exhibited an array of costume jewelry. Japan showed cultured pearls, and Czechoslovakia displayed an enticing assortment of synthetic stones. Since the end of World War II there had been huge growth and expansion in the costume jewelry industry. There had been a redistribution of national income and a decline in popularity of fine jewelry due partly to a high purchase tax. Once again people were spending money, and there was an expansion in both the amount and variety of consumer goods available.

World War II had ended half a decade before and people had enough leisure time to concern themselves with philosophical questions. Espresso and Existentialism were the new partners in coffeehouses all over Europe and the United States. Camus, Sartre, Malraux, and Simone de Beauvoir were widely read. Colette cast Audrey Hepburn as her Gigi for Broadway, and with her ponytail and luminescent dark eyes she was the perfect gamine.

The "ballerina look" was worn by many types of women. Chanel reopened her salon in 1954 and introduced a new collection of easy suits and an uncorseted body. Yves Saint Laurent created the "Trapeze," Givenchy the "A" line and the "sack dress," and Dior showed the "A" and "H" lines in 1955. The woman's counterpart to the man in the gray flannel suit was the cashmere twin sweater set over a tweed skirt worn with a simple string of pearls and a gold circle pin (or "virgin" pin, as the teenagers called it).

Tailored jewelry was worn by "career women." For casual wear in the suburbs, it was a madras skirt or Bermuda shorts with a simple round-collared blouse. The black cocktail dress was worn for evening, and red ballet slippers were a frivolous note to a conservative look. Marlon Brando and the beatniks wore T-shirts and black leather motorcycle jackets. Increased leisure time and the casual suburban life with occasional dress-up evenings led to a search for the new and the different, and gave women the freedom to wear costume jewelry for its own beauty. No longer did costume jewelry have to look real; frankly fake was chic.

Advertisements in 1958 showed a necklace and earrings set by Trifari with gold-speckled carved beads, a textured gold bangle bracelet with pointed ends, a large flower pin by Trifari, and "frankly fake copies of real gems." Tassel pins, an "antique" look by Benedikt, Greek crosses with large stones by Van S Authentics, Sandor enameled moon and stars, and pins by Lisner with iridescent stones were advertised in fashion magazines. Other Fifties companies whose creations are collectible today are HAR (particularly genies, Buddhas, dragons), Miriam Haskell, Chanel (Gripoix pieces), Napier, Schiaparelli, Coppola e Toppo, Hattie Carnegie, Nettie Rosenstein, Marcel Boucher, B.S.K., Kramer, Marvella, Robert, Zentall, Coro, Art, Regency, Florenza, Bartek, DeNicola, Sarah Coventry, Weiss, Schreiner, Renoir/Matisse, and Rebajes copper jewelry.

Coppola e Toppo glass necklace, bracelet, and earrings set. *Courtesy of Lorraine Wohl Collection, New York, NY. Photograph by Kenneth Chen.*

Coppola e Toppo Necklace, Bracelet, and Earrings Set. Triple-strand necklace, four-strand bracelet, elaborate motifs, large earrings, pale peach crystal beads, gold-plated clasps, marked "Coppola e Toppo Made in Italy," ca. 1950s. *Courtesy of Lorraine Wohl Collection.*

$1,000–$1,400

Coro heart necklace and earrings set. *Courtesy of Charles France, Divine Idea, New York, NY. Photograph by Kenneth Chen.*

Coro Necklace and Earrings Set. Three-dimensional heart pendant; simulated pearls; faux turquoises, amethysts, and citrines; simulated pearl chain; gold plated; 1950s. *Courtesy of Charles France, Divine Idea.*

$200–$300/set

HAR figural pin, Napier charm
bracelet. *HAR pin courtesy of Norman
Crider Antiques, New York, NY; Napier
bracelet courtesy of The Napier Co.*

HAR Pin. Smiling Asian, chunks of faux jade, aurora borealis rhinestone accents, antique gold plated, 1950s. *Courtesy of Norman Crider
Antiques.* $200–$300

Napier Bracelet. Charms, Asian motifs, multicolored beads, plastic and
metal, antique gold plated, 1950s. *Courtesy of The Napier Co.* $250–$350

Hattie Carnegie *tremblant*
necklace. *Courtesy of Joan
Orlen, Joan's Jewels, Lynbrook,
NY. Photograph by Steven D.
Freeman.*

Hattie Carnegie Necklace. Choker, *tremblant* leaf and floral design,
simulated pearls, clear round rhinestones, rhinestone chain, gold
plated, 1955. *Courtesy of Joan Orlen, Joan's Jewels.* $275–$325

Hollycraft pastel rhinestone pin and earrings. *Courtesy of Terry Rodgers, New York, NY. Photograph by Kenneth Chen.*

Hollycraft Pin and Earrings. Bow; round, marquise, square-cut, and baguette rhinestones in pastel shades of pink, blue, yellow, and green; gold plated; marked "Copr. 1955." Drop earrings in round and oval rhinestones in pastel shades of pink, blue, yellow, and green; gold plated; marked "Copr. 1950." *Courtesy of Terry Rodgers.*

Pin $75–$100; earrings $60–$90

Jomaz necklace, bracelet, and earrings set. *Courtesy of Charles France, Divine Idea, New York, NY. Photograph by Kenneth Chen.*

Jomaz Necklace, Bracelet, and Earrings Set. Choker, shield-shaped links, large faux Burma rubies, small square-cut faux sapphires, clear round rhinestone accents; bracelet, hinged cuff, matching faux rubies and sapphires; matching button earrings, textured gold plated, 1950s.
Courtesy of Charles France, Divine Idea. $1,200–$1,500/set

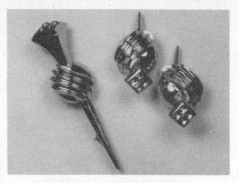

Marcel Boucher modernistic pin and earrings set.
*Courtesy of Alexandra Vangel. Photograph by John
Merowski.*

Marcel Boucher Pin and Earrings Set. Modernistic abstract design,
faux aquamarines, silver plated, 1950s. *Courtesy of Alexandra Vangel.*

$125–$150/set

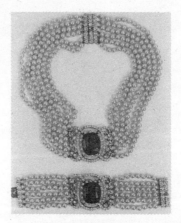

Marvella simulated pearl necklace
and bracelet set. *Courtesy of the
author. Photograph by Kenneth Chen.*

Marvella Necklace and Bracelet Set. Six strands of simulated pearls,
large antique rectangular-cut faux emerald, clear round rhinestones,
matching bracelet, silver plated, ca. 1950s. *Courtesy of the author.*

$500–$800/set

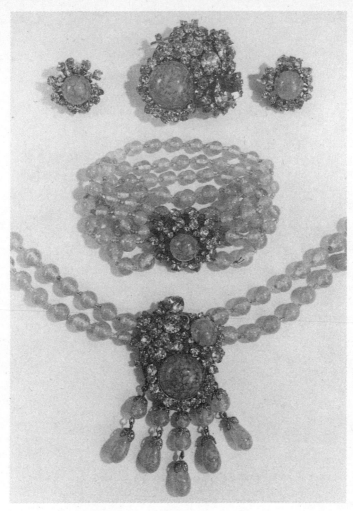

Miriam Haskell pink parure. *Courtesy of Robin Feldman Collectibles, New York, NY. Photograph by Kenneth Chen.*

Miriam Haskell Parure. Variegated pink round glass beads in a double-strand necklace, ornate pendant of blue round rhinestones and pink teardrop-shaped dangles; four-strand bracelet, ornate clasp of blue round rhinestones; matching pin and button earrings; gold plated; 1950s. *Courtesy of Robin Feldman Collectibles.* $1,400–$1,800/parure

Miriam Haskell "Bacchanalia" parure. *Courtesy of Susan Kelner Freeman, New York, NY. Photograph by Kenneth Chen.*

Miriam Haskell Parure. Rare, simulated pearl and rhinestone grape clusters, pavé rhinestone leaves, suspended from marquise rhinestone chain; necklace, pin, and earrings; gold plated; 1955. *Courtesy of Susan Kelner Freeman.* $5,000–$6,000/parure

NOTE: The necklace and earrings appear as part of the Miriam Haskell "Bacchanalia" collection in a full-page advertisement in *Harper's Bazaar*, October 1955, page 50.

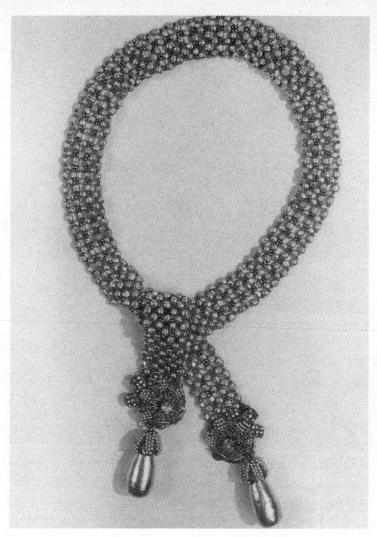

Miriam Haskell lariat necklace. *Courtesy of Susan Kelner Freeman, New York, NY. Photograph by Kenneth Chen.*

Miriam Haskell Necklace. Lariat style, interwoven simulated pearls, pair of seed pearl floral finials and caps, large simulated baroque teardrop-shaped pearls, gold plated, 1950s. *Courtesy of Susan Kelner Freeman.* $1,400–$1,600

Miriam Haskell simulated seed pearl necklace. *Courtesy of Lorraine Wohl Collection, New York, NY. Photograph by Kenneth Chen.*

Miriam Haskell Necklace. Fifteen strands, small simulated pearls, rose-shaped clasp, simulated seed pearls and flat-back clear rhinestones, gold plated, 1950s. *Courtesy of Lorraine Wohl Collection.*

$3,000–$3,500

Miriam Haskell pins and necklace. *Pins courtesy of Shirley Jaros, New York, NY; necklace courtesy of Charles France, Divine Idea, New York, NY. Photograph by Kenneth Chen.*

Miriam Haskell Pin. Round, large, simulated baroque pearls; overdesign of simulated seed pearls and rhinestone; gold plated, 1950s. *Courtesy of Shirley Jaros.* $300–$425

Miriam Haskell Necklace. Two strands, simulated baroque pearls, simulated pearl and gold-plated cut steel spacers, acorn caps, gold plated, 1950s. *Courtesy of Charles France, Divine Idea.* $350–$450

Miriam Haskell Pin. Doughnut shape, rare lava rock rhinestones set in radiating spokes, gold plated, 1950s. *Courtesy of Shirley Jaros.*

$225–$325

Miriam Haskell pins and necklace. *Round pin and necklace courtesy of the author; wing pin courtesy of Shirley Jaros, New York, NY. Photograph by Kenneth Chen.*

Miriam Haskell Pin. Round, simulated seed pearls and flat-back clear rhinestones, large central simulated pearl, gold plated, 1950s. *Courtesy of the author.* $150–$200

Miriam Haskell Pin. Simulated seed pearls, baroque pearls and rhinestones in a wing design, teardrop dangle, gold plated, 1950s. *Courtesy of Shirley Jaros.* $200–$350

Miriam Haskell Necklace. Pendant, floral medallion, simulated seed pearls; simulated baroque pearl necklace; gold plated, 1950s. *Courtesy of the author.* $250–$350

Miriam Haskell butterfly clasp necklace and Lucite pin and earrings set. *Necklace courtesy of Charles France, Divine Idea, New York, NY; pin and earrings set courtesy of Robin Feldman Collectibles, New York, NY. Photograph by Kenneth Chen.*

Miriam Haskell Necklace. Five graduated strands; simulated baroque pearls; gold-plated cut steel spacers; ornate butterfly-shaped clasp with simulated seed pearls; faux turquoises and coral, pink, blue, and clear round rhinestones; gold plated, 1950s. *Courtesy of Charles France, Divine Idea.* $900–$1,200

Miriam Haskell Pin and Earrings Set. Rare; leaf-shaped Lucite; clusters of glass beads forming flowers and leaves in pale and dark pink, yellow, light blue, and green; round green flat-back rhinestones; pink, blue, clear, and amethyst-colored rhinestones; matching earrings; gold plated; 1950s. *Courtesy of Robin Feldman Collectibles.* $800–$1,200/set

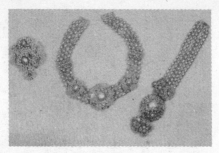

Miriam Haskell simulated pearl pin, neck-lace, and bracelet. *Jewelry and photograph courtesy of Maria Domont Collection, Beverly Hills, CA.*

(left to right)

Miriam Haskell Pin. Floral motif, intricate simulated seed pearl pin, gold plated, 1950s. *Courtesy of Maria Domont Collection.* $300–$450

Miriam Haskell Necklace. Four strands, simulated baroque pearls, three simulated seed pearl flowers, gold plated, 1950s. *Courtesy of Maria Domont Collection.* $900–$1,200

Miriam Haskell Bracelet. Five strands, simulated baroque pearls, intricate floral motif, simulated seed pearls, gold plated, 1950s. *Courtesy of Maria Domont Collection.* $700–$850

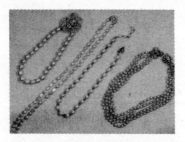

Miriam Haskell simulated pearl necklaces. *Jewelry and photograph courtesy of Maria Domont Collection, Beverly Hills, CA.*

Miriam Haskell Necklaces. Single to four-strand simulated pearls, simple to ornate simulated seed pearl clasps, gold plated, 1950s. *Courtesy of Maria Domont Collection.* $275–$450/each

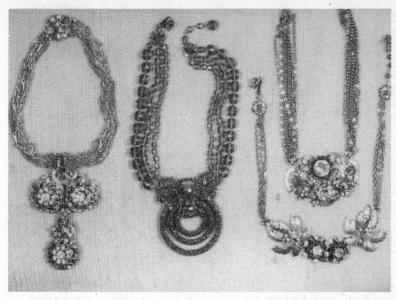

Miriam Haskell chain and glass bead necklaces. *Jewelry and photograph courtesy of Maria Domont Collection, Beverly Hills, CA.*

(left to right)

Miriam Haskell Necklace. Multistrand chains, clear rhinestone floral triple drop, antique silver plated, 1950s. *Courtesy of Maria Domont Collection.* $600–$750

Miriam Haskell Necklace. Three strands of gray crystal beads, cut steel beaded hoops, large hematite cabochon, silver plated, 1950s. *Courtesy of Maria Domont Collection.* $700–$850

Miriam Haskell Necklace (top right). Multistrand silver- and gold-plated chains, simulated baroque pearl and rhinestone floral drop, antique silver and gold plated, 1950s. *Courtesy of Maria Domont Collection.*
                                                                    $750–$950

Miriam Haskell Necklace. Choker, multistrand chains, leaf motif, clear rhinestones, silver plated, 1950s. *Courtesy of Maria Domont Collection.*
                                                                    $400–$500

Miriam Haskell necklace and earrings set and pins and earrings set. *Jewelry and photograph courtesy of Maria Domont Collection, Beverly Hills, CA.*

(left to right)

Miriam Haskell Necklace and Earrings Set. Triple strand, red glass beads and simulated baroque pearls, simulated pearl flowers, gold plated, 1950s. *Courtesy of Maria Domont Collection.* $750–$950/set

Miriam Haskell Pins and Earrings Set. Double and single flowers, simulated pearl petals,1950s. *Courtesy of Maria Domont Collection.*

$550–$650/set

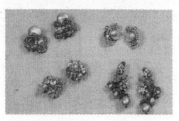

Miriam Haskell simulated pearl earrings. *Jewelry and photograph courtesy of Maria Domont Collection, Beverly Hills, CA.*

Miriam Haskell Earrings. Various designs, simulated pearls and seed pearls, rhinestones, 1950s. *Courtesy of Maria Domont Collection.*

$150–$275/each

Napier "fruits" bracelet, unsigned bead collar. *Bracelet courtesy of Robin Feldman Collectibles, New York, NY; collar courtesy of the author. Photograph by Kenneth Chen.*

Napier Bracelet. "Fruits"; pearlized glass beads in pink, blue, olive, garnet, amber, pale green, mulberry, amethyst, and topaz; gold plated; 1950s. *Courtesy of Robin Feldman Collectibles.* $225–$325

Unsigned Necklace. Collar; pink, orange, and clear iridescent beads; simulated pearls in a profusion of designs and materials; attached by silver-plated chain links; 1950s. *Courtesy of the author.* $125–$200

Napier ram's head dangle bracelet and earrings set. *Courtesy of Carol Moskowitz, New
York, NY. Photograph by Kenneth Chen.*

Napier Bracelet and Earrings Set. Bangle, ram's head, Venetian glass
dangles, yellow and multicolored bead, faux carnelian and turquoise
beads, simulated pearls, matching dangle earrings, silver plated, 1950s.
Courtesy of Carol Moskowitz. $400–$450/set

(top to bottom) Renoir copper
bracelet and earrings set, Castlecliff pin and earrings set. *Courtesy
of Tania Santé's Classic Collectables, Miami, FL. Photograph by
Phil Schlom.*

(top to bottom)

Renoir Bracelet and Earrings Set. Bangle, geometric, modernistic design,
light and dark green enameled squares on mesh, matching square earrings, copper, 1950s. *Courtesy of Tania Santé's Classic Collectables.*

$125–$150/set

Castlecliff Pin and Earrings Set. Abstract design, carved faux green jade, faux sapphire cabochon accents, gold plated, 1950s. *Courtesy of Tania Santé's Classic Collectables.* $95–$150/set

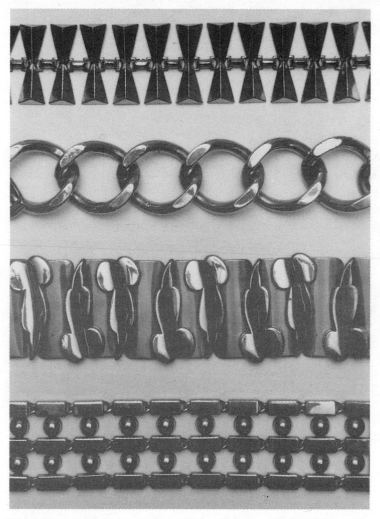

Renoir copper link bracelets. *Courtesy of Route 66 Antiques, Chatham, NY. Photograph by Kenneth Chen.*

Renoir Bracelets. Links, copper, 1950s. *Courtesy of Route 66 Antiques.*
$75–$150

Schiaparelli simulated pearl necklace and bracelet set. *Courtesy of Joan Orlen, Joan's Jewels, Lynbrook, NY. Photograph by Steven D. Freeman.*

Schiaparelli Necklace and Bracelet Set. Three-strand necklace, four-strand bracelet, simulated baroque pearls, mirror marquise and pear-shaped rhinestones, gold plated, 1950s. *Courtesy of Joan Orlen, Joan's Jewels.*

$800–$1,200/set

Schiaparelli pin and earrings set. *Courtesy of Alexandra Vangel.*
Photograph by John Merowski.

Schiaparelli Pin and Earrings Set. Rare, large faux citrines, simulated
yellow pearl centers in florets, antique gold plated, 1950s. *Courtesy of
Alexandra Vangel.* $900–$1,200/set

Schiaparelli bracelet and earrings set. *Courtesy of Muriel Karasik,*
Westhampton Beach, NY. Photograph by Kenneth Chen.

Schiaparelli Bracelet and Earrings Set. Links, kite-shaped faux emeralds and jet, round blue aurora borealis rhinestones, matching earrings, silver plated, marked "Pat. No. 156452," ca. 1950s. *Courtesy of
Muriel Karasik.* $750–$900/set

Schreiner bib necklace. *Courtesy of the Schreiner family collection.*
Photograph by Kenneth Chen.

Schreiner Necklace. Bib collar, clear marquise and round rhinestones, simulated pearls, round "burnt amber marble" stones, 1950s. *Courtesy of the Schreiner family collection.* $650–$900

|| **NOTE:** "Marble stones" were made by mixing metallic elements || into the glass. They were manufactured after the war in || Kaufbayern, Germany, and no two were exactly alike.

VOGUE

NOVEMBER 15

WHAT MAKES
A WOMAN MEMORABLE
by JOHN MASON BROWN

3-weeks Christmas shopping plan

Fashions in Living:
presents for the house

50 CENTS

Schreiner bib necklace and earrings set, *Vogue* cover of November 15, 1956. *Original editorial courtesy of the Schreiner family collection. Photograph of the page by Kenneth Chen.*

Schreiner Necklace and Earrings Set. Bib, simulated baroque pearls and clear rhinestones, matching large drop earrings, *Vogue* cover of November 15, 1956. *Courtesy of the Schreiner family collection.* $900–$1,200

Schreiner "Fire and Ice" fringe necklace and earrings set. *Courtesy of the Schreiner family collection. Photograph by Kenneth Chen.*

Schreiner Necklace and Earrings Set. "Fire and Ice" fringe bib, clear round rhinestones, round faux rubies, matching button earrings, sold at Neiman Marcus, used in Revlon ads, 1950s. *Courtesy of the Schreiner family collection.* $800–$1,000/set

Schreiner "Bubble" choker necklace and earrings set. *Courtesy of the Schreiner family collection. Photograph by Kenneth Chen.*

Schreiner Necklace and Earrings Set. "The Bubble" choker, Lucite ovals in handmade settings, matching earrings, gold plated, sold at Bonwit Teller, 1950s. *Courtesy of the Schreiner family collection.*

$400–$650/set

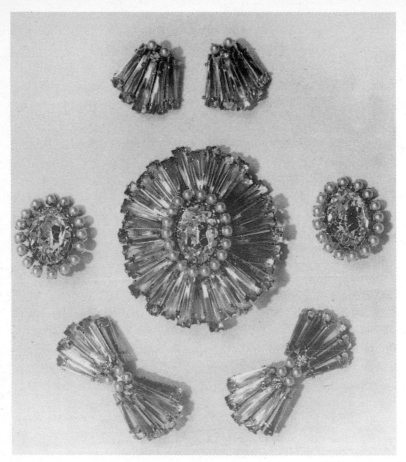

Schreiner "ruffle" pin and earrings. *Courtesy of the Schreiner family collection. Photograph by Kenneth Chen.*

Schreiner Pin and Three Pairs of Matching Earrings. "Ruffle" pin, "cracked ice" (clear) keystone-shaped rhinestones, clear round center rhinestones, simulated pearls, gold plated, 1950s. *Courtesy of the Schreiner family collection.* $350–$450/pin and earrings; $75–$150/earrings alone

NOTE: "Keystones," which are tapered at the bottom, were specially created to be used in the distinctive ruffle-shaped pin that was an exclusive Schreiner design. The ruffle pin was the signature piece on Originals coats.

Schreiner pins. *Courtesy of the Schreiner family collection. Photograph by Kenneth Chen.*

(clockwise from top)

Schreiner Pins. "Ike" pin, faux rubies, gunmetal plated; geranium pin, faux light Siam rubies, gold plated; petal pin, blue "carved" glass stones, central blue glass cabochon; butterfly quiver pin, pink glass stones; all 1950s. *Courtesy of the Schreiner family collection.* $75–$175/each

NOTE: Mrs. Eisenhower was given an "Ike" pin by Ms. Schreiner and she often wore it in official pictures. The "Ike" pin was given out as a gift to $100 donors to the Republican party. It is exhibited in the Eisenhower Museum collection.

Schreiner figural pins. *Courtesy of the Schreiner family collection. Photograph by Kenneth Chen.*

(left to right)

Schreiner Figural Pins. Penguin, jet glass body, chalk-white marquise and round glass stones in the wings and feet, gunmetal plated; butterfly multicolored opaque stones, chalk-white oval and round stones, gunmetal plated; "Henry the Mouse," pastel opaque stones, gold plated; all 1950s. *Courtesy of the Schreiner family collection.*

Penguin $75–$125; butterfly $60–$90; Henry $35–$50

Schreiner Maltese cross pin. *Courtesy of Charles France, Divine Idea, New York, NY. Photograph by Kenneth Chen.*

Schreiner Pin. Maltese cross, oval faux rose quartz dome cabochons, round faux rose quartz cabochon center surrounded by clear round rhinestones, pear-shaped faux amethyst accents, chain tassel, gunmetal plated, marked "Schreiner New York," 1950s. *Courtesy of Charles France, Divine Idea.* $350–$450

Trifari "carved" faux moonstone necklace, bracelet, and earrings set. *Courtesy of Tania Santé's Classic Collectables, Miami, FL. Photograph by Phil Schlom.*

Trifari Necklace, Bracelet, and Earrings Set. Short necklace, tulip-shaped "carved" pale blue faux moonstones, small round faux sapphire accents, rhodium plated, 1950s. *Courtesy of Tania Santé's Classic Collectables.* $400–$650/set

Trifari necklaces, bracelets, pins, and earrings. *Courtesy of Joan Orlen, Joan's Jewels, Lynbrook, NY. Photograph by Steven D. Freeman.*

Trifari Necklaces, Bracelets, Pins, and Earrings. Assortment of textured gold and simulated pearl pieces, ca. 1950s. *Courtesy of Joan Orlen, Joan's Jewels.* $45–$75/each

|| **NOTE:** These pieces are particularly popular among European || and English dealers and collectors.

Weiss flower pin and earrings set. *Courtesy of Alexandra Vangel. Photograph by John Merowski.*

Weiss Pin and Earrings Set. Flower, clear round rhinestones, faux pear-shaped emerald center, matching earrings, 1950s. *Courtesy of Alexandra Vangel.* $125–$150/set

Weiss rhinestone collar. *Courtesy of Ridgewood Antiques Shop, Ridgewood, NJ. Photograph by John Merowski.*

Weiss Necklace. Collar, round and marquise rhinestones, ca. 1950s. *Courtesy of Ridgewood Antiques Shop.* $200–$245

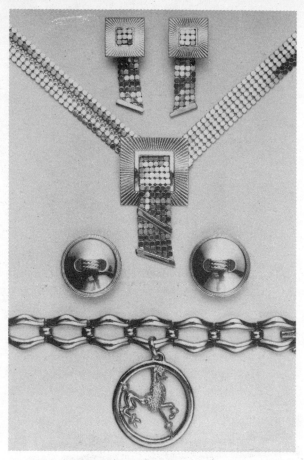

(top to bottom) Unsigned mesh necklace and earrings set, Monet button earrings, and poodle charm bracelet. *Necklace and earrings courtesy of author; Monet. Photograph by Kenneth Chen.*

(top to bottom)

Unsigned Necklace and Earrings Set. Mesh neckband, "engine turned" buckle pendant, matching earrings, gold plated. *Courtesy of the author.*

$50–$75/set

Monet Earrings. Button, gold plated, 1950s. *Courtesy of Monet.* $25–$45

Monet Bracelet. Poodle charm, gold plated, 1950s. *Courtesy of Monet.*

$40–$65

Unsigned Egyptian-inspired necklace, pin, and ear-rings set. *Courtesy of Rita Sacks, Limited Additions, New York, NY. Photograph by Kenneth Chen.*

Unsigned Necklace, Pin, and Earrings Set. Egyptian figures; brown, gray, yellow, black, red, and turquoise enameled features; triangular green Bakelite accents; gold plated; ca. 1950s. *Courtesy of Rita Sacks, Limited Additions.* $550–$750/set

Unsigned Cleopatra cameo necklace and bracelet. *Courtesy of Prudence Huang, New York, NY. Photograph by Kenneth Chen.*

Unsigned Necklace and Bracelet. Necklace, unusual Cleopatra glass cameos, green outline, simulated pearls, round faux emerald eyes in the asps, gold plated, each cameo is 1½ inches high; bracelet, links, ornate frame around each cameo, round faux jade stones, simulated pearls, silver plated; 1950s. *Courtesy of Prudence Huang.*

Necklace and bracelet $200–$300

. . . More Fifties

Boucher Pin and Earrings Set. Leaf-shaped pin with small round faux rubies and clear round rhinestones, matching wing-shaped earrings, rhodium plated, 1950s. *Courtesy of Metropolis.* $100–$175/set

Christian Dior Necklace and Earrings. Six florets of oval faux rubies and clear round rhinestones, oval faux rubies and clear round rhinestone chain, rhodium plated, marked "Christian Dior by Kramer," early 1950s. *Courtesy of Prudence Huang.* $200–$350/set

Coppola e Toppo Bracelet. Seven strands, faceted, faux amethyst beads, ornate beaded clasp, gold plated, 2¼ inches wide, ca. 1950s. *Courtesy of Prudence Huang.* $300–$400

Coppola e Toppo Necklace. Three strands with long dangles, simulated pearls, gold-plated spacers, 1950s. *Courtesy of Ginger Moro Archives.* $350–$450

Coppola e Toppo Bracelet and Earrings Set. Yellow Venetian glass, woven band with thick fringe, matching spikey drop earrings, gold plated, 1950s. *Courtesy of Ginger Moro Archives.* $350–$400/set

Hobé Necklace. Two strands of fuchsia, purple, and blue glass beads; 1950s. *Courtesy of Metropolis.* $150–$250

Jomaz Pin. Abstract floral design, large square faux sapphires surrounded by small clear round rhinestones, gold plated, 1950s. *Courtesy of Metropolis.* $125–$225

Jomaz Bracelet and Earrings Set. Narrow link bracelet, faux star sapphires, round clear rhinestones, matching earrings, rhodium plated, 1950s. *Courtesy of Tania Santé's Classic Collectables.* $150–$225/set

Kramer Necklace, Bracelet, and Earrings Set. Necklace, rectangular links, large rectangular faux rubies, surrounded by clear round rhinestones, round faux ruby and clear round rhinestone florets on rhinestone chain between each large link, faux ruby baguettes alternating with clear round rhinestones on the chain; matching earrings; bracelet of large rectangular links, large rectangular faux rubies and clear round rhinestones, rhodium plated, marked "Kramer New York," 1950s. *Courtesy of Prudence Huang.* $200–$300/set

Kramer for Christian Dior Necklace and Earrings Set. Pendant, faux sapphire surrounded by rows of round clear rhinestones, suspended from rhinestone chain, matching oval earrings, rhodium plated, 1950s. *Courtesy of Tania Santé's Classic Collectables.* $300–$500/set

Marvella Necklace, Bracelet, and Earrings Set. Triple-strand necklace and bracelet, simulated pink and white pearls, clear rhinestone rondelles, faux ruby cabochons on the clasps, silver plated, 1950s. *Courtesy of Metropolis.* $125–$175/set

Miriam Haskell Necklace. Two strands, small and medium simulated pearls, cut brass spacers, dove hook, gold plated, early 1950s. *Courtesy of the author.* $100–$150

Miriam Haskell Necklace. Choker, faceted, flat, oval faux amethyst beads filigree caps, bow-shaped medallion, flat-back clear rhinestones, round faux opal, faux sapphire cabochon, faux amethyst, round pink and green rhinestones, gold plated, 1950s. *Courtesy of Prudence Huang.* $200–$275

Miriam Haskell Necklace, Bracelet, and Earrings Set. Triple-strand necklace and bracelet; clear, round, pink, faceted glass beads alternating with round, pink, opaque beads; the bracelet's clasp and the earrings have a floral motif with triangular-shaped opaque glass petals, tiny clear pink beads in the centers; silver plated; 1950s. *Courtesy of Prudence Huang.* $225–$300/set

Miriam Haskell Pin. Floral design, opaque textured and smooth glass stones, pale green and topaz beads, gold plated, 1950s. *Courtesy of Shirley Jaros.* $250–$375

Miriam Haskell Pin. Floral design, large pink variegated central stone, pink opaque stones, aurora borealis, simulated pearls, pink glass bead and pink rhinestone dangle, gold plated, 1950s. *Courtesy of Shirley Jaros.* $350–$475

Miriam Haskell Necklace and Earrings Set. Lariat, eight strands of ruby-red Peking glass beads, jet glass spacers, marquise faux ruby flowers, five strands of smaller ruby-red glass bead dangles, ending in pear-shaped faux rubies and a large ruby Peking glass bead; matching flower earrings; gunmetal plated; the necklace is 33½ inches long, earrings are 1⅝ inches; 1950s. *Courtesy of Jane Gardener.* $2,500–$2,800/set

Robert Necklace, Bracelet, and Earrings Set. Single-strand necklace, double-strand bracelet, opaque pink beads and clear rhinestone spacers, ornate central motifs, matching earrings, gold plated, 1950s. *Courtesy of Metropolis.* $125–$175

Schiaparelli Necklace. Two strands of pink-and-green Venetian glass beads with copper-colored caviar bead spacers, 1950s. *Courtesy of Metropolis.* $150–$200

Schiaparelli Pin. Round floral design, small faux turquoises in the center, Venetian glass petals, gold plated, 1950s. *Courtesy of Metropolis.* $150–$225

Schiaparelli Bracelet and Earrings Set. Narrow bracelet, large pear-shaped faux amethysts and large round aurora borealis rhinestones; earrings are of round, oval, square, and pear-shaped faux amethysts and a round central aurora borealis rhinestone, 1⅝ inches diameter; gold plated; early 1950s. *Courtesy of the author.* $250–$325/set

Schreiner Pin. Round shape with the center recessed, round faux sapphire cabochons, marquise and pear-shaped gray rhinestones, simulated pearls, clear round rhinestones, antique silver plated, early 1950s. *Courtesy of the author.* $175–$250

Schreiner Necklace, Bracelet, and Earrings Set. Necklace, small and medium round orange rhinestones, faux pink/orange opals, coppery metallic stones; matching wide bracelet and button earrings; gunmetal plated; marked "Schreiner New York"; early 1950s. *Courtesy of the author.* $425–$600/set

Schreiner Pin. Abstract floral design; large rectangular faux topazes with inclusions; small marquise faux coral around the edges; the center with round and marquise faux coral and small rectangular, oval, and round faux citrines; gold plated; marked "Schreiner New York"; 1950s. *Courtesy of the author.* $150–$200

Schreiner Pin. Dome shape, deep pink round and pear-shaped cabochons, pink marquise rhinestones and pink aurora borealis stones, gunmetal plated, 1950s. *Courtesy of Shirley Jaros.* $200–$350

Unsigned Bracelet. Links, large clear pear-shaped rhinestones surrounded by clear round rhinestones with smaller pear-shaped rhinestones set above each link, antique silver plated, marked "Austria," 1950s. *Courtesy of Charles France, Divine Idea.* $200–$300

Unsigned Bracelet. Three strands, large faceted faux emerald, aurora borealis and gold metallic beads in floral shapes, the bottom row in loops, gold-plated clasp, early 1950s. *Courtesy of the author.* $200–$275

The Sixties

In the "Swinging Sixties" clothing and accessories took on a whole new social importance. The seeds of the sexual revolution had been sown and blossomed into full flower with the advent of "The Pill." There was a new body awareness, and tight-fitting hip-hugger bell-bottom dungarees were worn with an exposed midriff and a tiny top. Bralessness was rampant, with the ultimate style that shocked the conservative older generation—Rudi Gerneich's topless bathing suit. For those women who insisted on some coverage, Rudi invented the "no-bra" bra, the forerunner of today's unconstructed styles. For the truly modest, Band-Aids were used to cover one's nipples in Rudi's figure-revealing knit designs. Panty hose replaced the cumbersome garter belt and stockings, and *Hair* debuted on Broadway, exposing both men and women in the first display of frontal nudity on the legitimate stage. Women outlined their eyes in kohl and wore pale or white lipstick and bouffant hairstyles. Bill Blass, Anne Klein, Geoffrey Beene, and Donald Brooks were the leading designers of ready-to-wear.

The nation was shocked by the assassination of young President Kennedy, Vietnam went from being an unfamiliar name to headline news, and women had a new heroine in Audrey Hepburn's Holly Golightly.

The mothers of the braless and barefoot young women were

wearing the wildly patterned, beautifully colored, ubiquitous Pucci dresses and their copies. Puccis became the first fashion status symbol. Young matrons affected the "Jackie Kennedy" look, and Lilly Pulitzer wallpapered the horsey set with huge pastel and neon floral patterned clothing for men and women. In 1964, Courrèges showed a "space age" geometric look with a white helmet, white sculptural tunic, and white boots that caught on like crazy. Women of all ages wore the majorette lookalikes and they were knocked off by nearly every shoe manufacturer. The "London Look" spread to the United States and everyone wanted to wear the same things as the English "birds." Mary Quant, Zandra Rhodes, Thea Porter, and Jean Muir led the group of English designers who found an audience in the States. Miniskirts and tights were the foremost sellers in the boutiques of Chelsea. Going shopping for clothes became a form of entertainment that both sexes enjoyed. London boutiques Biba, Bus Stop, and Just Looking had their American counterpart on Madison Avenue at a chrome-and-Lucite store called Paraphernalia. Its next-door neighbor was the Vidal Sasson hair salon, with imported young English hairdressers giving everyone short, shiny, geometric cuts.

In Paris, women were wearing minis, the "baby doll" look, Yves Saint Laurent's retro Forties look, and Paco Rabanne's dresses made from metal or plastic disks linked together with rings and worn over flesh-colored body stockings. Boots were worn with everything; patterned stockings covered the part of the leg exposed by the mini. For evening, silver dresses, silver lamé shoes and stockings, and glittery materials and brocades were the rage.

Everywhere, men and women were experimenting with costumey outfits—caftans; antique dresses; floral and embroidered shirts; Indian headbands and beads; studded, patched, and embroidered denim; military surplus uniforms; and fantasy creations from the harem to outer space. Africa, ethnicism, psychedelia, and signs of the zodiac permeated clothing and jewelry. Hallucinogenic drugs inspired music, art, and fashions in wild patterns and colors. The most adventurous fashion leaders substituted body paint for clothing and wore paper dresses and jumpsuits. Models were the new celebrities of the Sixties, with Jean Shrimpton ("The Shrimp"), Twiggy, and Verushka setting the pace in the pages of *Vogue* and *Harper's Bazaar*.

Costume jewelry ranged from Kenneth Jay Lane's fabulous fakes and Chanel-inspired jewels to massive Lucite dome rings, tiered mobile earrings, and belts made out of electronic templates and silver chain by Harrison and Garrison (the author's own company).

Advertisements in the fashion magazines showed Lisner-painted flower pins, a Brania sunburst pin of mock turquoise and gold, a DeNicola medallion pin with a gold coin center, Giovanni roses, mesh jewelry by Wells, Kramer revivals of Victorian pins, Adele Simpson necklaces, and Weiss rhinestone pins. Corocraft, Krementz, Vêndome space pins with large colored rhinestones, Bergère rhinestone pins, Chanel, Danecraft perfume pins, François enameled flowers, and a Hattie Carnegie faux coral and rhinestone pin and textured gold choker for Carnegie Originals were also advertised.

Newspaper ads highlighted Nettie Rosenstein, Joseph Mazer, Robert Originals, Panetta, Castlecliff, Joseph Warner intaglios, Mimi di N, Capri, Napier's Egyptian look, Laguna for beads, a Marcel Boucher faux turquoise and gold pin, replicas of antique European jewelry, and Albert Weiss's "Cleopatra Collection" with faux turquoise stones and tassels. Sandor Goldberger, Judith McCann, Scaasi earrings, a Miriam Haskell pin and collar of gold-plated metal and jet beads, Van S Authentics, a Berger dog collar, jewelry by Shannon Rodgers for Jerry Silverman for Vêndome, and a white collar and bib by Vogue were in other ads.

Today the most collectible Sixties costume jewelry is some of the prettiest—Kenneth Jay Lane oversized earrings, large necklaces, animal bracelets and bold pins, Mimi di N enameled bracelets and striking pendants, Hattie Carnegie "primitives," Chanel "poured glass" pieces by Gripoix, Miriam Haskell pearl sets, Schreiner, Stanley Hagler, Arnold Scaasi, Coppola e Toppo, William de Lillo dramatic necklaces and pins, Christian Dior, and jewelry by the other designers mentioned in the preceding paragraphs.

Castlecliff Lucite necklace and earrings
set. *Courtesy of Marjorie Levin. Photograph
by Kenneth Chen.*

Castlecliff Necklace and Earrings Set. Clear Lucite balls 1¼ inches in
diameter, silver-plated clasp with pavé rhinestones, matching drop
earrings. *Courtesy of Marjorie Levin.* $150–$225/set

Christian Dior flower pin. *Courtesy of
Robin Feldman Collectibles, New York,
NY. Photograph by Kenneth Chen.*

Christian Dior Pin. Flower, faux ruby center surrounded by tiny faux
emeralds, pavé rhinestone petals, green enameled stem, silver plated,
marked "Christian Dior 1960." *Courtesy of Robin Feldman Collectibles.*

$1,200–$1,500

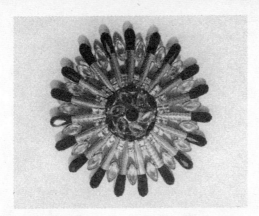

R. F. Clark and William de Lillo spoke pin. *Courtesy of Rita Sacks, Limited Additions, New York, NY. Photograph by Kenneth Chen.*

R. F. Clark and William de Lillo Pin. Large sunburst design, hand constructed, marquise Swarovski crystals and jet stones, gold plated, ca. 1969. *Courtesy of Rita Sacks, Limited Additions.* $1,500–$1,800

R. F. Clark and William de Lillo balloon pin and earrings set. *Courtesy Marene Weinraub, Teaneck, NJ. Photograph by Kenneth Chen.*

R. F. Clark and William de Lillo Pin and Earrings Set. Balloons, faux turquoises, clear round rhinestones, gold plated, 1967. *Courtesy of Marene Weinraub.* $150–$300/set

Jacques fringe necklace. *Courtesy of Prudence Huang, New York, NY. Photograph by Kenneth Chen.*

Jacques Necklace (unsigned). Fringed bib, garnet-red and pink rhinestones, oval faux jet, clear marquise rhinestones, pear-shaped faux rubies at the tips of clear rhinestone chain, silver plated, 1960s.
Courtesy of Prudence Huang. $300–$500

Kenneth Jay Lane collar. *Courtesy of Prudence Huang, New York, NY. Photograph by Kenneth Chen.*

Kenneth Jay Lane Necklace. Massive collar, large faux lapis lazuli domed cabochons, pear-shaped faux ruby cabochons, faux turquoise beads, octagon-cut faux lapis, mesh tube chain, chain tassels, gold plated, marked "KJL Laguna," each section is 2½ inches high, 1960s. *Courtesy of Prudence Huang.* $600–$800

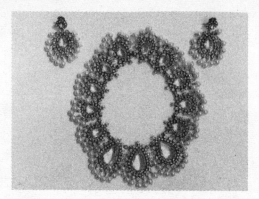

Kenneth Jay Lane necklace and earrings set.
Courtesy of E & J Rothstein Antiques, West Chester, PA.
Photograph by Kenneth Chen.

Kenneth Jay Lane Necklace and Earrings Set. Bib, linked-together motifs, graduated pear-shaped rhinestones, surrounded by clear round rhinestones and simulated pearl dangles, matching earrings, antique silver plated, marked "K.J.L.," 1960s. *Courtesy of E & J Rothstein Antiques.* $2,000–$2,500

|| **NOTE:** The previous owner of this set had one of the motifs || made into a pin.

Kenneth Jay Lane embroidered earrings
and acorn bracelet. *Earrings courtesy of*
Kenneth Jay Lane Vintage Collection, New
York, NY; bracelet courtesy of Ilene Chazanof,
Decorative Arts, New York, NY. Photograph
by Kenneth Chen.

Kenneth Jay Lane Earrings. Exotic drop earrings; embroidered on both sides; tiny glass beads of faux topazes, turquoises, and emeralds;

small and medium simulated pearls; gold-plated earring backs; marked "K.J.L.," 1964. *Courtesy of Kenneth Jay Lane Vintage Collection.*

$400–$650

Kenneth Jay Lane Bracelet. Acorn motif, Schlumberger-inspired design, pavé rhinestones, gold plated, marked "K.J.L.," late 1960s. *Courtesy of Ilene Chazanof.* $250–$400

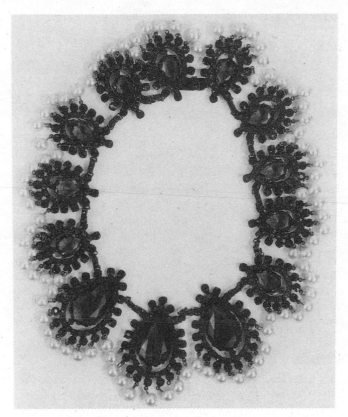

Kenneth Jay Lane Gloria Swanson necklace. *Courtesy of Kenneth Jay Lane Vintage Collection, New York, NY. Photograph by Kenneth Chen.*

Kenneth Jay Lane Necklace. Gloria Swanson necklace, large pear-shaped faux emeralds outlined with a row each of round faux sapphires and emeralds, simulated pearl dangles, gunmetal plated, marked "K.J.L.," 1960s (purchased from Gloria Swanson's estate). *Courtesy of Kenneth Jay Lane Vintage Collection.* $1,200–$1,500

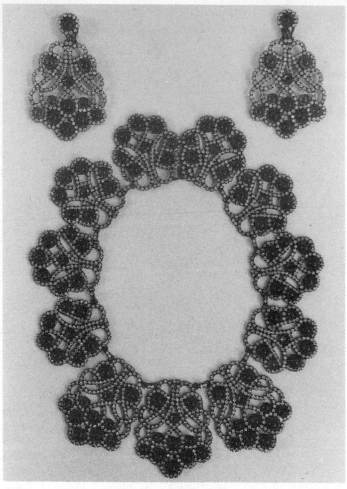

Kenneth Jay Lane Rosalind Russell necklace and earrings set. *Courtesy of Kenneth Jay Lane Vintage Collection, New York, NY. Photograph by Kenneth Chen.*

Kenneth Jay Lane Necklace. Rosalind Russell necklace, arabesque medallions of cabochon and faceted faux emeralds, outlined by clear round rhinestones, matching drop earrings, silver plated, marked "K.J.L.," 1966 (made for Rosalind Russell and purchased from her brother). *Courtesy of Kenneth Jay Lane Vintage Collection.* $3,500–$3,800

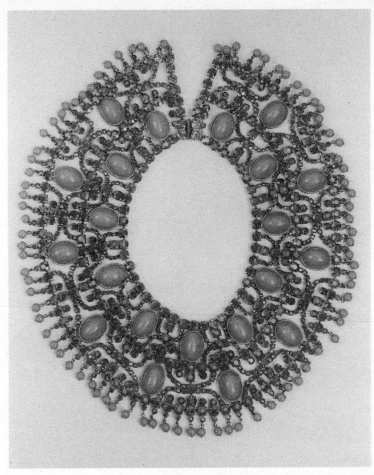

Kenneth Jay Lane necklace. *Courtesy of Kenneth Jay Lane Vintage Collection, New York, NY. Photograph by Kenneth Chen.*

Kenneth Jay Lane Collar (unsigned). Necklace, metallic gold round rhinestone chain soldered together, forming a 3½-inch deep collar, large faux coral cabochons and dangles, gold plated, 1960s. *Courtesy of Kenneth Jay Lane Vintage Collection.* $2,500–$2,800

||**NOTE:** Some faux citrines have been used to replace the gold|| ||metallic stones.||

Kenneth Jay Lane figural pins. *Courtesy of Only Yesterday, Hudson, NY. Photograph by Kenneth Chen.*

(top to bottom)

Kenneth Jay Lane Pin. Cupid, orange enameled torso, pavé rhinestones, gold plated, marked "K.J.L.," 1960s. *Courtesy of Only Yesterday.*

$200–$300

Kenneth Jay Lane Earrings. Faux coral cabochons, clear round rhinestones, gold plated, marked "K.J.L.," 1960s. *Courtesy of Only Yesterday.*

$60–$90

Kenneth Jay Lane Pin. Chameleon, reversible belly, pavé rhinestones on one side, faux turquoises on the other, faux emerald cabochon eyes and on top of head, gold plated, marked "K.J.L.," 1960s. *Courtesy of Only Yesterday.*

$300–$425

Kenneth Jay Lane Pin. Reindeer, pavé rhinestones, faux emerald cabochons, simulated pearl drop, textured gold plated, silver-plated horns and leaves, marked "K.J.L.," 1960s. *Courtesy of Only Yesterday.*

$200–$300

Kenneth Jay Lane Pin. Sea goddess, pavé rhinestones, white enameled tail, gold plated, marked "K.J.L.," 1960s. *Courtesy of Only Yesterday.*

$200–$300

Kenneth Jay Lane Pin. Two-headed unicorn, cream enameled body, faux emerald cabochon eyes, clear round rhinestone accents, gold plated, marked "K.J.L.," 1960s. *Courtesy of Only Yesterday.* $175–$250

Kenneth Jay Lane Pin. Walrus, gray enameled body, white enameled tusks, large central faux coral cabochon, gold plated, marked "K.J.L.," 1960s. *Courtesy of Only Yesterday.* $200–$300

Kenneth Jay Lane Pin. Fish, pavé rhinestones, faux emerald cabochon eye, gold plated, marked "K.J.L.," 1960s. *Courtesy of Only Yesterday.*

$200–$300

Kenneth Jay Lane pin and earrings set. *Courtesy of Alexandra Vangel.* Photograph by John Merowski.

Kenneth Jay Lane Pin and Earrings Set. Pin, faux turquoise, clear round rhinestone accents, matching drop earrings, gunmetal plated, 1960s. *Courtesy of Alexandra Vangel.* $180–$250/set

Mimi di N necklace with detachable pin. *Courtesy of Norman Crider Antiques, New York, NY. Photograph by Kenneth Chen.*

Mimi di N Necklace with Detachable Pendant/Pin. Ornate chain of marquise faux sapphires and emeralds and pale blue round rhinestones, ending in deep blue stretched octagon cabochon rhinestones; the pendant/pin has matching stones with a very large blue stretched octagon central stone and a pear-shaped faux emerald drop, silver plated, 1960s. *Courtesy of Norman Crider Antiques.* $600–$750

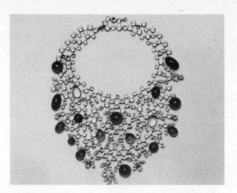

Pauline Trigère bib necklace. *Courtesy of Pauline Trigère. Photograph by Kenneth Chen.*

Pauline Trigère Necklace (unsigned). Bib, large round and marquise rhinestones, multicolored cabochons, silver plated, 1960s. *Courtesy of Pauline Trigère.* $600–$900

Robert banjo pin and earrings set. *Courtesy of Alexandra Vangel. Photograph by John Merowski.*

Robert Pin and Earrings Set. Banjo, round faux sapphires and emeralds, matching banjo earrings, gold plated, 1960s. *Courtesy of Alexandra Vangel.* $175–$350/set

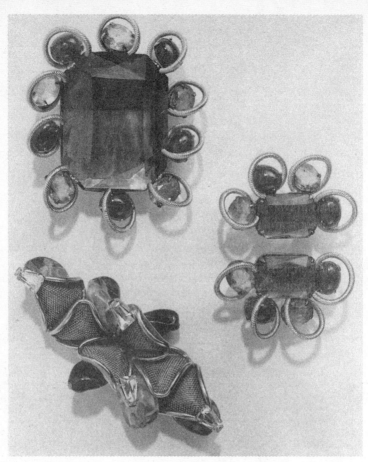

Arnold Scaasi abstract pin and pin and earrings set. *Pin and earrings set courtesy of Rita Sacks, Limited Additions, New York, NY; pin courtesy of Shirley Jaros, New York, NY. Photograph by Kenneth Chen.*

Arnold Scaasi Pin and Earrings Set. Abstract design, stretched octagon-cut faux topaz in the center, oval faux peridots and carnelians inside wiry loops, gold plated, 1960s. *Courtesy of Rita Sacks, Limited Additions.*

$250–$375

Arnold Scaasi Pin. Abstract design of mesh triangles, trapezium-cut clear rhinestones, light blue and navy glass beads, gold plated, marked "Scaasi," 1960s. *Courtesy of Shirley Jaros.* $150–$375

Schreiner bib necklace, *Glamour. Courtesy of the Schreiner family collection.*
Photograph of original page by Kenneth Chen.

Schreiner Necklace. Bib, crystal and faux turquoise drops, *Glamour*
magazine, 1960s. *Courtesy of the Schreiner family collection.* $700–$950

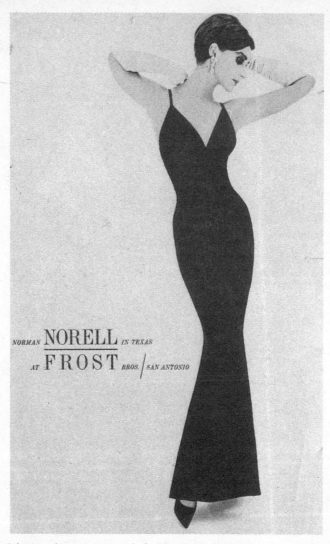

NORMAN NORELL IN TEXAS
AT FROST BROS. / SAN ANTONIO

Schreiner drop earrings made for Norman Norell, *Vogue*.
Courtesy of the Schreiner family collection. Photograph of original page by Kenneth Chen.

Schreiner Earrings. Drops, simulated pearls and clear rhinestones, made for Norman Norell, *Vogue*, 1961. *Courtesy of the Schreiner family collection.* $150–$225

Schreiner bib necklace and earrings set. *Courtesy of the Schreiner family collection. Photograph by Kenneth Chen.*

Schreiner Necklace and Earrings Set. Elaborate bib collar, simulated gray baroque pearl drops, clear round rhinestones, originally sold in the Park Avenue Room at Saks Fifth Avenue, New York City, 1960s.
Courtesy of the Schreiner family collection. $750–$1,000/set

Schreiner drop earrings, *Harper's Bazaar. Courtesy of the Schreiner family collection. Photograph of original page by Kenneth Chen.*

Schreiner Earrings. Yellow bead drop earrings, marquise clear rhine-stones, shown on the cover of *Harper's Bazaar*, February 1963. *Courtesy of the Schreiner family collection.* $125–$225

Schreiner wing earrings, *Vogue. Courtesy of the Schreiner family collection. Photograph of original page by Kenneth Chen.*

Schreiner Earrings. Rhinestone wing earrings, "winged brilliance at the ear," worn by Marisa Berenson on the cover of *Vogue*, September 1, 1965. *Courtesy of the Schreiner family collection.* $150–$225

EVENINGS—SLICED THIN

TWO LENGTHS OF EVENING, TWO KINDS OF PANELLING. BUT BOTH HAVE TH
YEAR'S NARROW LOOK, ARE WORN WITH THIS SEASON'S IMPORTANT COIFFUR

Short evening dress of black peau de soie, cloaked under a huge, wingy panel that points down to the hem at back, and pinned with an explosion of glitter. (Only

Chiffon with hardly a flutter, right—narrow, high-waisted, panelled. By Oleg Cassini, of bright, dark-blue silk chiffon; about $185. Meyers Make kidskin gloves. San-

Schreiner spoke pin made for Pauline Trigère, *Harper's Bazaar. Courtesy of the Schreiner family collection. Photograph of original page by Kenneth Chen.*

Schreiner Pin. Spoke crystal pin, made for Pauline Trigère, rhodium plated, shown in *Harper's Bazaar*, 1960s. *Courtesy of the Schreiner family collection.* $225–$325

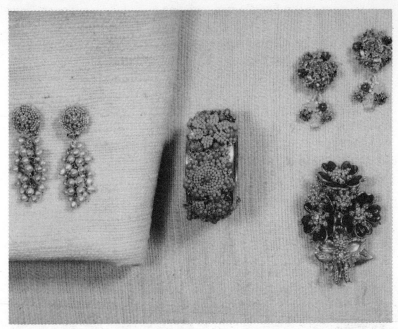

Stanley Hagler bracelet, pin, and earrings. *Jewelry and photograph courtesy of Maria Domont Collection, Beverly Hills, CA.*

(left to right)

Stanley Hagler Earrings. Grape cluster drop, simulated seed pearl tops and simulated baroque pearls, gold plated, 1960s. *Courtesy of Maria Domont Collection.* **$175–$225**

Stanley Hagler Bracelet. Hinged wide bangle, simulated coral beaded flowers, gold plated, 1960s. *Courtesy of Maria Domont Collection.* **$450–$550**

Stanley Hagler Earrings. Basket drops, simulated seed pearls and multicolored glass beaded flowers, gold plated, 1960s. *Courtesy of Maria Domont Collection.* **$150–$200**

Stanley Hagler Pin. Pansy, large faux sapphire flowers, simulated seed pearls, gold plated, 1960s. *Courtesy of Maria Domont Collection.* **$200–$300**

Stanley Hagler key necklace and earrings. *Original photograph courtesy of Stanley Hagler.*

Stanley Hagler Necklace and Earrings. Pendant, giant wine steward's keys, black-and-white florets and trim; earrings are from "shadow and substance" collection, one black and one white; plastic; 1960s.
Original photograph courtesy of Stanley Hagler.

Necklace $200–$300; earrings $40–$60

Stanley Hagler bib necklace. *Original photograph courtesy of Stanley Hagler.*

Stanley Hagler Necklace. Bib, chrysanthemums joined by scalloped bars, overlaid with simulated seed pearls, 1960s. *Original photograph courtesy of Stanley Hagler.* $700–$900

Stanley Hagler pendant necklace. *Original photograph courtesy of Stanley Hagler.*

Stanley Hagler Necklace. V-pendant, Swarovski crystals, simulated baroque and seed pearls, gold plated, 1966 (winner of Swarovski's Great Design in Jewelry Award). *Original photograph courtesy of Stanley Hagler.* $400–$500

Stanley Hagler breastplate. *Original photograph courtesy of Stanley Hagler.*

Stanley Hagler Necklace. Breastplate, Swarovski crystals and pavé rhinestones, fringed with rhinestone tassels, 1969. *Original photograph courtesy of Stanley Hagler.* $1,500–$2,500

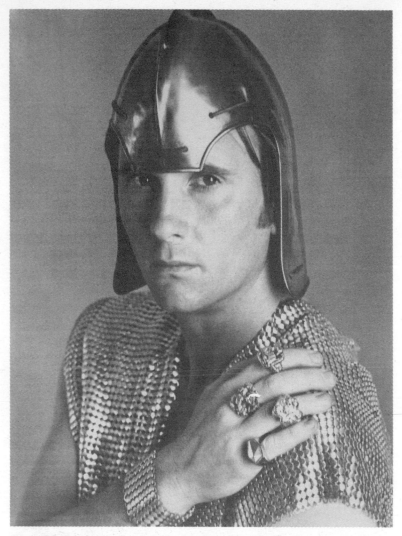

Stanley Hagler helmet, vest, wristband, and rings. *Original photograph courtesy of Stanley Hagler.*

Stanley Hagler Helmet, Vest, Wristband, and Rings. "The newest thing in motorcycle helmets," a grouping of aluminum men's creations designed in medieval style, free-form rings, 1963–1964. *Original photograph courtesy of Stanley Hagler.*   Rings $75–$125/each

Stanley Hagler whistle necklaces. *Original photograph courtesy of Stanley Hagler.*

Stanley Hagler Necklaces. Whistles, train, siren, bobby, bosun, police, gold plated, 1960s.   *Original photograph courtesy of Stanley Hagler.*

$35–$50/each

Stanley Hagler earrings.
Both robes, so dazzling they could only be Paris, are worn here by Princess Ira Furstenberg, a lightning fire Paris beauty and star of Dead Run, third and sexiest of her four films all within the year. Princess Ira's makeup and coiffures more magnificent than any headdress—are by Carita.

Stanley Hagler chandelier earrings on photo of Princess Ira Furstenberg wearing Stanley Hagler floral drop earrings. *Chandelier earrings courtesy of the author; original photograph courtesy of Stanley Hagler. Photograph by Kenneth Chen.*

Stanley Hagler Earrings. Large floral drops, worn by Princess Ira Furstenberg; chandeliers, simulated pearls, clear round rhinestones; gold plated; 1960s. *Original photograph courtesy of Stanley Hagler; chandelier earrings courtesy of the author.* $150–$200/each

Stanley Hagler drop earrings, *Vogue. Courtesy of Stanley Hagler. Photograph of the page by Kenneth Chen.*

Stanley Hagler Earrings. Huge simulated pearl drops, shown on the cover of *Vogue*, March 1, 1967. *Courtesy of Stanley Hagler.* $125–$200

Trifari "jade belly" swan and dragon pins. *Courtesy of Tania Santé's Classic Collectables, Miami, FL. Photograph by Jessica Michael.*

Trifari Pin. Large swan, orange enameled feathers, faux "carved" jade body, pavé rhinestones, gold plated, 1960s. *Courtesy of Tania Santé's Classic Collectables.* $500–$750

Trifari Pin. Large dragon, orange enameled body, faux "carved" jade center, pavé rhinestones, gold plated, 1960s. *Courtesy of Tania Santé's Classic Collectables.* $500–$750

Vêndome flower pin. *Courtesy of Ridgewood Antique Shop, Ridgewood, NJ. Photograph by John Merowski.*

Vêndome Pin. Flower, clear round and marquise rhinestones, pear-shaped simulated pearl center, 1960s. *Courtesy of Ridgewood Antique Shop.* $125–$165

Vogue abstract pin and earrings set. *Courtesy of Alexandra Vangel. Photograph by John Merowski.*

Vogue Pin and Earrings Set. Abstract design, light and dark pink rhinestones, matching drop earrings, gold plated, 1960s. *Courtesy of Alexandra Vangel.* $200–$280

Weiss drop necklace and earrings set. *Courtesy of Rita Sacks, Limited Additions, New York, NY. Photograph by Kenneth Chen.*

Weiss Necklace and Earrings Set. Unusual; large oval faux aquamarines, citrines, peridots, emeralds, and jet; aurora borealis and clear round rhinestones in an ornate pendant design; matching large drop earrings; gold plated; pendant and matching earrings are 5 inches high; 1960s. *Courtesy of Rita Sacks, Limited Additions.* $900–$1,200

Unsigned polka dot flower pin and neon fish
pin. *Courtesy of Rita Sacks, Limited Additions,
New York, NY. Photograph by Kenneth Chen.*

Unsigned Pin. Large black-and-white polka dot flower pin, metal,
4½ inches high, 1960s. *Courtesy of Rita Sacks, Limited Additions.* $100–$150

Unsigned Pin. Neon pink fish, turquoise and purple dots, white
metal, 1960s. *Courtesy of Rita Sacks, Limited Additions.* $75–$100

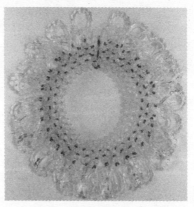

Unsigned Lucite collar. *Courtesy of Joan
Paley, Chicago, IL. Photograph by Kenneth
Chen.*

Unsigned Necklace. Lucite collar, oval loops, round faceted beads, gold
plated spacers, ca. 1960s. *Courtesy of Joan Paley.* $750–$1,000

(top to bottom) Unsigned pin and Jacques necklaces. *Courtesy of the author and Prudence Huang, New York, NY. Photograph by Kenneth Chen.*

Unsigned Pin. Huge round pin, faux gray moonstones, clear round rhinestones, silver plated, 1960s (from the estate of Doris Lilly). *Courtesy of the author and Prudence Huang.* $100–$175

Jacques Necklace (unsigned). Collar, rhinestone fringe tassel, large clear oval rhinestones, silver plated, ca. 1960s. *Courtesy of the author and Prudence Huang.* $150–$200

Jacques Necklace (unsigned). Huge elaborate collar, clear rhinestones in many shapes, wide front plaquette, silver plated, 1960s. *Courtesy of the author and Prudence Huang.* $200–$300

Unsigned choker and Jacques necklaces. *Unsigned necklace courtesy of the author; Jacques necklaces courtesy of the author and Prudence Huang, New York, NY. Photograph by Kenneth Chen.*

(top to bottom)

Unsigned Necklace. Choker, oval and pear-shaped pink rhinestones, gold plated, ca. 1960s. *Courtesy of the author.* $100–$200

Jacques Necklace (unsigned). Choker; stretched-octagon-cut faux emeralds, sapphires, and clear rhinestones; silver plated; 1960s. *Courtesy of the author and Prudence Huang.* $175–$275

Jacques Necklace (unsigned). Bib, dangles, round and pear-shaped jet and clear rhinestones, gold plated, 1960s. *Courtesy of the author and Prudence Huang.* $160–$250

Unsigned rhinestone collar from the estate
of Doris Lilly. *Courtesy of the author and
Prudence Huang, New York, NY.
Photograph by Marcelo Maia.*

Unsigned Necklace. Ornate collar, clear marquise rhinestones, large
stretched-octagon-cut faux rubies, silver plated, 1960s (from the estate
of Doris Lilly). *Courtesy of the author and Prudence Huang.* $350–$450

Unsigned fringe collar from the estate
of Doris Lilly. *Courtesy of the author
and Prudence Huang, New York, NY.
Photograph by Marcelo Maia.*

Unsigned Necklace. Collar with four rows of large clear round rhinestones, graduated fringe of rhinestones with teardrop-shaped simulated pearl drops, silver plated, 1960s (from the estate of Doris
Lilly). *Courtesy of the author and Prudence Huang.* $150–$250

Unsigned massive bib. *Courtesy of the author. Photograph by Marcelo Maia.*

Unsigned Necklace. Large bib with multiple strands of clear round and rectangular rhinestones, silver plated, 1960s. *Courtesy of the author.*

$500–$750

. . . More Sixties

Anne Klein Pendant. Heraldic figure, pavé rhinestone suit of armor, faux ruby cabochons on the headdress, faux emerald cabochons at the top of the headdress and the middle of the chest, faux ruby and clear crystal bead dangles, suspended from a flat link chain, gold plated, 1960s. *Courtesy of Rita Sacks, Limited Additions.* $250–$350

Boucher Bracelet. Rigid bangle, clear melon-cut rhinestones and clear round rhinestones set between each large stone, silver plated, marked "01167," 1960s. *Courtesy of Shirley Jaros.* $500–$750

Chanel Bracelet. Unusual gauntlet bangle with "CHANEL" embossed and filled in with black enamel, green "poured glass" pea pods, simulated pearl pea dangles, gold plated, ca. 1960s. *Courtesy of Joan Paley.*

$1,200–$1,500

Kenneth Jay Lane Necklace. Pendant; square, oval, and round cabochons in faux (plastic) emeralds, rubies, sapphires, and fuchsia stones; clear round rhinestones and baguettes; suspended from a chain of narrow baguette links; gold plated; marked "K.J.L.," pendant 4½ inches in diameter; 1960s. *Courtesy of E & J Rothstein Antiques.*

$350–$500

Kenneth Jay Lane Pin. Donkey, faux turquoise cabochon eyes, faux ruby cabochon buttons, pavé rhinestone bow tie and ivory enamel pants and ears, gold plated, marked "K.J.L.," 1960s. *Courtesy of Rita Sacks, Limited Additions.*

$300–$400

Kenneth Jay Lane Necklace. Multistrand, green and pink glass beads, clear rhinestone rondelles, enameled clasp, gold plated, marked "K.J.L.," 1960s. *Courtesy of Metropolis.*

$100–$150

Kenneth Jay Lane Necklace and Earrings Set. Large bib, faux turquoises, simulated pearls, medium and large clear round rhinestones, gold plated, 4¼ inches at the widest point, matching drop triangular-shaped earrings 3¾ inches long, 1960s. *Courtesy of Prudence Huang.*

$800–$1,200/set

Lucien Piccard Necklace. Pendant with chain dangles, faux lapis lazuli, gold plated, 1960s. *Courtesy of Metropolis.*

$75–$125

Mimi di N Pin and Earrings Set. Dome-shaped, pear-shaped faux turquoises, central domed faux ruby cabochon, round clear rhinestone accents, simulated pearls with round clear rhinestone tips, matching earrings, 1960s. *Courtesy of Tania Santé's Classic Collectables.*

$150–$300/set

Miriam Haskell Pin and Earrings Set. Floral design, large faux emerald cabochon petals, each surrounded by clear round flat-back rhinestones, clear round rhinestone florets in the centers, melon-cut faux emerald center, coordinating earrings, gold plated, 1960s. *Courtesy of Prudence Huang.* $250–$350/set

Miriam Haskell Pin. Floral design, large faux emerald central cabo-chon, surrounded by leaves edged with blue-and-green flat-back rhinestones, green glass bead dangles with larger irregularly shaped green glass beads, gold plated, 1960s. *Courtesy of Shirley Jaros.* $350–$650

Yves Saint Laurent Necklace. Cross, simulated baroque pearls, designed by Roger Scemama, France, 1960s. *Courtesy of Ginger Moro Archives.* $300–$450

The Seventies

The Seventies were a short chapter in the annals of costume jewelry. Manufacturers in Providence shrugged their shoulders, designers in New York muttered something about chains, and women we interviewed couldn't exactly remember what they wore around their necks except love beads, peace symbols, puka shells, and huge medallions.

Space exploration; discos; flower children; women returning to the office with new status as lawyers, corporate vice presidents, and heads of their own companies; the end of the Vietnam non-war; unisex; and most important, the do-your-own-thing credo all greatly influenced fashion and costume jewelry. The height of ridiculousness was reached with men's chest wigs advertised for those who were embarrassed about their hairless chests, newly bared under shirts open to the waist, all the better to show off gold chains.

For a while there was a fashion-is-dead movement when long floral skirts, vests, and imported caftans from Pakistan and India seemed to take over the fashion scene. The midi skirt in 1970 gave way to the micro-mini in 1972, only to give way to a softer silhouette and lower hemline by 1975. Designer Mary McFadden based her dress designs on historical periods or cultural phenomena, with accessories in hammered shapes, disks, and abstract designs in golden tones. She showed necklaces draped across the shoulder or worn as one huge pendant. Zandra Rhodes's prints were freewheeling and spirited, with the shape of the dress inspired by the fabric. She parodied the street punks with a "conceptual chic" collection.

Very American designers Calvin Klein, Ralph Lauren, and Halston were joined by Louis Dell'Olio and Donna Karan to form the new couturier ready-to-wear group. Diane Von Furstenberg wrapped women of all ages and sizes in her go-everywhere dress. Pantsuits, bell-bottoms, platform shoes, and man-made silk, and the *Annie Hall* look were widespread.

In the late Seventies, Laura Ashley emerged with a flourish, showing a country gentlewoman look that tapped into a longing for the simpler life, while Yves Saint Laurent's woman wore a man's tuxedo and other women borrowed their lovers' Nehru suits. Catherine Deneuve's man-tailored style typified the menswear look for women.

At the office, women discovered the feminine counterpart to the executive's "uniform" and wore two- or three-piece conservative skirt suits with full silk bow ties at their throats, leaving no room for necklaces or pins. The earrings they wore were tiny, almost invisible studs or classic pearl buttons. Bracelets were gold bangles worn singly, if at all, and watches were the size of men's.

Away from the office, everything was worn, with skirt lengths varying from maxi to midi and some mini leftovers. Hot pants were worn by the young and the thin—and by some who were neither. Anklets, once considered trashy, were shown with the new, sexy, feminine clothing styles. Looks were ethnic, peasant, cowboy, hippy, Gypsy, arty, and others created innovatively by their wearers. The "Rich Gypsy" look originated with Millicent Rogers's wardrobe exhibit at the American Women of Style show at the Metropolitan Museum of Art in New York. At popular discos such as Studio 54 and at art openings at the then-hip Jewish Museum in New York City, one could see every major style at once, including people who came with their bodies painted "Yves Klein blue" in honor of his exhibit. Women were exercising their bodies and showed them off with bare shoulders, bare arms, bare backs, see-through dresses with or without body stockings underneath, and skinny dresses that hugged the body.

Romantic necklines were even prettier with beaded chokers and jeweled bibs. Longer necklaces with rhinestones and carved beads were in proportion for leggy jumpsuits. Gimmicky designs flowed from Paris. Yves Saint Laurent showed a "Can-Can" bride and "Carmen" outfits with cinched waists and huge blousons. Everyone took a stab at the African tribal look, Moroccan caftan styles, fanny wrappers, see-through fabrics, wrapped ankles, plunging necklines front and back, and gold lamé dresses with gold trim and gold jewelry.

John Travolta heated everyone up with *Saturday Night Fever* and *tout le monde* went disco dancing after midnight. Jewelry and pocketbooks were scaled down to fit the nightlife. Unobtrusive accessories that didn't interfere with dancing complemented wild and crazy disco outfits. Earrings became very important and were shown bulky, hammered, textured, and in the shape of drops, hoops, door knockers, buttons, and elaborate pendants. Bracelets got lost in long sleeves made of floaty fabrics but large rings made a big comeback. Necklaces were dog collars, chokers, wooden beads, macramé bibs, ethnic amulets, and large heavy medallions. For evening, big "headlight" crystals, long pendants, dressy dog collars, and gold beads were worn. In the mid Seventies, neck rings with suspended ornaments and crescent-shaped necklaces were made by all the big manufacturers. Once again, initials and zodiacs were everywhere—answering the favorite California question of "What's your sign?" In 1977, a pyramid pendant was sold with an accompanying booklet extolling its mysterious powers. In 1979 the King Tutankhamen exhibit traveled across the country, sparking yet another Egyptian revival in jewelry.

Ripped black stockings, bruised-looking eye makeup, rainbow-hued hair, and otherworldly music were hot at the punk Mudd Club in New York. Bicycle chains, safety pins, and pointed studs on leather collars that were usually worn by killer dogs passed for jewelry on all sexes.

Now is a great time to collect Seventies jewelry. Pieces can still be found at reasonable prices. Eisenberg enamels, Kenneth Jay Lane figurals and large necklaces, Art Deco revivals, Nettie Rosenstein, Diane Love pieces designed for Trifari, Chanel, Christian Dior, Yves Saint Laurent, Hattie Carnegie, Panetta, Ciner, Pierre Cardin, and amusing, unsigned, painted flower and animal pins are all collectible.

WENDY GELL   *Wendy Gell*

WENDY GELL
©DISNEY CO

In 1975, Wendy Gell, a young New York songwriter, created her first "wristy," gluing together some bits and pieces she found in remnant bins on Canal Street. Rhinestones, plastic palm trees, and flamingos were artistically arranged on an expandable copper bracelet and presented to a friend for his birthday. It was love at first sight and he became her partner. They showed their first samples out of a wooden wine case and were a huge success.

Through the Seventies and on into the Eighties, Wendy Gell's designs were on the cover of *Vogue* and in thousands of editorials in magazines all over the world. Wendy created sequinned Disney characters, jeweled Roger Rabbits and his friends, *Wizard of Oz* jewelry, and masks from *The Phantom of the Opera*. She designed special pieces for Bill Blass, Oscar de la Renta, and Louis Dell'Olio. Her company specialized in a "different" look. Many of the fabulous large cuff bracelets were one-of-a-kind or part of a limited edition.

Wendy's pieces are collected by Marisa Berenson, who showed them in her book, Liza Minnelli, Elizabeth Taylor, Elton John, and the late Liberace. Collectors of Wendy Gell jewelry can tell the older pieces by the glue around the edge of the cuff, which yellows with age. The early signature was made by an electric pen, or may have been signed "Wristies by Wendy™." It was replaced in 1986 by an oval disk that was soldered into the piece. Detailed beadwork is finer in the more recent pieces. The Wendy Gell company closed in 1992.

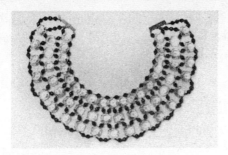

Miriam Haskell bib necklace. *Courtesy of the author. Photograph by Marcelo Maia.*

Miriam Haskell Necklace. Unusual bib, Lucite and jet glass, silver-plated clasp, early 1970s. *Courtesy of the author.* $500–$750

Napier bracelets and necklace, (center) Pierre Cardin necklace. *Napier pieces courtesy of The Napier Company; Pierre Cardin necklace courtesy of Sloane Miller. Photograph by Kenneth Chen.*

(top to bottom)

Napier Bracelet. Open cuff, textured and smooth metal, gold and silver plated, 1970s. *Courtesy of The Napier Co.* $75–$100

Pierre Cardin Necklace. Double pendant, black and silver-plated metal, silver-plated chain, marked "Pierre Cardin Made in France," 1970s. *Courtesy of Sloane Miller.* $75–$125

Napier Necklace. Pendant, snake chain, silver and gold plated, 1970s. *Courtesy of The Napier Co.* $50–$75

Napier Bracelet. Links, gold and silver plated, 1970s. *Courtesy of The Napier Co.* $35–$50

Nettie Rosenstein rose pin. *Courtesy of Dr. Raymond Carol. Photograph by Kenneth Chen.*

Nettie Rosenstein Pin. Rose, pale amber translucent plastic petals, pavé rhinestone leaves, gold plated, 4 inches high, ca. early 1970s. *Courtesy of Dr. Raymond Carol.* $150–$225

Nettie Rosenstein Ferdinand and
Isabella pins. *Original advertisement
and jewelry courtesy of Dr. Raymond
Carol. Photograph of original page by
Kenneth Chen.*

Nettie Rosenstein Pins. Ferdinand and Isabella, faux ruby cabochon
faces, pavé rhinestones, gold plated, 1¾ inches high, ca. early 1970s.
Courtesy of Dr. Raymond Carol. $200–$250/pair

Nettie Rosenstein figural pins. *Courtesy of Dr. Raymond Carol.*
Photograph by Kenneth Chen.

Nettie Rosenstein Pins. Fighting cocks, red enameled cockscomb,
opaque red glass eyes, pavé rhinestones, gold plated, 2¼ inches high,
ca. early 1970s. *Courtesy of Dr. Raymond Carol.* $200–$250/pair

Nettie Rosenstein Pin. Monkey in a palm tree, simulated ivory head, pavé rhinestone accents, gold plated, 2¾ inches high, ca. early 1970s. *Courtesy of Dr. Raymond Carol.* $125–$175

Nettie Rosenstein Pin. Giraffe, pavé rhinestones, gold plated, 3⅜ inches high, ca. early 1970s. *Courtesy of Dr. Raymond Carol.* $125–$175

|| NOTE: The Nettie Rosenstein pieces described above are from the private collection of Dr. Raymond Carol, whose late wife, Lois, designed jewelry for Nettie Rosenstein from the late Fifties through the early Seventies. ||

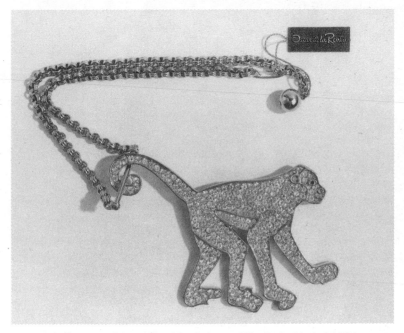

Oscar de la Renta monkey pendant/pin. *Courtesy of Rita Sacks, Limited Additions, New York, NY. Photograph by Kenneth Chen.*

Oscar de la Renta Pendant/Pin. Monkey hanging from a bar, pavé rhinestone body, faux ruby eye, gold plated, marked "OR" inside an oval, ca. 1970s. *Courtesy of Rita Sacks, Limited Additions.* $400–$600

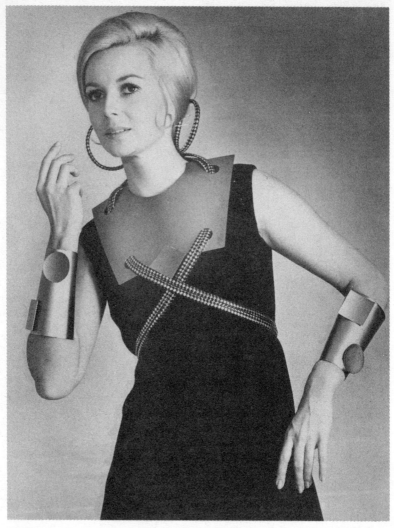

Stanley Hagler body sculpture and bracelets. *Original photograph courtesy of Stanley Hagler.*

Stanley Hagler Body Sculpture and Bracelets. Combination breastplate and harness, 5½ inch tapered cuff bracelets, stainless steel, made for the Chase Maid of Metals, 1970s. *Original photograph courtesy of Stanley Hagler.* $300–$500/set

Stanley Hagler pendant necklace and headpiece. *Original photograph courtesy of Stanley Hagler.*

Stanley Hagler Necklace and Headpiece. Pendant, "Order of the Superstar," Swarovski crystals, Lucite, suspended from a band of silver bugle beads; headpiece, egret feathers, Swarovski crystals; 1970s. *Original photograph courtesy of Stanley Hagler.*

Necklace $300–$400; headpiece $150–$200

Stanley Hagler metal cuff, drop earrings, and watch fob pin. *Original photograph courtesy of Stanley Hagler.*

Stanley Hagler Bracelet, Pin, and Earrings. Cuff bracelet and coordinated drop earrings, sculptured watch fob pin, gold plated, made for Chase Metals Service, 1970s. *Original photograph courtesy of Stanley Hagler.*

Cuff $125–$175; Earrings $75–$125; Pin $150–$225

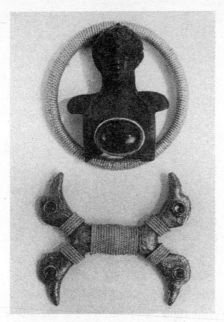

Trifari pins designed by Diane Love. *Courtesy
of Ilene Chazanof, Decorative Arts, New York,
NY. Photograph by Kenneth Chen.*

Trifari Pin. Bust of a man, white metal, painted green patina, large
oval faux jet cabochon in a gold plated setting, gold-plated wire
wrapped around frame, designed by Diane Love, 1969–1970. *Courtesy
of Ilene Chazanof, Decorative Arts.* $150–$250

Trifari Pin. Four duck heads, pewter-plated white metal, a pair each
of round faux sapphire and ruby cabochon eyes, wrapped in gold-
plated wire, designed by Diane Love, 1969–1970. *Courtesy of Ilene
Chazanof, Decorative Arts.* $150–$250

NOTE: Ms. Love brought pieces back from her world travels.
The pieces were then cast in white metal and plated in an
antique gold finish. Sometimes the pieces were painted black or
plated with a dark finish and then the plating was partly rubbed
off for contrast. Ms. Love worked directly with the modelmaker
in creating these designs.

Unsigned elephant pin. *Courtesy of Rita Sacks, Limited Additions, New York, NY. Photograph by Kenneth Chen.*

Unsigned Pin. Elephant; jeweled howdah; pavé rhinestones; faux rubies, emeralds, citrines, and amethysts; simulated pearls on the feet; silver plated; 5 inches wide; 1970s. *Courtesy of Rita Sacks, Limited Additions.*

$300–$400

. . . More Seventies

Unsigned Chatelaine. Frog under a toadstool connected by a chain to two smaller frogs; green-and-yellow enameled frogs; red, yellow, and green enameled toadstool; clear round rhinestone eyes and accents on the toadstool; gold plated; 1970s. *Courtesy of Rita Sacks, Limited Additions.*

$75–$150

Trifari Watch/Bracelet. Black bezel, Asian figure carrying a gilt fan, gilt geometric and bamboo designs on a textured gold bangle, designed by Diane Love, early 1970s. *Courtesy of Rita Sacks, Limited Additions.*

$200–$300

Unsigned Pin. Jointed Pierrot with a red, white, and blue enameled costume; holding a large red enameled heart; copper plated; marked with script initials and " '78"; 1978. *Courtesy of Rita Sacks, Limited Additions.*

$100–$175

The Eighties

The Eighties—the peak of the self, the "me" generation, health clubs and oat bran, Reaganomics, total freedom in dress, hemlines that were fine wherever they fell, Madonna's global fashion influence, First Lady Barbara Bush's pearls by Kenneth Jay Lane, and the old mirror, mirror question now being "Who is the thinnest of them all?" answered by Tom Wolfe's social X-rays and Nancy Reagan, the reigning Queen of Thin.

Important designers made their marks—Norma Kamali's wonderful use of fabrics and her own line of costume jewelry based on her collection of vintage costume jewelry, Betsey Johnson's forever-young fashions, "couture ready-to-wear" by Isaac Mizrahi, Mark Jacobs, Oscar de la Renta, Carolyne Roehm, Carolina Herrera, and Bob Mackie competed in popularity with workout gear. Women at work were now executives, and mail-order catalogs filled a need for the busy working mom/wife/lover/friend.

Costume jewelry was practically a religion, with devotees numbering among the millions. Accessories shows overflowed huge convention halls, women didn't even bother to use the excuse of traveling to wear costume jewelry with ball gowns, and people collected vintage costume jewelry with a vengeance, waiting hours in line for estate sales to begin. Copies of copies were sold on street corners for the price of a magazine. Every major fashion designer had a line of costume jewelry that accessorized each season's line.

Women wore multiples of everything. Earrings were worn in a series along the outer edge of pierced ears, bracelets were worn in clusters, and groups of necklaces combined old, new, real, and costume. Diane Smith, senior fashion editor at *Glamour*, collected multiple strands of beads in every color to fill in a collar or a neckline. She thought it was great to mix everything—chains, gold lockets, and costume jewelry that gave it the look of importance. Diane believed that the simple way of dressing required elegant, glamorous jewelry. The basic, double-breasted dark evening suit needed a spectacular piece to dress it up—it had to be basic, yes, but big *important* basic. Diane noted that the Eighties woman wanted to be able to wear something over and over and not tire of it. She didn't want to be bothered with fussy or fragile jewelry. She wanted jewelry that could be relied on all the time.

In the fall of 1985, Donna Karan, a leading designer of contemporary clothing, started her own clothing line including a line of costume jewelry. She said:

> Jewelry is important because it gives a woman a chance to express her individuality. We can all buy the same black pants, the same black bodysuit, but accessories make it your own.
>
> We design for the woman who does it all, is always on the go and thinking about twenty million things at once. She wants to look fabulous and have everything work—including the jewelry. The clothing can take her from day to evening just by adding or changing the jewelry. It's a very important part of each collection. If a woman wants to spark up her wardrobe and can buy just one thing, often it's a piece of jewelry.
>
> Costume jewelry is great because it's accessible, you can have fun with it, it's more relaxed than precious jewelry. Our line is mostly 24K-gold-plated brass. We design pieces for specific times of the year. For winter we'll have heavy collars or neck pieces and the holiday line will be softer, more feminine, ethnic. The jewelry line is based on the clothing for that season. We love jewelry that makes noise. In the way a woman has a scent, she also has a sound. We do lots of charm bracelets that move and produce a sound.
>
> Our inspiration is the elements—stones, pebbles, sand, the colors of the sunset. My husband is a sculptor and he works with shapes and forms and the body and movement, and I'm inspired by his work. We're also influenced by vintage costume jewelry and we wear it for fun. Sometimes an old belt buckle or a clasp on a handbag becomes a detail in a necklace.

What's wonderful about our jewelry is that it's timeless—it could easily be from another decade or another century. It's definitely not "throwaway jewelry" because of this classic quality. We encourage retailers to carry the jewelry with the clothing in their Donna Karan New York boutique so that our customers can coordinate a complete look.

Besides clothing designers, artists were turning to jewelry design as an outlet for their creative energies. In 1986, Maria Snyder, a young, former Yves Saint Laurent model who had studied art in Paris and received a master's degree in art history, started her own costume jewelry company. Maria said:

I'm a born sculptor. I see jewelry as an extension of sculpture. I use plastic that I mold with my hands. I never draw my designs, I sculpt them in plastic or clay. I also cast white metal and resin and use free-form plastics. The pieces are plated in 24K gold or gold leafed by hand.

I entered jewelrymaking so innocently; I knew nothing about the industry. I made my first bracelets over my own wrist and they didn't fit anyone else. Some things I do are truly experimental. I just say to myself, "Wouldn't it be fun to try that!" I've designed jewelry for Giorgio di Sant'Angelo, Geoffrey Beene, Carolina Herrera, and Isabel Toledo for their fashion shows. My rings are worn by Jody Watley on her album cover and the model Paulina is wearing my earrings in the Estée Lauder ads. I did a piece for the National Glaucoma Trust in brass. I recently designed a piece for a Revlon ad. My jewelry is in fifty or sixty stores. I love to design and I love working with different materials. The important thing for me is the grace of the line.

Maria's jewelry and sculptures have been exhibited in art galleries in New York and Florida. The direction her work took was an important one in the designs of the Eighties—bold, well crafted, and innovative with an excellent use of materials that satisfied form, function, and design.

Maria talked about vintage costume jewelry:

What is really interesting is there was so much creativity in costume jewelry. There were such fabulous experimental pieces—all that wonderful enamel work, designers like Schlumberger in the Thirties and Forties. Sometimes I feel really wild and think of the weirdest color schemes and something I want to do that's really outrageous that I wouldn't dare do in gold and I do it in costume!

Artisan jewelry, replicas of estate jewelry, and "theme" jewelry based on movies or plays were the outstanding design motifs of the Eighties. Street jewelry, with its roughness refined for the ready-to-wear crowd, and crystals designed by Tina Chow and Yves Saint Laurent sold at precious jewelry prices, and rhinestone pins adorned jeans jackets again. Marcasite jewelry made in the Far East, heavy-looking Byzantine and Renaissance-inspired jewelry, enameled revivals of animal pins and bracelets, and charm bracelets with fertility symbols were popular and collectible.

What people are collecting from the Eighties are mostly the couture or runway pieces by Yves Saint Laurent, Chanel, Dior, Lacroix, Lanvin, Karl Lagerfeld, and other designers. Costume jewelry designers Isabel Canovas, Robert Lee Morris, Herve van der Straeten, Eric Beamon, Steven Vaubel, Maria Snyder, Donna Karan, Kenneth Jay Lane, and Bill Schiffer made pieces that collectors find interesting.

Butler & Wilson hand and spider pins. *Courtesy of Charles France, Divine Idea, New York, NY. Photograph by Kenneth Chen.*

Butler & Wilson Pin. Hand, clear round rhinestones, pear-shaped jet fingernails and bracelet, gunmetal plated, 1980s. *Courtesy of Charles France, Divine Idea.* $125–$175

Butler & Wilson Pin (unsigned). Spider, clear round rhinestones, black plated, 1980s. *Courtesy of Charles France, Divine Idea.* $125–$175

Carolee flamingo pin. *Photograph courtesy of Carolee.*

Carolee Pin. Flamingo; channel-set faux rubies, sapphires, and emeralds in the tail; faux sapphire eye; pavé rhinestones; from the Estate Collection inspired by the Duchess of Windsor's jewels; gold plated; 1987. *Original photograph courtesy of Carolee.* $75–$125

Chanel tie earrings and charm
bracelet. *Earrings courtesy of the
author; bracelet courtesy of Robin
Feldman Collectibles, New York,
NY. Photograph by Kenneth Chen.*

Chanel Earrings. Ties, double "C" insignia, suspended from circles with a
double "C" insignia, gold plated, 1980s. *Courtesy of the author.* $185–$250

Chanel Bracelet. Charms suspended from a heavy chain, gold plated,
marked "CHANEL" in block print, 1980s. *Courtesy of Robin Feldman
Collectibles.* $650–$800 (sold for $700 in early 1993)

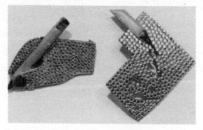

Gourdji pins. *Courtesy of Rita Sacks, Limited
Additions, New York, NY. Photograph by
Kenneth Chen.*

Gourdji Pin. Hand holding a pencil, pavé flat-back rhinestones, red,
transparent, yellow-and-black pencil, red enameled fingernail,
pewter plated, 1980s. *Courtesy of Rita Sacks, Limited Additions.* $75–$125

Gourdji Pin. "I lov" design; pavé flat-back rhinestones; yellow, brown, and black enameled pencil; gold plated; 1980s. *Courtesy of Rita Sacks, Limited Additions.* $75–$125

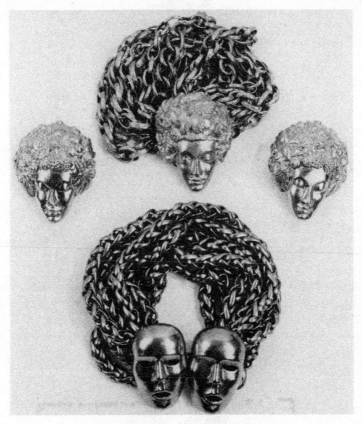

Isabel Canovas mask bracelet and "summer and winter" bracelet and earrings set. *Mask bracelet courtesy of Robin Feldman Collectibles, New York, NY; bracelet and earrings set courtesy of Joan Paley, Chicago, IL. Photograph by Kenneth Chen.*

Isabel Canovas Bracelet and Earrings Set. "Summer and winter" design, faces, eight strands of chain, matching earrings, gold plated, 1988. *Courtesy of Joan Paley.* $600–$800/set

Isabel Canovas Bracelet. Masks, several strands of chain, gold plated, 1980s. *Courtesy of Robin Feldman Collectibles.* $400–$500

Lanvin couture necklace. *Courtesy of the author. Photograph by Kenneth Chen.*

Lanvin Necklace (unsigned). Couture piece, gold leather-like curls, Lucite cubes, black satin ribbon, early 1980s. *Courtesy of the author.*

$300–$450

Yves Saint Laurent Lucite necklace and earrings set. *Courtesy of the author. Photograph by Kenneth Chen.*

Yves Saint Laurent Necklace (unsigned) *and Earrings Set*. Lucite pyramid domed cabochons in shades of topaz and raspberry, strung on wire, gunmetal plated, earrings marked "YSL," early 1980s. *Courtesy of the author.*

$600–$900/set

. . . More Eighties

Yves Saint Laurent Necklace. Collar, ten strands, gunmetal-colored flat-back beads, simulated baroque pearls, one blue, one orange and one pink large round rhinestone, three vertical rows of large square-cut clear crystals, gunmetal plated, from the Couture Collection, early 1980s. *Courtesy of the author.* $400–$700

Yves Saint Laurent Necklace. Pendant on a heavy link chain; 1⅝ inch hexagon cut faux tourmaline; gold plated, marked "YSL," early 1980s. *Courtesy of Prudence Huang.* $200–$275

The Nineties

The Nineties—the decade when Baby Boomers have come into their own politically, with President "Billary" Clinton and Vice President Gore leading a nation that has high hopes for meaningful social and environmental changes. Fashion is still mandated by a handful of European couturiers—Chanel, Yves Saint Laurent, and Balmain (even though Karl Lagerfeld and Oscar de la Renta are designing for Chanel and Balmain, respectively, the originators' power still reigns).

We're seeing the Gapping of America, Timberland stores opening in Europe, home shopping networks being the answer to hungry vendors' prayers, Armani's "reasonable" jeans snapped up at $140 per, and couture suits selling for $10,000 to $20,000 without the blouse! Cartier's Love Bracelet, $350 in 1969, is now $3,500. Restaurants are enjoyed as theater and no one cares about the food, and cross-sexual club gear and "Grunge" amuse the fashion avant-garde. Madonna has escalated herself to a money-making machine, with her hot hot picture book *Sex* selling over half a million copies at $50 apiece. Every man and woman's fifteen minutes of fame is happening on tell-all talk shows. The Soviet Union is no more, Somalia is starving, and the newest jewel of the decade is the red ribbon made of satin, sequins, rhinestones or rubies, worn by supporters of the fight against AIDS.

Skirts have gone down well past the knees and come back up again; Gianni Versace's bandage dresses suggest the dominatrix's duds worn on public access TV; and newcomers Todd Oldham, Isaac Mizrahi, and Anna Sui are now part of the Old Guard. The Seventies are hot—bell-bottoms, ruffled blouses, and platform shoes are part of every designer's "new" look. Donna, Calvin, and Ralph dominate men's and women's markets. Elvis is sighted at Macy's in New York in the Elvis Lives in the Arcade boutique. Elvis pins, watches, T-shirts, and sunglasses perpetuate the fixation. In the *New York Times*, Bill Cunningham finds a photo-worthy fad in pin-decorated jeans and leather jackets—everything is there, from Hard Rock Cafe mementos, Marine Corps insignia, and trendy miscellania to vintage collections of jeweled flies and insects.

Creeping connoisseurism has invaded the vintage costume jewelry collector. A small but growing minority has reached the big time, and phones and faxes hum from California to New York to London and Milan and back again. How did we ever sell jewelry without a copier and a fax machine? Important pieces are being "ordered" using picture books on costume jewelry as catalogs. The prices reflect the global markets, and dealers who attempt to join this crowd are as aware of the dollar's fluctuations as the commodity traders who deal in currency. The pieces flying back and forth across the big pond are often the rarest and most expensive.

Costume jewelry collectors are buying couture pieces by Chanel (particularly the limited editions made by Gripoix using "poured glass"), Christian Dior, and Yves Saint Laurent, as well as contemporary couture designers Christian Lacroix, Karl Lagerfeld, Moschino, Gianni Versace, Nina Ricci, Valentino, Louis Feraud, Givenchy, Emanuel Ungaro, and others. Costume jewelry aficionados are buying for their collections the most fabulous pieces made by very current costume jewelry designers Gerard Yosca, Iradj, Maria Snyder, Kenneth Jay Lane, Simon Tu, Jay Strongwater, Butler & Wilson, and Isabel Canovas (who went out of business in 1992).

Carolee

See the chapter called Designers and Manufacturers We Know and Love.

Iradj Moini

See the chapter called Designers and Manufacturers We Know and Love.

Jay Strongwater

Jay Strongwater, formerly Jay Feinberg Limited, is a successful family-run company whose distinctive costume jewelry designs are sold in major department and specialty stores and are often featured in the pages of fashion magazines.

I was studying clothing design at the Rhode Island School of Design. The summer between my sophomore and junior years, I started painting beads for my mother to wear. A local store in New Jersey gave me an order for some. I was encouraged by this and took some beads in a little bag to Bergdorf's, where I got an order. Next came Bendel's, Bonwit's, and Saks. When I went back to school I was doing my schoolwork by day and filling orders at night. By October the orders were filled and I figured I was finished. Then the buyers called and wanted to see my spring collection! *New York Magazine* had shot a piece for the fashion issue and I decided to leave school and start a business with my parents' blessing. They actually helped me get the business going.

By 1983, we were shipping $80,000 in orders! The buyer from Saks placed an order for fifteen stores. I had to hire students to help me. I was now Jay Feinberg Limited and took a small space in Manhattan, where buyers came to see my collections. Saks put some of my pieces in the windows on Oscar de la Renta's clothing. I kept bothering him to see me and finally his assistant in charge of jewelry, who was Carolyne Roehm, said to come up and asked me to do some runway pieces for the resort collection.

The two things that were really important to me in the business were working with Saks Fifth Avenue and the visibility of doing Oscar's runway jewelry. Now all the magazines had seen my work.

When my parents retired from their business I asked them to work with me full-time. Penny works in the showroom with the buyers and magazines and Marty heads production and the business end. By 1987–1988 it was a two-million-dollar business with over thirty employees. Neiman Marcus, I. Magnin, Bloomingdale's, and great specialty stores across the country sold my jewelry.

In order to take the business to the next level, we got a backer in 1989. That didn't work out well, so we regrouped, but the name went to the backer. We realized the important thing was the jewelry, not the name. We opened again as Jay Strongwater, which is my mother's maiden name. Again, a success!

I make a lot of personal appearances and I get to meet women who are excited by the jewelry. When I design jewelry, I have women like my mother in mind. She has great style and a terrific fashion sense. She has always worn designer clothing. It is for that kind of woman I design, the one who likes something bold and new and different; the one with a particular look—who stands out in a crowd. She's not a shy person; she's gutsy. My designs are somewhat clothes-driven. I am aware of the clothing of the season and I think about accessorizing them.

My ideas come from everywhere. I look at old pieces of jewelry and auction house catalogs and go to flea markets. I was very inspired by the Vienna show at the Modern Museum of Art. I love beads, their different techniques and finishes. I can build an entire collection around one bead.

We have beads designed for us. It's important that my collection be unique. I have resin dyed to my specifications in Germany. All our castings are done from my sketches each season. I work with model-makers to execute them. My line has no bought pieces.

My materials are resin, glass, casted metal, wood—the tortoise is all faux painted wood from the Philippines. I think the trend now is toward the real look, rather than high-fashion—smaller earrings, more intricate details, greater use of enameling, pearl studding, and crystals. We're not producing thousands of these pieces. Each one is handmade right here. We're making limited runs and we can make something special to suit a customer's request.

It's nice having a family company. Many of our employees have been with us for years, since the Jay Feinberg company. We even think of our stores as part of the family.

Gerard Yosca

We spoke to Gerard Yosca, whose pieces are sold in major department stores and appear on the covers of *Vogue* and *Harper's Bazaar*:

I always painted, sculpted, and did arts and crafts—anything with my hands. I love color. I went to Parsons School of Design and majored in advertising because I also love to write. I was in that field for about eight years. I was creative director at Christie's and worked in auction houses, advertising agencies, and taught advertising at Parsons. About ten years ago I decided to go into fashion. It has taken about ten years to figure out what I'm doing. Now I'm more in command of my craft. I do things in very unorthodox ways because there was no one to teach me how to do it properly. I developed my own methods. But now I make things that look uniquely mine, so that's good!

The first five years were really rough. I was making things in sterling and brass, then I made the pieces in white metal. I started playing with stones. I had to find a design vocabulary. When I started I didn't even know where to buy pearls or who could do my plating!

I think accessories are the most important part of the fashion scene. What else can you pull out of your pocketbook that changes the way you look, from sitting in an office all day to going out at night? Accessories are the fastest way to get this season's look.

I am aware of the fashions, but I keep going ahead on my own. My wife, Susan, who runs the business, tells me she can't figure out how I know how to do something that's right for the moment. There is a jet stream with ideas floating around. All of a sudden, blue looks good and it never looked good before. I'll do things in blue and I'll see three other designers doing things in blue at the same time.

My inspiration is really inner. I read and travel and go antiquing all the time. I design for the woman who is European in attitude, who has a lust for life and understands a grand gesture. I design for the woman who is confident in showing who she is, who wears hats and shawls but also ties a scarf around her waist and goes to the beach.

What makes a piece of mine collectible is when it just all comes together—the inspiration, the timing, the color. I love the bumblebee earring, for example. I don't revive pieces, I'm always doing new pieces. I walk a tightrope with the more forward pieces—we're always really ahead. I see things going in a more casual direction—jewelry to accessorize weekend wear. If a person can afford to relax in the Nineties, he or she should do it well.

Butler & Wilson pin, necklace, bracelet, and earrings set.
Courtesy of Fragments. Photograph by Kenneth Chen.

(top to bottom)

Butler & Wilson Pin. Blackamoor; black enameled face; faux rubies, sapphires, and emeralds; clear round rhinestones; gold plated; early 1990s. *Courtesy of Fragments.* $220

Butler & Wilson Necklace. Pendant medallion, faux rubies, black-and-red enameled accents, black grosgrain ribbon, gold plated, early 1990s. *Courtesy of Fragments.* $185

Butler & Wilson Pins. Segmented lizard, jet eyes, clear round rhine-stones, silver plated, 7½ inches long; dragonfly, pavé rhinestones, gold plated; both early 1990s. *Courtesy of Fragments.*

Lizard $385; dragonfly $325

Butler & Wilson Bracelet and Earrings Set. Planets and stars, iridescent red enameled links, pavé rhinestones, gold plated, early 1990s. *Courtesy of Fragments.*   Bracelet $250; earrings $170

Chanel "poured glass" leaf necklace. *Courtesy of Joan Paley, Chicago, IL. Photograph by Kenneth Chen.*

Chanel Necklace. "Green poured glass" leaves, simulated pearls, gold plated, 1992. *Courtesy of Joan Paley.* $2,200–$2,500

Christian Dior Boutique Collection bee necklace, earrings, and pins; crown/heart pin; and Dior letter pins. *Photograph courtesy of Grosse Jewels, New York.*

(top to bottom)

Christian Dior Boutique Collection Necklace, Earrings, and Pins. Bee motif, pear-shaped hand-set European crystals, clear round crystals, 18K gold electroplated, 1992. *Courtesy of Grosse Jewels.*

Necklace $1,665;
earrings $170;
pins $95/each

Christian Dior Boutique Collection Pin. Crown/heart with "Dior" worked into the design, hand-set pavé European crystals, pear-shaped and round crystals in the crown, 18K gold or rhodium electroplated, 1992. *Courtesy of Grosse Jewels.* $945

Christian Dior Boutique Collection Pins. "D," "I," "O," "R"; hand-set European pavé crystals on the "D" and "R"; large round crystal dotting the columnar "I"; 18K rhodium electroplated, 1992. *Courtesy of Grosse Jewels.* "D" $210; "I" $125; "O" $60; "R" $125

Ciner figural pins. *Photograph courtesy of Ciner.*

Ciner Pins. Seashell, roses, dragonfly; pavé rhinestones; gold plated; early 1990s. *Photograph courtesy of Ciner.* $200–$335

Ciner geometric necklace, bracelet, and earrings set. *Photograph courtesy of Ciner.*

Ciner Necklace, Bracelet, and Earrings. Geometric pattern, simulated pearls, pavé rhinestones, black enamel, 18K gold plated, early 1990s. *Photograph courtesy of Ciner.*

Necklace $775; bracelet $375; earrings $200

Donna Karan necklace, bracelet, and ring set. *Courtesy of Donna Karan, New York, NY. Photograph by Pierre Schreman.*

Donna Karan Necklace, Bracelet, and Ring. Scripture tube choker with medallion, 24K gold plated and leather; matching cuff and ring, 24K gold plated; all 1993. *Photograph courtesy of Donna Karan.*

Choker $135; cuff $395; ring $80

Gerard Yosca cross and zebra pin and earrings set. *Courtesy of Gerard Yosca. Photograph by Kenneth Chen.*

(top to bottom)

Gerard Yosca Necklace. Cross pendant, brown wooden link chain, green enameled cross, faux turquoise beads, orange crystals, brown enameled center, dark green enameled star, gold plated, 1990s. *Courtesy of Gerard Yosca.* $200

Gerard Yosca Pin and Earrings Set. Zebra, brown-and-white enameled stripes, clear green enameled plume, green crystal eye, faux turquoise beads, matching door knocker earrings, green glass tops, small orange crystals, gold plated, part of Circus Collection, early 1990s. *Courtesy of Gerard Yosca.* Pin $125; earrings $150

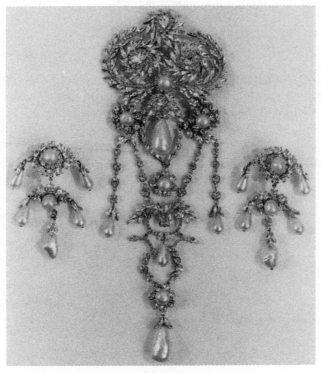

Iradj Moini Empress Eugenie pin and earrings set. *Courtesy of Charles France, Divine Idea, New York, NY. Photograph by Kenneth Chen.*

Iradj Moini Pin and Earrings Set (unsigned). Ornate design of marquise, pear-shaped, round, and square-cut clear crystals; teardrop-shaped smooth and baroque simulated pearls; silver plated, 1992. Fashioned after Empress Eugenie's jewelry. *Courtesy of Charles France, Divine Idea.* $800–$850/set

Iradj Moini fruit pins. *Courtesy of Iradj Moini.*
Photograph by Kenneth Chen.

Iradj Moini Pins (unsigned). Group of fruits: bananas, orange, lemon, and lime with appropriate colors of round and marquise opaque glass cabochons; the lemon, lime, and orange have octagon and pear-shaped faux emeralds; the bananas have large, clear round rhinestones; gold plated; the lime is 3¾ inches high, the orange is 5 inches high; 1991. *Courtesy of Iradj Moini.*

Two-bananas pin $600 (also available as a
three-bananas pendant, $750);
orange and lemon $350/each; lime $250

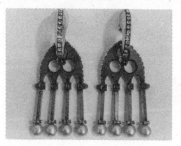

Iradj Moini mosque-shaped earrings.
Courtesy of Iradj Moini. Photograph by
Kenneth Chen.

Iradj Moini Earrings (unsigned). Mosque-shaped design with faux ruby and emerald cabochons, clear round rhinestones on the edges of the earring top and clear crystal rondelles above the simulated pearl drops, gold plated, 1992. *Courtesy of Iradj Moini.* $450

Iradj Moini bow pin. *Courtesy of Iradj Moini. Photograph by Kenneth Chen.*

Iradj Moini Pin (unsigned). Large bow; designed to be worn at the hip; with square-cut, round, and pear-shaped clear crystals; gold plated; 12½ inches high, 6¾ inches wide; 1992. *Courtesy of Iradj Moini.*

$2,500

Kenneth Jay Lane earrings, pins, and bracelets. *Courtesy of Kenneth Jay Lane. Photograph by Kenneth Chen.*

(top to bottom)

Kenneth Jay Lane Earrings. Large drops, large oval crystal in the center surrounded by clear round rhinestones and marquise jet stones; top is a round jet stone ringed by clear round rhinestones; silver plated; early 1990s. *Courtesy of Kenneth Jay Lane.* $140

Kenneth Jay Lane Pin. "Tiffany" bow, pavé crystal and black enameled edges, gold plated, early 1990s. *Courtesy of Kenneth Jay Lane.* $220

Kenneth Jay Lane Bracelet. Hinged bangle, channel-set clear crystals, alternating stripes of black enamel, gold plated, early 1990s. *Courtesy of Kenneth Jay Lane.* $395

Kenneth Jay Lane Bracelets. Hinged bangle, alternating enameled diagonal stripes, faux coral and turquoise concentric circles, gold plated, early 1990s. *Courtesy of Kenneth Jay Lane.* $150

Kenneth Jay Lane Earrings. Part of the Let Them Eat Cake Collection, ornate bow design, teardrop dangles, clear round and pavé crystals, silver plated, 4 inches high. *Courtesy of Kenneth Jay Lane.* $265

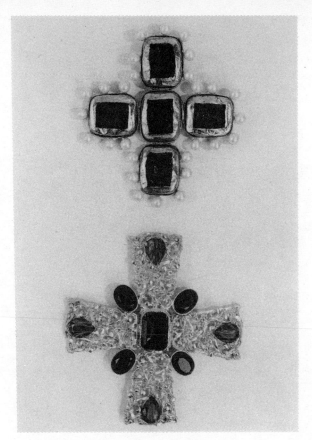

Kenneth Jay Lane crosses. *Courtesy of Kenneth Jay Lane.*
Photograph by Kenneth Chen.

(top to bottom)

Kenneth Jay Lane Pin. Maltese cross; irregular square faux rubies, emeralds, and a central faux sapphire; overgilded; surrounded by simulated pearls; gold plated; 4¾ inches high. *Courtesy of Kenneth Jay Lane.* $140

Kenneth Jay Lane Pin. Maltese cross, filigree design, stretched octagon central faux sapphire, oval faux rubies and pear-shaped faux emeralds, gold plated, 5¼ inches high, early 1990s. *Courtesy of Kenneth Jay Lane.* $150

Kenneth Jay Lane figural pins. *Courtesy of Kenneth Jay Lane. Photograph by Kenneth Chen.*

(clockwise from top)

Kenneth Jay Lane Pin. Frog, black enameled body, gold plated, early 1990s. *Courtesy of Kenneth Jay Lane.* $50

Kenneth Jay Lane Earrings. Frogs, green enameled bodies, pavé crystal legs, gold plated, 1 inch high, early 1990s. *Courtesy of Kenneth Jay Lane.* $100

Kenneth Jay Lane Pin. Sea monster, faux emerald cabochon eye, a simulated pearl in its mouth, pavé crystal fins and body, gold plated, early 1990s. *Courtesy of Kenneth Jay Lane.* $95

Kenneth Jay Lane Pin. Turtle, oval simulated pearl back, round faux emerald eyes, pavé crystal body and neck, gold plated, early 1990s. *Courtesy of Kenneth Jay Lane.* **$100**

Kenneth Jay Lane Pin. Bee; faux sapphire cabochon body; pavé crystal wings, head, and body; silver plated; early 1990s. *Courtesy of Kenneth Jay Lane.* **$90**

Kenneth Jay Lane Pin. Butterfly, large pear-shaped simulated pearl wings, jet cabochon head, gold plated, early 1990s. *Courtesy of Kenneth Jay Lane.* **$75**

Kenneth Jay Lane Pin. Large hinged frog, faux emerald cabochon eyes, gold plated, 6⁷⁄₁₆ inches high, early 1990s. *Courtesy of Kenneth Jay Lane.* **$80**

Alison Mager cherub necklace. *Courtesy of Fragments. Photograph by Kenneth Chen.*

Alison Mager Necklace and Earrings Set. Florentine-inspired cherubim, gold-plated pewter, early 1990s. *Courtesy of Fragments.*

Necklace $180; earrings $60

Christina McCarthy leopard cross; Herve van der Straeten earrings.
Courtesy of Fragments. Photograph by Kenneth Chen.

(top to bottom)

Christina McCarthy Necklace. Lucite leopard-patterned cross, gold-plated brass chain, early 1990s. *Courtesy of Fragments.* $220

Herve van der Straeten Earrings. Hands, simulated pearl drops; large spikey hoops; both gold plated; early 1990s. *Courtesy of Fragments.*

Hand earrings $225; hoops $200

Maria Snyder crosses. *Courtesy of Maria Snyder. Photograph by Kenneth Chen*.

(left to right)

Maria Snyder Necklace. Maltese cross pendant, Maltese cross link chain, silver plated, 1992. *Courtesy of Maria Snyder*. $180

Maria Snyder Necklace. Cross, black casted resin, gold metallic accents and red streaks, glazed epoxy, round faux topazes and faux rubies, braided black soutache necklace, August 1992. *Courtesy of Maria Snyder*. $120

Maria Snyder Necklace. Cross, cut-out link chain, 24K gold plated, 1992. *Courtesy of Maria Snyder*. $180

Maria Snyder floral necklace and earrings set, "The Lovers" pendant. *Courtesy of Maria Snyder. Photograph by Kenneth Chen*.

(top to bottom)

Maria Snyder Necklace and Earrings Set. Flowers, green enameled leaves, pink enameled centers, gold plated, matching drop earrings, January 1992. *Courtesy of Maria Snyder*.   Necklace $210; earrings $105

Maria Snyder Necklace. "The Lovers" pendant, black-and-yellow enameled hair, gold plated, August 1990. *Courtesy of Maria Snyder.* $250

Napier "X" necklace, bracelets, and earrings. *Courtesy of The Napier Co. Photograph by Jim Brill.*

Napier Necklace, Bracelets, and Earrings. "Monte Carlo" choker, simulated pearls, "X" design; matching bracelet; narrow bracelet and button earrings; gold plated; 1992. *Courtesy of The Napier Co.*

Necklace $75;
wide bracelet $35;
narrow bracelet $18;
earrings $22.50

Napier necklace and earrings. *Courtesy of The Napier Co. Photograph by Scott Osman.*

Napier Necklace and Earrings Set. "Starlight" adjustable necklace, clear marquise crystals, matching drop earrings, 1992. *Courtesy of The Napier Co.*   Necklace $200; earrings $40

Yves Saint Laurent "Sevilla" necklace and earrings. *Courtesy of Yves Saint Laurent*.

Yves Saint Laurent Necklace and Earrings (two styles). "Sevilla" engraved golden hearts necklace and earrings with chain tassels, the necklace with a simulated pearl, matching loop earrings, gold plated, fall/winter 1992. *Courtesy of Yves Saint Laurent*.   Necklace $470;
heart earrings $150;
hoop earrings $110

. . . More Nineties

Carolee Pin. Panther, faux jet spots, pavé crystals, gold plated, limited edition of 1,500, 1992. *Courtesy of Carolee.*

Ciner Necklace. Collar, two cougar heads in the front, enameled black-and-white stripes, pavé rhinestones, 18K gold plated, early 1990s. *Courtesy of Ciner.* $450

Ciner Bracelets. Cuffs; ivory and tortoise enameled zebra; giraffe in either enameled ivory and tortoise or black and tortoise; pavé rhinestones; 18K gold plated; early 1990s. *Courtesy of Ciner.* $250

Gerard Yosca Pin and Earrings Set. Elephant head, matching button earrings, gold plated, part of the Circus Collection, 1990s. *Courtesy of Gerard Yosca.* Pin $125; earrings $150

Iradj Moini Earrings/pin (unsigned). Parrot head; pale green opaque glass cabochons; large oval faux turquoise cheek; round faux amethyst cabochon eye; clear round crystals on the beak, mouth, and neck; faux carnelian dangles; gold plated; 1992. *Courtesy of Iradj Moini.* $650

Isabel Canovas Earrings. Elephant hanging from an African mask, gold plated, 1990. *Courtesy of the author.* $225–$400

Isabel Canovas Necklace and Earrings. Deck of cards motif, engraved red-and-black enameled assorted card designs, single card for each earring, gold plated, 1991. *Courtesy of the author.* $600–$800

Swarovski Pins. Whale, large oval blue crystal in the head, two small marquise blue crystals in the tail, silver plated; angelfish, blue-and-green enameled, pavé crystals, silver plated; goldfish, orange enameled red crystal eye, silver plated; fish, emerald-and-blue enameled, blue crystal eyes, gold plated; fish, large oval crystal body, blue crystal eye, pavé rhinestone trim on the fins; 1992. *Courtesy of Swarovski.*

Whale $37.50; angelfish $42;
goldfish $15;
emerald/blue fish $15;
blue crystal fish $40

Swarovski Pins. Violin and harp, simulated pearls, pavé crystals, gold plated, Swarovski's Jeweler's Collection, 1992. *Courtesy of Swarovski.*

Violin $175;
harp $120

Swarovski Pins and Bracelet. Clowns on one leg and standing on hands, red-and-blue enameled, multicolored crystals, matching bracelet, blue-and-green crystal bead, Savvy Collection, 1992. *Courtesy of Swarovski.*

Pins $30–$32;
bracelet $70

Swarovski Pin and Bracelet. Teapots, cups, and saucers; blue-and-green enameled; gold plated; Savvy Collection; 1992. *Courtesy of Swarovski.*

Pin $22;
bracelet $70

REFERENCES

Dealers' Directory

For this edition, we sent out questionnaires to many hundreds of vintage costume jewelry dealers we've met, heard from, and heard about. In the questionnaire, we attempted to ascertain the quantity and quality of the jewelry they sell.

The dealers are listed by state and country. Shops are listed with full addresses and phone numbers; call for business hours. Dealers who don't have shops are listed "by appointment only." Because of busy show schedules and buying trips, write or call these dealers in advance, when possible. If there are dealers out there who would like to be included in the next edition, please write to the author in care of the publisher.

The United States

ARIZONA

Sandi Fuller
PZAZ
2528 E. Camelback Road
Phoenix, AZ 85016
(602) 956-4402
FAX: (602) 956-3297

CALIFORNIA

Acanthus—Nothing Ordinary
20470 Broadway
Sonoma, CA 95476
(707) 935-7950

Patsy Comer's Antiques & Jewelry
7445 Reseda Boulevard
Reseda, CA 91335
(818) 345-1631

Domont
8661 Sunset Boulevard
West Hollywood, CA 90069
(310) 289-9500
fax (310) 276-3952

Rissie & Sid Fischer
San Mateo, CA
(415) 347-3577
(by appointment only)

Gail Freeman
Antiquarius Center
8840 Beverly Boulevard
West Hollywood, CA 90048
(818) 340-0655
(310) 273-5199
(by appointment only)

Diane Keith
P.O. Box 1814
Beverly Hills, CA 90213
(310) 273-2020
(by appointment only)

Madame Butterfly
5474 College Avenue
Oakland, CA 94618
(510) 653-1525

Ginger Moro
Showcase Antiques #417
13603 Ventura Boulevard
Sherman Oaks, CA 91423
(818) 905-5007
(310) 475-2802
(by appointment only)

Connie Parente's Accessories
Los Angeles, CA
(213) 650-6882
(by appointment only)

Pure Gold
625 State Street
Santa Barbara, CA 93101
(805) 962-4613

Reincarnation
214 Seventeenth Street
Pacific Grove, CA 93950
(408) 649-0689

Vintage Silhouettes
1420 Pomona Street
Crockett, CA 94525
(510) 787-7274

Yesterday's Memories
Old Towne Pomona Antique Mall
260 Pomona Mall East, space #9
Pomona, CA 91766
(714) 622-1011

CONNECTICUT

Belles Choses
The Ridgefield Antique Center
109 Danbury Road
Ridgefield, CT 06877
(203) 438-2777

Chelsea Antiques
293 Pequot Avenue
Southport, CT 06490
(203) 255-8935

Dud's Vintage Clothing & Jewelry
Loft
10 Marietta Street
Hamden, CT 06514
(203) 248-8675

Joann Narkis
Vintage Associates—Jewelry with
Past
Charcoal Woods
(P.O. Box 385)
Middlebury, CT 06762
(203) 758-1363
(by appointment only)

One of a Kind, Inc.
21 Main Street
(Rte. 9, exit 6)
Historic Chester, CT 06410
(203) 526-9736

Remember When
66 Main Street
Torrington, CT 06790
(203) 489-1566

DELAWARE

Merrill's Antiques & Jewelry
100 Northern Avenue
Wilmington, DE 19805
(302) 994-1765
(by appointment only)

FLORIDA

A Consignment Gallery
251 North Federal Highway
Boca Raton, FL 33432
(407) 338-4706

Deane Granoff
P.O. Box 403201
Miami Beach, FL 33140
(305) 673-5515
(by appointment only)

Sticks 'N Stones
180 South Federal Highway
Boca Raton, FL 33432
(407) 394-8761

Tania Santé's Classic Collectables
6556 Bird Road
Miami, FL 33155
(305) 662-4975

Terri's Treasures
743 Lincoln Road
Miami Beach, FL 33139
(305) 534-3322

Winkie Arflin
290 Park Avenue
Satellite Beach, FL 32937
(407) 777-3058
(also does rhinestone replacement and
minor repairs)

GEORGIA

Celie's Pretty Things
2942 Lynda Lane
Columbus, GA 31906
(706) 561-3953

ILLINOIS

Flashy Trash
3524 North Halsted
Chicago, IL 60657
(312) 327-6900

Kelly's Vintage Fashions
5152 Harlem Road
Loves Park, IL 61125
(815) 654-1610

Oswego Antique Markets
Route 34 & Main Street
Oswego, IL 60543
(708) 554-3131/3788/9779

Joan Paley
Chicago, IL
(312) 327-8147
(by appointment only)

Riverfront Antique Mart
2929 North Western Avenue
Chicago, IL 60618
(312) 252-2500

Studio V
672 North Dearborn
Chicago, IL 60610
(312) 440-1937

Zig Zag
3419 North Lincoln Avenue
Chicago, IL 60657
(312) 525-1060
(specializing in Bakelite jewelry)

LOUISIANA

Blackamoor
324 Chartres
New Orleans, LA 70130
(504) 523-7786

MAINE

Orphan Annie's
96 Court Street
Auburn, ME 04210
(207) 782-0638

MARYLAND

Angels in the Attic, Ltd.
P.O. Box 70
4105 Seventh Street
North Beach, MD 20714
(410) 257-1069

Liz Vilas Antiques
Olney Antique Village
16650 Georgia Avenue
Olney, MD 20832
(301) 924-0354

MASSACHUSETTS

Andrea Stuart Industries
P.O. Box 67194
Chestnut Hill, MA 02167-9998
(617) 469-0697
(by appointment only)

Berkshire Hills Coins and Antiques, Inc.
111 South Street (Rte. 7)
Pittsfield, MA 01201
(413) 499-1400

Bird Cage Antiques
Rte. 23 (next to the Post Office)
South Egremont, MA 01258
(413) 528-3556

Blackbird Antiques and Collectibles
152 North Main Street (Rte. 7)
Great Barrington, MA 01230
(413) 528-8278

Cambridge Antique Market
201 Monsignor O'Brien Highway
East Cambridge, MA 02139
(617) 868-9655

Carriage Trade Antiques
159 South Undermountain Road
(Rte. 41)
Sheffield, MA 01257
(413) 229-2870

Elizabeth's 20th Century
41 State Street
Newburyport, MA 01950
(508) 465-2983

Geffner/Schatzky Antiques and
Varieties
Rte. 23 (at the sign of the Juggler)
South Egremont, MA 01258
(413) 528-0057

Frederick A. Hatfield Antiques
South Main Street (Rte. 7)
Sheffield, MA 01257
(413) 229-7986

Olde Antiques Market
Jennifer House Commons
Rte. 7 (Stockbridge Road)
Great Barrington, MA 01230
(413) 528-1840

Remembrances of Things Past
376 Commercial Street
Provincetown, MA 02657
(508) 487-9443

Saturday Sweets
507 South Main Street (Rte. 7)
Great Barrington, MA 01230
(413) 528-6661

Snyder's Store
945 South Main Street (Rte. 7)
Great Barrington, MA 01230
(413) 528-1441

The Kahn's Antique and Estate
Jewelry
38 Railroad Street
Great Barrington, MA 01230
(413) 528-9550

MICHIGAN

Herman D. Lawson
2528 Lake Shore Drive
Niles, MI 49120
(616) 684-5402
(by appointment only)

Plaza Antique Mall
1410 28th Street SE
Grand Rapids, MI 49508
(616) 243-2465

NEW JERSEY

A.N.D. Antiques
Leonia, NJ 07605
(201) 592-6251
(by appointment only)

Another Fine Mess
62 Overlook Avenue
Dover, NJ 07801-4832
(201) 366-5733
(by appointment only)

Karwen's Jewelry & Antiques
68 Raritan Avenue
Highland Park, NJ 08904
(908) 828-5575

Rob-lynn
P.O. Box 232
Livingston, NJ 07039
(201) 992-8952

Pamela D. Smith
Ridgewood, NJ
(201) 445-1174
(by appointment only)

The Collector
85 Passaic Street
Garfield, NJ 07026
(201) 473-1377

The Jewel Table
877 Prospect Street
Glen Rock, NJ 07452
(201) 612-9027

Marene Weinraub
Teaneck, NJ
(201) 692-9515
(by appointment only)

NEW HAMPSHIRE

Knotty Pine Antique Market
Rte. 10
West Swanzey, NH 03469
(603) 352-5252

NEW YORK

New York City:

Frances Cavaricci
New York, NY
(212) 758-9400 (daytime)
(212) 517-0098 (evening)
(by appointment only)

Ilene Chazanof
Decorative Arts
7 East 20th Street
New York, NY 10003
(212) 254-5564
(by appointment only; Saturdays no
appointment necessary)

Ann M. Cohen
New York, NY
(212) 838-2114
(by appointment only)

Norman Crider Antiques
Trump Tower
725 Fifth Avenue
New York, NY 10022
(212) 832-6958

Dullsville
143 East 13th Street
New York, NY 10003
(212) 505-2505

Robin Feldman Collectibles
New York, NY
(212) 717-1667
(by appointment only)

Barbara Flood
New York, NY
(212) 348-6233
(by appointment only)

Charles France
Divine Idea
New York, NY
(212) 362-9243
(by appointment only)

Susan Kelner Freeman
New York, NY
(212) 473-0294
(by appointment only)

Virginia M. Fuentes
New York, NY
(212) 362-2199
(by appointment only)

Jane L. Gardner
Somewhere in Time
New York, NY
(212) 982-1668
(by appointment only)

Pauline Ginnane-Gasbarro
New York, NY
(212) 598-9136, fax (212) 598-9136
(by appointment only)

Elayne Glotzer
Chelsea Antiques Building
3rd Floor
110 West 25th Street
New York, NY 10001
(212) 348-5221
(212) 647-9284

Prudence Huang
New York, NY
(212) 559-6096
(by appointment only)

Shirley Jaros
New York, NY
(212) 866-3763
(by appointment only)

Joia
1151 Second Avenue
New York, NY 10021
(212) 754-9017

Kenneth J. Lane Vintage Collection
677 Fifth Avenue
New York, NY 10019
(212) 750-2858

Harriet Love
126 Prince Street
New York, NY 10012
(212) 966-2280

Harrice Miller Collection
300 East 33rd Street #11J
New York, NY 10016
(212) 532-1394
(by appointment only)

Linda Morgan Antiques
152 East 70th Street
New York, NY 10021
(212) 628-4330

Carole Moskowitz
Chelsea Antiques Building
3rd Floor
110 West 25th Street
New York, NY 10001
(212) 647-9284

Mullen & Stacy
375 West Broadway
New York, NY 10012
(212) 226-4240

Panache
525 Hudson Street
New York, NY 10014
(212) 243-5009

Roslyn Raphan
New York, NY
(212) 362-5631
(by appointment only)

Terry Rodgers
Manhattan Art and Antiques Center
Gallery #30
1050 Second Avenue
New York, NY 10022
(212) 758-3164

Rover & Lorber NYC
Gallery #45
Manhattan Art and Antiques Center
1050 Second Avenue
New York, NY 10022
(212) 838-1302

Rita Sacks
Limited Additions (Gallery #66)
Manhattan Art and Antiques Center
1050 Second Avenue
New York, NY 10022
(212) 421-8132

Ira Scheck
Chelsea Antiques Building
110 West 25th Street
2nd Floor
New York, NY 10001
(212) 647-0044

Lorraine Wohl Collection
150 East 70th Street
New York, NY 10021
(212) 472-0191

New York State:

Ambience Antiques
145 Montauk Highway
Westhampton, NY 11977
(516) 288-6930

Another Time Antiques
P.O. Box 1414
765 Hill Street
Southampton, NY 11969-1414
(516) 283-6542
(closed during winter)

Another Time
P.O. Box 135
Clarendon, NY 14429
(716) 638-8496
(mail-order and by appointment)

Beverly Austrian
Tarrytown Antique Center
25 Main Street
Tarrytown, NY 10591
(914) 631-9710

Matthew Burkholz
Route 66 Antiques
P.O. Box 198
Chatham Center, NY 12184
(518) 392-9177
(by appointment only)

Edinburgh Enterprises
97 Edinburgh Street
Rochester, NY 14608
(716) 546-6383

Libby Goldschmidt
Binghamton, NY
(607) 722-6577
(by appointment only)

Irene Grundman
287 Chestnut Ridge Road
Rochester, NY 14624
(716) 889-4329
(by appointment only)

Joan's Jewelry
P.O. Box 616
Lynbrook, NY 11563
(516) 887-1765
(by appointment only)

Jessica Lex
The Gilded Lily
Huntington, NY
(516) 421-3685, (717) 635-5885 (summer)

Metropolis
44 Central Avenue
Albany, NY 12206
(518) 427-2971

Muriel Karasik Gallery
2 Jobs Lane
Southampton, NY 11968
(516) 287-4780
(closed during winter)
92 Main Street
Westhampton Beach, NY 11968
(516) 288-1372
(closed during winter)

Rennie Myers
Rennie's Jewels & Treasures
Rochester, NY 14616
(716) 663-7186
(by appointment only)

Maria Nanni
636 North Terrace Avenue 2E
Mount Vernon, NY 10552
(914) 668-6134
(will do mail-order approvals)

Elizabeth Nyland
The Irish Princess
537 Warren Street
Hudson, NY 12534
(518) 828-2800, (518) 851-7865
(by appointment only)

Partners in Time
66 Jobs Lane
Southampton, NY 11968
(516) 287-1143
(closed during winter)

Port Chester Antiques Mall
27 South Main Street
Port Chester, NY 10573
(914) 937-4800

Rhinebeck Antique Center
7 West Market Street and Rte. 9
Rhinebeck, NY 12572
(914) 876-8186

Something Grand Antiques
155 Main Street
Northport, NY 11768
(516) 754-6016

NORTH CAROLINA

Designs on You
16 South Front Street
Wilmington, NC 28401
1-800-704-1133
(901) 251-1133

Wilson Antique Mall
Highway 301 South
Wilson, NC 27893
(919) 291-6020

OHIO

Steeplechase Antiques Mall
111 Main Street
Chardon, OH 44024
(216) 729-2790

OREGON

Mary Alice Chessman
Avalon
318 S.W. 9th
Portland, OR 97205
(503) 224-7165

PENNSYLVANIA

Antique Treasures
West Main Street
Shartleville, PA 19554
(215) 488-1545

Bosha
(215) 579-1113
(by appointment only)

Elizabeth Hine
Lancaster, PA
(717) 396-9527
(by appointment only)

M. Klein
P.O. Box 473
Wynnewood, PA 19096
(215) 896-8664
(by appointment only)

Mod-Girl
615 South Sixth Street
Philadelphia, PA 19147
(215) 592-0256

E & J Rothstein Antiques
611 North High Street
West Chester, PA 19380
(610) 696-1500
(by appointment only)

Esther Schwartz
Den of Antiquity
Scranton, PA 18510
(717) 347-8026

Something Special
North Hills Antique Gallery
251 Church Road
Wexford, PA 15090
(412) 935-9804

TENNESSEE

Geraldine's Antiques
150 Public Square
Lebanon, TN 37087
(615) 449-8113

Peggy's Pretties in the Pink
1712 South Mount Juliet Road
Mount Juliet, TN 37122
(615) 758-8255

VIRGINIA

WASHINGTON

Marigold Fine Arts
P.O. Box 19234
Alexandria, VA 22320-0234
(703) 548-8096
(by appointment only)

Michael Wm. Farrell Jeweler
5420 Sand Point Way NE
Seattle, WA 98105
(206) 524-8848
324 15th Avenue E
Seattle, WA 98112
(206) 324-1582

Shirley Shier
The Jewellery Lady
Antique Center II
Leesburg, VA 22075
(703) 338-4956

Victoria Village
1108 First Street
Snohomish, WA 98290
(206) 568-4913

VERMONT

WEST VIRGINIA

Frederique Edelman
Antique Group Shop
Rte. 7, Tennebrook Square
Shelburne, VT 05482
(802) 985-2903

Watzman's Old Place
709 Charles Street
Wellsburg, WV 26070
(304) 737-0711

Canada

Carole Tanenbaum
The Incurable Collector
15 Forest Wood
Toronto, Ontario
Canada M5N 2VS
(416) 782-1555

England

LONDON

Beauty & The Beasts
Stand Q9-10
Antiquarius Antiques Centre
131-141 Kings Road
London SW3
UK
(071) 351-5149

Cobra & Bellamy
149 Sloane Street
London SW1
UK
(071) 730-2823

Hilary Conquy
Antiquarius Antiques Center
131-141 Kings Road
London
UK
(071) 352-2366

Cristobal
Unit G 133-134
Alfies Antique Market
13–25 Church Street
London NW8 8DT
UK
(071) 724-7789, fax (071) 724-7789
(071) 625-5314

Lynette Gray
No. 1 Georgian Village
Camden Passage, Islington
London N1
UK
(071) 226-7835

Gillian A. Horsup
York Arcade
Camden Passage
80 Islington High Street
London N1 8EQ
UK
(071) 833-2640

Marianne Landau
York Arcade
Camden Passage
80 Islington High Street
London N1 8EQ
UK
(071) 833-2640

Le Paul Bert
198 Westbourne Grove
London W11
UK
(071) 727-8708

Ian Lieber
29 Craven Terrace
Lancaster Gate
London W2 3EL
UK
(071) 262-5505

Lynn Waller
Spectus Gallery
298 Westbourne Grove
Portobello
Saturday only
(0932) 220-593

Monika
16 The Mall
Camden Passage
London N1
UK
(071) 354-3125/(081) 546-2807

Linda Morgan
26 The Mall
Camden Passage
London N1 OPD
UK
(071) 359-0654

Paladium Jewels
London
UK
(081) 346-4790

Ritzy
7 The Mall
Camden Passage, Islington
London N1
UK
(071) 704-0127

Steinberg & Tolkien
183 Kings Road
Chelsea London SW3 5EB
UK
(071) 376-3660

William Wain
20th Century Costume Jewellery
2 York Arcade
Camden Passage, Islington
London N1
UK
(071) 833-2640

France

PARIS

Olwen Forest
Marché Serpette, Allée 3, Stand 7
110, rue des Rosiers
93400 Saint Ouen, Paris
France
40 11 96 38

L'Heure du Bijou
70, rue Bonaparte
75006 Paris
France
43 54 21 45

Sophie
SR Antiquities
Marché Serpette, Allée 3,
Stand 20
93400 Saint Ouen, Paris
France
40 12 00 75

Carolle Thibaut-Pomerantz
54 Rue de L'Université
75007 Paris
France
42 22 83 41

Italy

MILAN

Demaldé
Piazza del Carmine 1
Milan 20121
Italy
02 86460428

VENICE

Antiquariato SILGAB
Via Fusinato, 20/AB
Mestre (VE)
Italy
(041) 988810

Riflessi
Ramo Fuseri 1801
Venezia
Italy
(041) 5225744

Switzerland

GENEVA

L'Arcade
18, rue de la Corraterie
1204 Genève
Switzerland
(022) 311-1554, fax (022) 311-1554

Germany

WIESBADEN

Wirth Antik
Barenstrasse 2
6200 Wiesbaden
Germany
0 61 21/30 02 86

Show Promoters' Directory

The following list of promoters, arranged alphabetically by the states in which they produce shows, is compiled of those promoters who answered our questionnaire, plus those promoters we know to have a reasonable number of vintage costume jewelry dealers at their shows. We suggest calling or writing to specific promoters for show schedules and to ascertain whether or not they expect to have costume jewelry dealers at any particular show. We welcome additions to our listing for the next edition of the book.

To find promoters in your area who aren't listed in this section, contact the Professional Show Managers Association (PSMA), (203) 243-3977. This association has 150 members who are show managers and associate members who support the antiques business, from both the United States and Canada. They abide by the following Code of Ethics:

- Show managers adhere to high ethical and business standards.
- Exhibitors in PSMA events are required to maintain high ethical standards.
- All merchandise exhibited in PSMA shows must be represented honestly by those offering it for sale.
- Contracts pertaining to the production of antiques shows must be adhered to by PSMA members.
- PSMA members use their activities to promote the business interests of their exhibitors.

- PSMA members are encouraged and expected to show professional respect in the trade.
- PSMA members support their customers' rights.

The PSMA Customers' Bill of Rights states that customers have the right to a written receipt that states the following:

- Condition of the item with special reference to repairs, replacements, repaint, and restoration.
- Approximate age of the item.
- Make of the item, if known.

Customers should be sure the receipt includes the name and address or phone number of the exhibitor.

CALIFORNIA

The Miller Production Group, Inc.
P.O. Box 967
Rancho Santa Fe, CA 92067
(619) 436-3844

*The Prestigious Anaheim Antiques
    Show and Sale*
Anaheim Stadium Exhibition
Center
2000 Gene Autry Way
Anaheim, CA
(February and June shows)

*The Prestigious Ventura Antiques
    Show and Sale*
10 West Harbor Boulevard
(Ag/Commercial Building)
Ventura, CA
(March, June, and November
shows)

*The Prestigious Santa Barbara
    Antiques Show and Sale*
Earl Warren Showgrounds
(#101—Las Positas exit)
Santa Barbara, CA
(February, May, and October shows)

*The Prestigious San Diego
    Antiques Show and Sale*
1895 Camino del Rio South
(Mission Valley)
I-8 at Mission Valley exit
San Diego, CA
(January, April, July, and October
shows)

R. G. Canning Attractions
P.O. Box 400
Maywood, CA 90270
(213) 587-5100

Long Beach Antique Show
Long Beach Arena
Long Beach, CA
(October show)

Vintage Expositions
Box 391
Alamo, CA 94507
(510) 653-1087

Vintage Fashion Expo
Convention Center,
Broadway & 10th
Oakland, CA
(January and September shows)

Vintage Fashion Expo
Civic Auditorium
1855 Main (& Pico)
Santa Monica, CA
(October, December, and
February shows)

Vintage Fashion Expo
The Concourse
8th & Brannan
San Francisco, CA
(March show)

COLORADO

Walt and Nancy Johnson
P.O. Box 692
Des Moines, IA 50303
(515) 262-6714

Collectors' Extravaganza
Currigan Hall—14th & Champa
Denver, CO
(January and June shows)

CONNECTICUT

The Maven Company, Inc. and
The Young Management
Company
P.O. Box 1538
Waterbury, CT 06721
(203) 758-3880

Semiannual Show and Sale of
Vintage Clothing, Jewelry,
and Textiles
National Guard Armory
Armory Road & Route 108
Stratford, CT
(September and March shows)

Wendy Management
Diane and Meg Wendy
5 Harbor Lane
Rye, NY 10580
(914) 698-3442

Greenwich Antiques Show
Convent of the Sacred Heart
School
King Street
Greenwich, CT
(October show)

Stamford Antiques Show
Italian Center
Newfield Avenue
Stamford, CT
(February show)

*Lockwood-Mathews Mansion
    Antiques Show*
Lockwood-Mathews Mansion
Norwalk, CT

Revival Promotions, Inc.
P.O. Box 388
Grafton, MA 01519
(508) 839-9735

Farmington Antiques Weekends
Farmington Polo Grounds
Farmington, CT
(Second Weekend in June and
Labor Day Weekend)

Robert Cottler
46 Kohary Drive
New Haven, CT 06515
(203) 387-7006

*Annual Spring New Haven
    Antiques Show*
New Haven Coliseum
215 South Orange Street
New Haven, CT
(Spring and Fall shows)

Cord Shows, Ltd.
23-D Whippowill Road
Armonk, NY 10504
(914) 273-4667

Holiday Stocking Stuffer Sale
Civic Center
I-95, exit 5
Old Greenwich, CT
(December show)

Jacqueline Sideli Antiques Show
P.O. Box 67
Malden Bridge, NY 12115
(518) 766-4968

Greenwich Antiques Market
Hyatt Regency
Old Greenwich, CT
(October, November, December,
January, and February shows)

Barrows Show Promotional, Ltd.
Box 141
Portland, CT 06480
(203) 342-2540

*Greater Hartford Vintage Clothing
    and Jewelry Show and Sale*
West Hartford, CT
(November, January, and June
shows)

DISTRICT OF COLUMBIA

Wendy Management
Diane and Meg Wendy
5 Harbor Lane
Rye, NY 10580
(914) 698-3442

*District of Columbia Antiques
    Show*
Omni Shoreham Hotel
2500 Calvert Street, NW
Washington, DC
(November show)

McHugh Presentations, Inc.
1500 Providence Highway
Norwood, MA 02062
(617) 255-9120

> *Antiques on the Potomac*
> St. Albans School
> Washington, DC
> (May show)

FLORIDA

Colonel Larry Stowell
P.O. Box 175
Mendon, NY 14506
(716) 924-4530

> *Fort Myers Spring Antique and
>   Collectible Show*
> 2254 Edwards Drive
> Fort Myers, FL
> (March show)

> *Sanibel Island Antique and
>   Collectible Show*
> 2173 Periwinkle Way
> Sanibel, FL
> (April and December shows)

> *Tampa Fall, Winter, Spring
>   Convention Center Show*
> 333 South Franklin Street
> Tampa, FL
> (November, December, and
> January shows)

> *Venice Antique and Collectible Show*
> 326 Nokomis Avenue, South
> Venice, FL
> (January and February shows)

Beverly A. August
August Antiques
5333 North Tamiami Trail
Sarasota, FL 34234
(813) 351-6666

> *Sarasota Antique Show*
> Sarasota Exhibition Hall
> Sarasota, FL
> (August, September, November,
> January, March, April, and May
> shows)

> *Winter Park Antique Show*
> Winter Park Civic Center
> Winter Park, FL
> (January show)

> *Bradenton Antique Show*
> Bradenton City Auditorium
> Bradenton, FL
> (February show)

> *Tampa Antique Show*
> Tampa Garden Center
> Tampa, FL
> (March show)

Piccadilly Antiques and
Collectibles
P.O. Box 41381
St. Petersburg, FL 33743
(813) 345-4431, fax (813) 343-8977

> *Fall, Winter, Spring, Summer,
>   Holiday Antique Extravaganzas*
> South Florida Fairgrounds
> West Palm Beach, FL
> (October, November, December,
> February, March, July, and August
> shows)

Shador/Dolphin Management
P.O. Box 7326
Fort Lauderdale, FL 33338
(305) 563-6747

Antiques World
Fort Lauderdale Convention
Center
S.E. 17th Street at the Intracoastal
(January show)

*Miami National Antiques Shows
    and Sale*
Miami Radisson Center
(adjacent to Miami International
Airport)
N.W. 72nd Avenue at 836
Expressway
(January show)

Baron Antique Shows
Lou Baron
266 N.E. 70th Street
Miami, FL 33138
(305) 754-1716/4931

*Miami Beach Antique Show and
    Sale*
Miami Beach Convention Center
Miami Beach, FL
(November and March shows)

*The Original Winter Miami Beach
    Antique Show*
Miami Beach Convention Center
Miami Beach, FL
(January and February shows)

Gem Shows
Bud and Muriel Maron
P.O. Box 350185
Fort Lauderdale, FL 33335
(305) 565-3484

Fort Lauderdale Antique Show
Broward County Convention
Center
17th Street Causeway
Fort Lauderdale, FL
(November and February shows)

Fort Myers—Naples Antique Show
Harborside Convention Center
Fort Myers, FL
(January show)

Orlando Antique Show
Tupperware Convention Center
Orlando, FL
(February show)

D. S. Clarke Miami Antique Show
Coconut Grove Convention
Center
Coconut Grove, FL
(February show)

GEORGIA

Gem Shows
Bud and Muriel Maron
P.O. Box 350185
Fort Lauderdale, FL 33335
(305) 565-3484

D. S. Clarke Atlanta Antique Show
Georgia Dome Stadium
Atlanta, GA
(October and January shows)

Savannah Antique Show
Savannah Civic Center
Savannah, GA
(January show)

ILLINOIS

Cat's Pajamas Productions
(708) 428-8323

Vintage Clothing and Jewelry Show
Elgin Holiday Inn Ballroom
I-90 & Rte. 31
Elgin, IL
(January and June shows)

Robert C. Lawler
1510 North Hoyne
Chicago, IL 60622
(312) 227-4464

Sandwich Antiques Market
Fairgrounds, Rte. 34
Sandwich, IL
(May, July, August, September,
and October shows)

Wendy Management
Diane and Meg Wendy
5 Harbor Lane
Rye, NY 10580
(914) 698-3442

*Sacred Heart of Chicago Antiques
  Show*
Convent of the Sacred Heart
School
6250 Sheridan Road
Chicago, IL
(October show)

IOWA

Walt and Nancy Johnson
P.O. Box 692
Des Moines, IA 50303

Collectors' Extravaganza
Vets Auditorium—833 5th
Avenue
Des Moines, IA
(November and April shows)

MARYLAND

Zita Waters Bell, Inc.
Zita Waters Bell
P.O. Box 340103
Boca Raton, FL 33434
(407) 483-4047

Antique and Fine Arts Festival
Baltimore Convention Center
Baltimore, MD
(April show)

MASSACHUSETTS

J&J Promotions
Jill Reid Lukesh and Judith Reid
Mathieu
Rte. 20, P.O. Box 385
Brimfield, MA 01010

> *J&J Promotions Antiques and*
> *Collectibles Shows*
> Rte. 20, Auction Acres
> Brimfield, MA
> (May, July, and September shows)

Bernice P. Bornstein
P.O. Box 421
Marblehead, MA 01945
(508) 744-2731

> *New Years' Day Antique Show*
> *Park Plaza Castle*
> Arlington Street at Columbus
> Avenue
> Boston, MA
> (January show)

> *Berkshire Antiques Show*
> Barrington Fairgrounds
> Great Barrington, MA 01803
> (Last Weekend in July)

Sonia Paine Antiques
Promotions, Inc.
Sonia Paine, Manager
1198 Boylston, State Rte. 9
Chestnut Hill, MA 02167
(617) 566-9669

> *Fall Antique Show and Sale*
> The Northeast Trade Center
> Exit 35 off Rte. 128
> Woburn, MA
> (October show)

> *Presidents' Birthday Antique Show*
> *and Sale*
> The Northeast Trade Center
> Exit 35 off Rte. 128
> Woburn, MA
> (February show)

> *Sonia Paine Antique Show and Sale*
> *at Copley Plaza*
> Boston, MA
> (January show)

> *Sonia Paine Antique Show and Sale*
> *at Buckingham Browne &*
> *Nichols School*
> Cambridge, MA
> (March show)

> *The Brimmer May School Annual*
> *Antique Show and Sale*
> Chestnut Hill, MA
> (March show)

The Textile Show Associates
Linda Zukas
384 Union Street
Portsmouth, NH 03801
(603) 430-8588

> *Sturbridge Textile Shows*
> Host Hotel, Rte. 20
> Sturbridge, MA
> (May, July, September, and
> December shows)

McHugh Presentations
1500 Providence Highway
Norwood, MA 02062
(617) 255-9120

> *The Vineyard Antique Show*
> Martha's Vineyard Regional High
> School
> Oak Bluff, MA
> (July show)

MICHIGAN

Robert C. Lawler
1510 North Hoyne
Chicago, IL 60622
(312) 227-4464

> *Caravan Antiques Market*
> Fairgrounds, Rte. 86
> Centreville, MI
> (Sundays in May, June, July,
> August, and October)

MISSISSIPPI

Connie Miller
P.O. Box 821
Crystal Springs, MS 39059
(601) 892-5487

> *Christmas Faire*
> Mississippi Street Trademart
> Fairgrounds
> Jackson, MS
> (Saturday and Sunday after
> Thanksgiving)

MISSOURI

Walt and Nancy Johnson
P.O. Box 692
Des Moines, IA 50303
(515) 262-6714

> *Collectors' Extravaganza*
> Kansas City Market Center
> Exhibit Hall (I-435 at front)
> Kansas City, MO
> (November show)

NEW JERSEY

Brimfield Associates
P.O. Box 1800
Ocean City, NJ 08226
(609) 926-1800

> *Atlantique City Show*
> Atlantic City Convention Hall
> Florida Avenue & Boardwalk
> Atlantic City, NJ
> (Semiannually—Third Weekends
> in March and October)

JD Promotions
105 39th Street
Avalon, NJ 08202
(609) 967-7737

> *Atlantic City Race Course Winter*
>   *Antique Extravaganza*
> Atlantic City Race Course
> Rte. 322 (Black Horse Pike)
> Atlantic City, NJ
> (January show)

Morgenstein Enterprises, Ltd.
P.O. Box 6
New City, NY 10956
(914) 634-9663

Meadowlands Antiques Show
Giant Stadium, Meadowlands
Sports Complex
East Rutherford, NJ
(January show)

Stella Show Management
163 Terrace Street
Haworth, NJ 07641
(201) 384-0010

*Garden State International
Antiques and Jewelry
Show*
Garden State Exhibit Center
Somerset, NJ
(February and August
shows)

Meadowlands Antiques Expo
Meadowlands Convention Center
Secaucus, NJ
(March and November
shows)

Liberty Collectibles Expo
Liberty State Park
Jersey City, NJ
(June show)

Labor Day Street Fair
Park Avenue
Rutherford, NJ
(September show)

Wendy Management
Diane and Meg Wendy
5 Harbor Lane
Rye, NY 10580
(914) 698-3442

Morristown Antiques Show
National Guard Armory
Western Avenue
Morristown, NJ
(January, April, and
October shows)

NEW YORK

Stella Show Management
163 Terrace Street
Haworth, NJ 07641
(201) 384-0010

New York Coliseum Antiques Show
New York Coliseum
Columbus Circle
New York, NY
(January show)

Manhattan Triple Pier Expo
Passenger Ship Terminals 88, 90, &
92
New York, NY
(February and November
shows)

Wendy Management
Diane and Meg Wendy
5 Harbor Lane
Rye, NY 10580
(914) 698-3442

*White Plains Winter Antiques
    Shows*
Westchester County Center
Bronx River Parkway
White Plains, NY
(January, April, and November
shows)

*Convent of the Sacred Heart
    of NYC*
1 East 91st Street
New York, NY
(January show)

*New York Armory Holidays
    Antiques Shows*
7th Regiment Armory
Park Avenue at 67th Street
New York, NY
(December, February,
 March, May, and September
shows)

White Plains Antiques Show
Westchester County Center
Bronx River Parkway
White Plains, NY
(May show)

St. Ignatius Loyola Antiques Show
Park Avenue at 84th Street
New York, NY
(October show)

Morgenstein Enterprises, Ltd.
P.O. Box 6
New City, NY 10956
(914) 634-9663

Collectors' Expo
Rockland Community College
NYS Thruway, exit 14B
Suffern, NY
(April and November shows)

Westchester County Center Show
Bronx River Parkway & Rte. 100
White Plains, NY
(June, July, and August shows)

A Gloria Rothstein Show Inc.
Box J
Highland Mills, NY 10930
(914) 928-9494

*Westchester Jewelry/Gem/Mineral
    Show/Sale*
Westchester County Building
Bronx River Parkway, Central
Avenue
White Plains, NY 10605
(October, April, and December
shows)

Depasquale Enterprises
P.O. Box 278
Selden, NY 11784
(516) 736-0995

Stony Brook Antiques Show
SUNY at Stony Brook
Nichols Road
Stony Brook, NY
(April show)

Westhampton Beach Antique Show
Montauk Highway
Westhampton Beach, NY
(June show)

*Southampton Classic Antique
    Market*
Rte. 27, Southampton Elks Lodge
Southampton, NY
(June, July, and September shows)

McHugh Presentations, Inc.
1500 Providence Highway
Norwood, MA 02062
(617) 255-9120

*The New York Double Pier
    Antique Show*
Piers 90 & 92
12th Avenue & 50–55th Streets
New York, NY
(April show)

The South Shore Antique Show
Southampton Campus, L.I.U.
Southampton, NY
(June show)

The Southampton Antique Show
Southampton Campus, L.I.U.
Southampton, NY
(August show)

The McHugh's Pier Extravaganza
Pier 92
55th Street & 12th Avenue
New York, NY
(September show)

*The January Winter Pier Antique
    Show*
Pier 92
55th Street & 12th Avenue
New York, NY

Antiques on the Hudson
Pier 92
55th Street & 12th Avenue
New York, NY
(January show)

OREGON

Palmer/Wirfs and Associates, Inc.
4001 N.E. Halsey
Portland, OR 97232
(503) 282-0877

Antique and Collectible Sales
Portland Exposition Center
Portland, OR
(March show)

PENNSYLVANIA

Nadia
P.O. Box 156
Flourtown, PA 19031
(215) 643-1396

*Antique Vintage Clothing, Textiles
    and Accessories Show and Sale*
Adams Mark (Grand Ballroom)
City Avenue & Monument Road
Philadelphia, PA
(November and February shows)

Chambers Associates
122 North 5th Street,
P.O. Box 1786
Allentown, PA 18105
(215) 437-5534

*Eastern National Antiques Show
    and Sale*
State Farm Show Complex
Cameron Street (I-81 at exit 23)
Harrisburg, PA
(April and November shows)

Great Eastern U.S. Antique Show
R.D. #2, Box 141
Zionsville, PA 18092
(215) 967-2181

*Jewelry, Vintage Fashions and
    Textile Show and Sale*
Agricultural Hall
Allentown Fairgrounds
17th & Chew Streets
Allentown, PA
(May show)

Renningers Promotions
27 Bensinger Drive
Schuylkill Haven, PA 17972
(717) 385-0104

Renningers Mid-Winter Classic
Valley Forge Convention Center
King of Prussia, PA
(February and March shows)

VIRGINIA

Heritage Promotions
P.O. Box 3504
Lynchburg, VA 24503
(804) 846-7452

Shenandoah Antiques Expo
Expoland (I-64 at exit 91)
Fishersville, VA
(Second Weekend in October
and Third Weekend in May)

Commonwealth Promotions
P.O. Box 7003
Charlottesville, VA 22906
(804) 296-8018

*Norfolk Summer/Winter Show at
    the Scope*
St. Paul's Boulevard
Norfolk, VA
(July and January shows)

*Charlottesville Show
    at Foxfield*
Foxfield Race Course
Charlottesville, VA
(September show)

WASHINGTON

Somewhere in Time Promotions
P.O. Box 88892
Seattle, WA 98138
(206) 848-5420

*Pacific Northwest Vintage Fashion
    Market*
Seattle Center Flag Pavilion
Seattle, WA
(September and March shows)

Glossary of Terms

Art Deco   Refers to the style of design that succeeded Art Nouveau in Europe in the Twenties and Thirties and was exhibited at the Exposition Internationale des Arts Decoratifs et Industriels Modernes in Paris in 1925: geometric, streamlined, rectilinear interpretations of roses, garlands and baskets of flowers, fountains, deer, and nudes; followed by austere, Cubistic, "Machine Age" motifs.

Aurora borealis   Rhinestones that have been treated with various metals to produce iridescent effects; originally used in the 1950s.

Baguette   A narrow, rectangular-cut rhinestone, usually used in conjunction with other rhinestones.

Bakelite   The name for phenolic resin (phenol formaldehyde) coined by Dr. Leo Baekeland in 1908; used in the Thirties for necklaces, bracelets, and pins, with popular motifs of animals, fruits and vegetables, flowers and leaves, Asian subjects, hearts, sporting themes, polka dots, and whimsical designs.

Baroque pearl   An irregularly shaped pearl.

Base metal   Alloy or nonprecious metal; for example, brass.

Batch   A mixture of lead oxide, potash, quartz sand, and soda that is heated to make crystal.

Bezel setting   A setting that circles the entire stone with flanges soldered and folded over, or burnished over the edge.

Bracelet
>   *Bangle*—a rigid, circular bracelet that slips over the hand.
>   *Charm*—a link bracelet with various charms suspended.
>   *Cuff*—an oval or round bracelet with a hinge and clasp.
>   *Flexible*—made of metal or mesh, set with rhinestones or pearls.
>   *Indian or gauntlet*—a rigid oval with an opening at the underside of the wrist.
>   *Spiral*—a long span of rhinestones, metal, beads, or pearls that wraps around the wrist or upper arm.
>   *Tab*—a rigid bracelet with a suspended charm.

Brilliant   Usually refers to a round-shaped rhinestone.

Brooch   An alternate name for a pin; from the French *broche*, meaning a spit or skewer; often used when describing pins made before the Fifties.

Cabochon   A smooth, unfaceted, dome-shaped stone with a flat back.

Cap   A tube- or cone-shaped cup closed at one end; holds a bead or pearl.

Carnelian (cornelian)   A translucent, dull red quartz with a waxy finish; often used in Art Deco jewelry, seals, and intaglios.

Casting   Jewelry formed by the "lost wax" method: pouring a metal into a mold, usually rubber, that makes an impression when it hardens, producing a piece with weight and depth.

Celluloid   A name for the highly flammable composition cellulose nitrate, patented in 1869, called Xylonite in London. An early translucent plastic used for haircombs, bangles, and pins in the Twenties; imitated ivory, bone, tortoiseshell, coral, and pearls.

Champlevé   Enamel fused over a metal base with colors that blend; sections are cut.

Channel setting   Rhinestones are placed in a channel cut into the metal, with the top edge of the channel bent over the stones to retain them.

Charms   Objects worn initially for their protective properties, attracting good luck or averting ill health; now worn to commemorate an event or as a fashion object.

Chatelaine   Formerly used to describe a chain attached to an ornamental brooch or hook worn at the waist, from which was suspended various objects useful to the wearer, such as keys, a watch, a purse, or grooming items; later used to describe pins connected by a chain.

Chaton cut   Round stone with eight facets surrounding the surface table and eight facets on the back, which is pointed.

Choker   A short necklace, usually 15 inches long, worn high on the neck; popular in the Fifties, revived in the Seventies with the addition of ornaments cascading to cover the chest.

Citrine   Yellow quartz that ranges from pale yellow to a reddish hue.

Clip   Ornamental piece that attaches to shoes, a dress, or a fur; held in place by spring pressure; may have teeth or two prongs.

Cloisonné   Enamel divided by sections of metal (*cloisons*) on a metal base.

Deposé   A word often found on the back of jewelry made in France, similar to a copyright or patent stamp.

Die stamping   Dies are created from models made according to designers' drawings, then machines stamp out stampings of brass, sterling silver, or other metals that are then trimmed, soldered, polished, plated, and lacquered.

Dog collar   A broad necklace worn tightly around the neck; popular in the 1960s.

Drop   A small ornament suspended from a chain, earrings, or another piece of jewelry.

Earrings   Buttons, clusters, hoops, drops, pendants, or chandeliers with spring clips, screw-backs, earwires, or posts.

Electroplating   A method of depositing a thin layer of precious metal on base metal using an electronic device. Articles are immersed in a chemical solution and bonded with electric current.

Enamel   Colored glass or glaze fused onto a metal base; the method reached a height of artistry in the Forties and was revived in the Sixties.

Facet   A small, flat surface cut into a stone or glass; refracts the light in order to enhance the brilliance of the stone.

Filigree   Twisted and soldered fine strands of wire in intricate, lacy patterns; often used as backings for earrings and pins.

Findings   Functional parts of jewelry: catches, joints, ear clips, wires, and settings.
Closings—findings used to close parts of a piece of jewelry: catches, clasps, hooks, rings, springs.
Fastenings—findings used to hold jewelry to clothing or the body: clips, clutches, pins.
Joinings—findings that hold parts of jewelry together: bails, bezels, bolts, caps, cords, chains, eyes, head-and-eye pins, loops, jump rings, nuts, rivets, screws, stone settings, swivels, wires.

Foil Reflective metal coating put under a rhinestone to enhance its shine or color.

German silver Term used to describe an alloy of nickel, zinc, and copper with no silver content; also called nickel silver.

Girandole A type of drop earring with three pendants; similar earrings were worn by eighteenth-century Spanish noblewomen.

Gold filled A "sandwich" of two thin slices of gold with another metal in between; jewelry is marked with the fraction of gold content and the initials "g.f." The jewelry standard in the United States is a minimum of 12 karats, as accepted by the Manufacturing Jewelers and Silversmiths Association.

Grisaille Enamel with a monochromatic effect obtained by using dark and light colors of similar hue.

Gutta percha A natural substance obtained from the bark of the Malayan palaquilm tree; used to make jewelry in the 1800s.

Hematite A blue-black stone used for intaglio and beads.

Intaglio An engraving cut into a stone; if the stone is pressed into a softer material, an image is produced in relief.

Japanned The result of a process that blackens metal; originally used for mourning jewelry, later used to blacken a setting for decorative purposes.

Jet Black lignite; used extensively in Victorian jewelry, originally worn to express mourning, now may refer to any black stone used in jewelry.

Karat (K) Standard weight for precious metal.

Lapis lazuli An opaque silicate; dark blue with white dots, often simulated for costume jewelry.

Lariat Necklace with open ends that are looped or knotted instead of clasped; popular in the 1940s and 1950s.

Lavalliere A necklace with a drop of a single stone suspended from a chain, also called a *negligé*; derived its name from Louise de la Valliere, a mistress of Louis XV.

Locket A pendant made in two parts that opens to reveal photographs, a lock of hair, or a charm.

Marcasite White iron pyrite cut to look like diamonds, also available in "gold"; cut steel can be mistaken for marcasites; used extensively in the Twenties and Thirties, usually set in sterling silver in fanciful pins.

Marquise cut Faceted, elongated stone, pointed at both ends. Also known as navette cut.

Matinee Necklace 24 to 26 inches long; in Europe, 30 to 35 inches.

Millefiori Glass rods of various colors fused and then sliced across to form cubes.

Moonstone Bluish translucent stone; used in jewelry in the Thirties and Forties, often simulated.

Niello Alloys of silver, copper, or lead with sulfur, producing a deep black color used to "shadow" a design.

Opera Necklace 28 to 30 inches long; in Europe, 48 to 90 inches, can extend to 120 inches.

Papier-mâché   A process patented in 1772 using layers of paper and glue placed in a mold and allowed to harden or dry in an oven; painted or plated when used in jewelry.

Parkesine   Early celluloid developed by Alexander Parkes in the 1840s; used in jewelry through the Twenties.

Parure   A matching set of jewelry consisting of a necklace, bracelet, pin, and earrings. A partial set—for example, a bracelet and earrings—is a demi-parure.

Pate-de-verre   A paste made with crushed glass that is colored with metal oxides, fused, molded, and then fired; the result is an opaque, dense glass used in jewelrymaking.

Pavé   Small rhinestones set into metal without prongs; "nicked in" to metal beads using a special tool, secured with glue, or a combination of both, producing a "paved" effect; from the French word meaning "paved."

Pear-shaped cut   Stone in the shape of a pear or teardrop; rounded at one end and pointed at the other.

Pendant   A movable ornament suspended from a chain or another part of the same piece of jewelry.

Princess   Necklace 20 to 21 inches long.

Plique-a-jour   Enamel over an open design, allowing the light to strike it from the back.

Prong setting   Prongs made of four to six teeth bent over to hold the jewelry stone in place.

Repoussé   Using a hammer and punches to produce a design in reverse relief in metal.

Rhodium   A hard, white, metallic element derived from platinum; used for electroplating onto casted metal.

Rock crystal   Clear quartz that is harder, colder, and has double the refraction of glass; often used in jewelry as beads or frosted in Art Deco pins.

Rondelles   Small, round jeweled beads; often used as spacers.

Rose monteé   A faceted rhinestone with a flat base; also known as a "flat back."

Sautoir   A long necklace popular in the 1920s; usually made of chains, beads, or pearls and ending in a tassel or fringe.

Scarf pin   A pin, often with tassels, used to secure a scarf.

Scatter pins   Small pins—usually birds, insects, or flowers—worn in groups; popular in the Fifties.

Soldering   Using solder to join metals, pronounced "sodder."

Stamping   Marking a texture on metal with a die or hammer, cutting out a shape; also refers to the cut pieces of metal that become part of a piece of jewelry.

Tassels   A pendant with free-hanging chains, pearls, or other ornaments; common in the Twenties and revived in the Fifties.

Tremblant   When a part of the jewelry is set on a spring, causing it to "nod" or "tremble"; often used in the Forties on pins of flowers, birds, and animals; from the French word for "trembling"; also called "nodders."

Torsade   A combination of several strands of pearls, chain, or beads twisted together into a single necklace.

Wire drawing   A production method in which pencil-size rods of cast metal are pulled through draw plates of various dimensions and styles to meet functional and decorative requirements.

Zircon   A silicate of zirconium; transparent crystals in various colors.

Bibliography

BOOKS

Baker, Lillian. *Fifty Years of Collectible Fashion Jewelry 1925–1975*. Paducah, Ky.: Collector Books, 1986.

Ball, Joanne Dubbs. *Costume Jewelers: The Golden Age of Design*. West Chester, Pa.: Schiffer Publishing Co., 1990.

_____ . *Jewelry of the Stars: Creations from Joseff of Hollywood*. West Chester, Pa.: Schiffer Publishing Co., 1991.

Batterberry, Michael and Ariane. *A Social History of Fashion*. New York: Holt, Rinehart & Winston, 1977.

Becker, Vivienne. *Fabulous Fakes*. London: Grafton Books, 1988.

_____ . *Rough Diamonds*. New York: Rizzoli, 1991.

Burkholz, Matthew L., and Kaplan, Linda Lichtenberg. *Copper Art Jewelry: A Different Lustre*. West Chester, Pa.: Schiffer Publishing, Ltd., 1992.

Cartlidge, Barbara. *Twentieth Century Jewelry*. New York: Harry N. Abrams, Inc., 1985.

Cera, Deanna Farneti, ed. *Jewels of Fantasy: Costume Jewelry of the 20th Century*. New York: Harry N. Abrams, Inc., 1992.

Culme, John, and Rayner, Nicholas. *The Jewels of the Duchess of Windsor*. New York: The Vendome Press, 1987.

Davidow, Corinne, and Dawes, Ginny Redington. *The Bakelite Jewelry Book*. New York: Abbeville Press, 1988.

DiNoto, Andrea. *Art Plastic: Designed for Living*. New York: Abbeville Press, 1984.

Dolan, Maryanne. *Collecting Rhinestone Colored Jewelry*. Alabama: Books Americana, Inc., 1989.

Duncan, Alistair, ed. *Encyclopedia of Art Deco*. New York: E. P. Dutton, Quarto Publishing, 1988.

Ellman, Barbara. *The World of Fashion Jewelry*. Highland Park, Ill.: Aunt Louise Imports, 1986.

Ettinger, Roseann. *Forties and Fifties Popular Jewelry*. Atglen, Pa: Schiffer Publishing, Ltd., 1994.

Ewing, Elizabeth. *History of 20th Century Fashion*. Totowa, N.J.: Barnes & Noble, 1974, 1986.

Fregnac, Claude. *Jewelry from the Renaissance to Art Nouveau*. London: Octopus Books Limited, 1973.

Gold, Annalee. *75 Years of Fashion*. New York: Fairchild Publications, 1975.

Gordon, Angie. *Twentieth Century Costume Jewellry*. New York: Adasia International, 1990.

Griendl, Gabriele. *Gems of Costume Jewelry*. New York: Abbeville Press, 1991.

Hall, Carolyn. *The Twenties in Vogue*. London: Octopus Books Ltd., 1983.

Hoffer, Otto. *Imitation Gemstones—Random Personal Reminiscences*. Published privately. 1980.

Keenan, Brigid. *Dior in Vogue*. New York: Harmony Books, 1981.

Kelley, Lyngerda, and Schiffer, Nancy. *Plastic Jewelry*. West Chester, Pa.: Schiffer Publishing Co., 1987.

Leese, Elizabeth. *Costume Design in the Movies*. New York: Dover Publications, Inc., 1991.

Leymarie, Jean. *Chanel*. Genéve, Switzerland: Albert Skira, 1987.

Marascutto, Pauline B., and Stainer, Mario. *Perle Veneziane*. Italy: Nuove Edizioni Dolomiti S.r.l., 1991.

Mason, Anita. *An Illustrated Dictionary of Jewellery*. New York: Harper & Row, 1974.

Mauriès, Patrick. *Jewelry by Chanel*. Boston, Mass.: Little, Brown and Company, 1993.

McClinton, Katharine Morrison. *Art Deco: A Guide for Collectors*. New York: Clarkson N. Potter, 1972.

Milbank, Caroline Rennolds. *Couture: The Great Designers*. New York: Stewart, Tabori & Chang, Inc., 1985.

Miller, Harrice Simons. *The Official Identification and Price Guide to Costume Jewelry*. New York: House of Collectibles, Ballantine Books, 1990.

Mulvagh, Jane. *Costume Jewelry in Vogue*. New York: Thames and Hudson Inc., 1988.

Proddow, Penny; Healy, Debra; and Fasel, Marion. *Hollywood Jewels*. New York: Harry N. Abrams, Inc., 1992.

Rose, Augustus F. *Jewelry Making and Design*. Worchester, Mass.: The Davis Press, Inc., 1949.

Sarett, Morton R. *The Jewelry in Your Life*. Chicago: Nelson-Hall, 1979.

Schiaparelli, Elsa. *Shocking Life*. New York: E. P. Dutton & Co., Inc. and London: J. M. Dent & Sons, Ltd., 1954.

Schiffer, Nancy. *The Best of Costume Jewelry*. West Chester, Pa.: Schiffer Publishing Co., 1990.

_____ . *Costume Jewelry: The Fun of Collecting*. West Chester, Pa.: Schiffer Publishing Ltd., 1988.

_____ . *Fun Jewelry*. West Chester, Pa.: Schiffer Publishing Ltd., 1991.

Shields, Jody. *All That Glitters*. New York: Rizzoli, 1987.

Steinberg, Sheila, and Dooner, Kate. *Fabulous Fifties: Designs for Modern Living*. Atglen, Pa: Schiffer Publishing, Ltd., 1993.

Untracht, Oppi. *Jewelry Concepts and Technology*. New York: Doubleday & Co., 1982.

Vautrin, Line, and Mauriès, Patrick. *Line Vautrin, Sculptor, Jeweller, Magician*. New York: Thames and Hudson, Inc., 1992.

Warren, Geoffrey. *Fashion Accessories Since 1500*. New York: Drama Book Publishers, 1987.

White, Palmer. *Elsa Schiaparelli: Empress of Paris Fashion*. New York: Rizzoli, 1986.

PERIODICALS

Ball, Joanne Dubbs. "Faux and Fabulous." *Art & Auction*, December 1990.

"Bakelite Envy." *Connoisseur*, July 1985.

"Costume Jewelry: High Style at Low Cost." *Mass Bay Antiques*, September 1982.

Fried, Eunice. "Faux but Fabulous—Joseff: Jeweler to the Stars." *Almanac*, November/December 1988.

Hoving, Nancy. "All That Glitters." *Connoisseur*, September 1989.

Klein, Mim. "Joseff of Hollywood." *Collectors Clocks and Jewelry*, Fall 1988.

Main, Eve. "Joseff, of Hollywood." *Modern Plastics*, September 1939.

Menkes, Suzy. "Fake, but Fabulous." *International Tribune*, May 19, 1992.

"Star Fashions." *Movie Mirror*, December 1938.

AUCTION AND MUSEUM CATALOGS

Couture, First Annual Auction of Couturier, Antique Clothing & Accessories. New York: William Doyle Galleries, September 30, 1993.

Couture, Antique Clothing, Accessories & Costume Jewelry. New York: William Doyle Galleries, April 27, 1994.

Fine Antique and Modern Jewelry. New York: Phillips, January 22, 1985.

Infinite Riches: Jewelry Through the Centuries. St. Petersburg, Fl.: Museum of Fine Arts, February 19–April 30, 1989.

The Diana Vreeland Collection of Fashion Jewelry. New York: Sotheby's, October 21, 1987.

Index

A.B., pin, 196
Age, determining, 23–24
Albert, Ambros, 63
Amourelle, earrings, 196
Antique Researchers, 24
ARPAD (Senior), 34
Athennic Arts, necklace, 141

B.S.K., pins, 106
Barclay, McClelland, pins, 152
Block, Fred A., 35
    pin, 142
Blumenthal, B.
    pin and clip, 99
    pins, 149
Body sculpture and bracelets, seventies, 288
Boucher, Marcel, 49
    bracelet and earrings set, 186
    bracelets, 151, 276
    clip, 185
    pin and earrings sets, 208, 236
    pins, 105–106, 150
Bracelet, clip, and earrings set, forties, 184
Bracelet and earrings sets
    forties, 186
    fifties, 220, 223, 236, 238
    sixties, 277
    eighties, 299
    nineties, 307
Bracelet and pin sets
    forties, 176, 196
    fifties, 109

Bracelets
    twenties, 127–28, 129, 133
    thirties, 85, 151, 164, 168, 169
    forties, 84, 85, 91, 117, 187, 195, 197
    fifties, 205, 216, 219, 221, 232, 234, 236, 238
    sixties, 247, 261, 276–77
    seventies, 97, 283, 284, 290
    eighties, 298, 299
    nineties, 307, 311, 312, 316, 322, 325, 326
Butler & Wilson
    bracelet, 307
    bracelet and earrings set, 307
    earrings, 307
    necklace, 307
    pins, 296–97, 307

Cadoro, 35
Calvaire, 35
    bracelet, 84
Canovas, Isabel
    bracelet and earrings set, 299
    bracelets, 299
    earrings, 325
    necklace, 325
Cardin, Pierre, necklace, 284
Carnegie, Hattie, 35
    clips, 171–72, 178, 185
    necklace, 205
    pins, 89, 100–101
Carolee, 35–37
    pins, 297, 325

369